Wittgenstein and the Vienna Circle

Wittgenstein and the Vienna Circle

conversations recorded by
Friedrich Waismann

Edited by Brian McGuinness

Translated by Joachim Schulte
and Brian McGuinness

BARNES & NOBLE

BOOKS

10 East 53d St., New York 10022
(a division of Harper & Row Publishers, Inc.)

Published in the U.S.A. by Harper and Row Publishers, Inc.,
Barnes & Noble Import Division

ISBN 0–06–497310–7

Library of Congress Catalog Number 78–6452

Printed in Great Britain

CONTENTS

n—Works cited   10
ace   11

I

Wednesday, 18 December 1929 (at Schlick's house)   33
  ⟨Proof in Mathematics⟩   33
  What Does Looking for Something Mean in Mathematics?   34
    Example: Trisection of an Angle   36
    Simile: Unravelling a Knot   37
  Geometry as Syntax I   38
  Consistency I   38

Sunday, 22 December 1929 (at Schlick's house)   38
  ⟨'All' I⟩   38
    Objects   41
    What Does 'All' Mean?   44
  Solipsism   45
    The Sense of a Proposition is its Verification   47
    Wheels Turning Idly   48
    ⟨'I cannot feel your pain'⟩   49
  ⟨Language and World⟩   50

Wednesday, 25 December (at Schlick's house)   51
  'All' II   51
  Time   53
    External—Internal   54
  Visual Space   55
    Addendum, 30 December 1929   59
  Geometry as Syntax II   61
  Physics and Phenomenology   63
  Colour-System   63
    Is Every Proposition Part of a System? I   65
    ⟨*The World is Red* I⟩   65

Addendum, Monday, 30 December 1929 66
Anti-Husserl 67

Monday, 30 December 1929 (at Schlick's house) 68
Apropos of Heidegger 68
Dedekindian Definition 69
Real Numbers I 71

Thursday, 2 January 1930 (at Schlick's house) 73
⟨Elementary Propositions⟩ 73
⟨'The Present State of Knowledge in Mathematics'⟩ 81
 Freely developing sequence 83
 ⟨*Miscellaneous*⟩ 84

Sunday, 5 January 1930 (at Schlick's house) 84
Positive and Negative Propositions 84
The Colour Blue in Memory 87
'The World is Red' II 88
Is Every Proposition Part of a System? II 89
Inference 91
Lecture on Ethics 92
Probability I 93
 Dice 95

II

22 March 1930 (at Schlick's house) 97
⟨Verification and the Immediately Given⟩ 97
 ⟨*Verification and Time*⟩ 98
Probability II 98
Hypotheses I 99
 Double Meaning of Geometry 100
 ⟨*Various Remarks about Hypotheses*⟩ 101

III

19 June 1930 (at Schlick's house) 102
⟨What to Say at Königsberg⟩ 102
 Formalism 103
 Equation and Tautology I 105

25 September 1930   107
  ⟨Miscellanea⟩   107
  Variables   108
  Proof   109
  Real Numbers II   109
  Idealization   113
  Interpretation   113

IV

Wednesday, 17 December 1930 (Neuwaldegg)   115
  On Schlick's Ethics   115
  Value   115
  Religion   117
  Ought   118
  Consistency II   119

Friday, 26 December 1930 (at Schlick's house)   121
  Style of Thinking   121

Sunday, 28 December 1930 (at Schlick's house)   121
  Consistency III   121
    Sheffer's Discovery   122
    ⟨Rules and Configurations of a Game⟩ 123
    What Does it Mean to Apply a Calculus? 126
    ⟨Independence I⟩   128

Tuesday, 30 December 1930 (at Schlick's house)   130
  ⟨Consistency IV⟩   130
    ⟨Frege and Wittgenstein I⟩   130
    Hilbert's Proof   137

Thursday, 1 January 1931 (at Schlick's house)   142
    America. The Institution of Colleges 142
  Consistency V   142
    Independence II   145
    Summary   148
    Hilbert's Axioms I.1 and I.2   148

⟨Calculus and Everday Prose⟩ 149
Frege and Wittgenstein II 150

Sunday, 4 January 1931 (at Schlick's house) 152
⟨Equation and Substitution-Rule I⟩ 152
⟨Equation and Tautology⟩ 158
⟨Verification of the Propositions of Physics⟩ 158
Hypotheses II 159
⟨Geometry as Syntax II⟩ 162
Addenda 163
Chess 163
Apropos of Königsberg 164
Definition of Number 164

V

Monday, 21 September 1931 (first Argentinierstrasse, then in
the street) 166
Intention, to Mean, Meaning 166
⟨Calculus and Application⟩ 170
⟨Looking Things Up in a Diary⟩ 171
Constructing a Boiler 171
Proof of Existence 172
⟨Consistency VI⟩ 173
Hidden Contradiction 173
Contradiction 175
⟨Equation and Substitution-rule II⟩ 178
Indirect Proof I 179

VI

Wednesday, 9 December 1931 (Neuwaldegg) 182
On Dogmatism 182
On Infinity 187
On Ramsey's Definition of Identity 189
Consistency VIII 192

Insertion from dictation	196
Consistency VIII	196
An Analogy—'The Expansion' of	201
⟨*The Concept of a Calculus*⟩	202
⟨Proof in Geometry and Arithmetic⟩	203
Bisection of an Angle	204
Generality in Geometry	206
Indirect Proof II	207

VII

1 July 1932 (Argentinierstrasse)	209
Hypotheses III	210

Appendix A

Totality and System	213
Equation and Tautology	218
Concept and Form	220
What is a Number?	221
Sense and Meaning	227
On Infinity	227
Dedekind's Definition	232

Appendix B

Theses by Friedrich Waismann (ca. 1930)	233
1. *States of Affairs, Facts, Reality*	233
2. *Language*	235
3. *Syntax*	239
4. *Symmetry, Asymmetry*	241
5. *Identity*	242
6. *Verification*	243
7. *Definition*	246
8. *Objects*	254
9. *Logical Space*	260

Index	263

WITTGENSTEIN: WORKS CITED

Abbreviation		Approximate date of composition
NL	*Notes on Logic (Notebooks 1914–1916*, Oxford 1961, pp. 93–106)	1913
Nb	*Notebooks* (ibid., pp. 2–91)	1914–1917
TLP	*Tractatus Logico-Philosophicus* (first published as *Logisch-Philosophische Abhandlung*, latest edition, London 1971)	1918–1919
LE	'Lecture on Ethics' (*Philosophical Review* lxxiv (1965), pp. 3–12)	1929
MS voll.	Manuscript volumes I–X (unpublished)	1929–1932
PR	*Philosophical Remarks* (Oxford 1975, first published as *Philosophische Bemerkungen*, Oxford and Frankfurt 1965) [contains material from MS voll. I–III and part of MS vol. IV]	1930
EM	Extract from the Manuscript volumes (unpublished) [a typescript of 770 pages; contains material from MS voll. V–IX]	1931–1932
BT	The 'Big Typescript' (unpublished) [a typescript of 768 pages; contains material from *EM* and other similar extracts, arranged in sections and chapters]	1932
GdM	*Grundlagen der Mathematik* [the last 240 pages of *BT*; for the most part published in *PG*]	1932
PG	*Philosophical Grammar* (Oxford 1974, first published as *Philosophische Grammatik*, Oxford and Frankfurt 1969) [contains *GdM* and reworkings of other parts of *BT*]	1932–1936
RFM	*Remarks on the Foundations of Mathematics* (Oxford 1956, fuller edition as *Bemerkungen über die Grundlagen der Mathematik*, Frankfurt 1974)	1937–1942
PI	*Philosophical Investigations* (Oxford 1953)	1937–1949

EDITOR'S PREFACE

I

The material translated in the present volume is practically all drawn from the papers of the late Friedrich Waismann (1897–1959). The exceptions are a few pages missing from Waismann's own copy of his *Theses* (Appendix B), which were supplied by Dr. Josef Schächter of Jerusalem, and some sections of the notes on the philosophy of mathematics (Appendix A), which exist only in the form of extracts made by Mr. Shimshon Stein, now of Tel Aviv. It was all first published in the original German jointly by the present publishers and by Suhrkamp of Frankfurt in 1967. The present edition follows as nearly as possible the pagination of that one.

None of the material can be described without qualification as Waismann's own work. All of it originated at a time when Wittgenstein, though with considerable misgivings, was willing to see his ideas propagated at any rate in Vienna by means of reports composed by Waismann. Gradually, however, as we shall see, he became dissatisfied with this method and had recourse to full collaboration with Waismann. When that too proved unsatisfactory, it seems that his philosophical ideas were communicated to his Viennese friends for the most part as a result of his meetings with Schlick and through the despatch of copies of the *Blue Book* and other dictated notes.

Waismann, for his part, was able to incorporated many of Wittgenstein's ideas on the philosophy of mathematics into his own *Einführung in das mathematische Denken (Introduction to Mathematical thinking),*[1] which first appeared in 1936 and is of course essentially a work of Waismann's. But his book *Logik, Sprache, Philosophie (Logic, Language, Philosophy),* which had been announced several times between 1929 and 1931, never appeared in Waismann's lifetime, despite or because of frequent revisions. It was finally published in

---

1 Vienna 1936, [2]1947, [3]Munich 1950; E. T. New York 1951. Wittgenstein's contribution to this work is described in detail in an appendix.

translation six years after Waismann's death under the title *Principles of Linguistic Philosophy*[2] in a form much altered from the original conception.

II

The earliest material published in the main part of this volume consists of the record of a conversation that took place in December 1929. Wittgenstein had spent that year in Cambridge: his return to philosophy as his main occupation can be dated to that time. But, as might be expected, there were several occasions earlier in the twenties when his interest in the subject began to revive, whether stimulated by others or of its own accord. F. P. Ramsey visited him several times in 1923 and also in 1924 over a period of six or seven months. The two men discussed the *Tractatus* and Wittgenstein proposed a number of changes in the English translation, which were in fact adopted for the second edition.[3] They also talked about the foundations of mathematics and about the changes to be wished for in a second edition of *Principia Mathematica*. On 24 March 1924, however, Ramsay wrote to Keynes saying that Wittgenstein obviously found thinking to be uphill work and needed someone like Ramsey himself to stimulate him. Wittgenstein[4] later (4 July 1924) wrote to Keynes saying, 'You ask in your letter whether you could do anything to make it possible for me to return to scientific work. The answer is, No: there's nothing that can be done in that line, because I myself no longer have any strong inner drive towards that sort of activity. Everything that I really *had* to say, I have said, and so the spring has run dry. That sounds queer, but it's how things are.' There the matter rested for the moment. A plan to induce Wittgenstein to spend in Cambridge the remainder of the time necessary to qualify him for a doctorate was

2 London, 1965. The German original was later published under the title *Logik, Sprache, Philosophie*, Stuttgart, 1976, with some account of the genesis of the work, for which see also Section IV below.
3 See C. Lewy's 'Note on the text of the *Tractatus*' in *Mind* 76 (1967) 416–423.
4 See L. Wittgenstein, *Letters to Russell, Keynes and Moore*, pp. 114–118, for both Ramsey's and Wittgenstein's letters at this time.

abandoned and the visit to England that he actually made in 1925 was devoted simply to visiting friends.

Meanwhile, in Vienna, the *Tractatus* had become an object of intense interest. The mathematician Hans Hahn gave a seminar on the work in 1922 and two professors newly arrived in Vienna —Moritz Schlick, the philosopher, and Kurt Reidemeister, the mathematician—were deeply impressed. One consequence was that Schlick wrote to Wittgenstein (25 December 1924):

> As an admirer of your *Tractatus Logico-Philosophicus* I have long intended to get in touch with you. My professorial and other duties are responsible for the fact that I have again and again put off carrying out my intention, though nearly five semesters have passed since I was called to Vienna. Every winter semester I have regular meetings with colleagues and gifted students who are interested in the foundations of logic and mathematics and your name has often been mentioned in this group, particularly since my mathematical colleague Professor Reidemeister reported on your work in a lecture which made a great impression on us all. So there are a number of people here—I am one myself—who are convinced of the importance and correctness of your fundamental ideas and who feel a strong desire to play some part in making your views more widely known . . . (Schlick proceeds to ask how to obtain copies of the *Tractatus*) . . . It would be an especially great pleasure for me actually to meet you and I should like to call on you sometime in Puchberg,[5] unless you let me know that you would rather not have your country retreat disturbed.

Wittgenstein found this letter in Otterthal on his return from the Christmas holidays and replied (7 January 1925) in most friendly terms, explaining that he himself had no copy of the *Tractatus*. He expressed great pleasure at the prospect of a visit from Schlick, who in his reply (14 January) once more expressed his intention of coming. In

5 Wittgenstein had in fact moved unexpectedly to Otterthal in the autumn. The Puchberg address was perhaps given to Schlick by Ramsey.

fact, it seems that he did not attempt the visit until after April 1926, for, when he and a few chosen pupils went to Otterthal, they found that Wittgenstein had given up his post as a teacher and left. For all Wittgenstein's good will towards Schlick, he was evidently too retiring to call on him, though Schlick had told him that he would of course be delighted to see him if he ever came to Vienna.

From the autumn of 1926 Wittgenstein was in Vienna engaged on the building of the house in the Kundmanngasse for his sister, Mrs. Margaret Stonborough. Mrs. Stonborough was well known in social and intellectual circles in Vienna and, in the event, it was through her that Schlick came to meet Wittgenstein. He had sent Wittgenstein one of his writings and he proposed a meeting with one or two other persons to discuss logical problems. Mrs. Stonborough wrote (19 February 1927):

> He asks me to give you his warmest regards and to make his excuses to you, since he still feels quite unable to concentrate on logical problems as well as doing his present work, which demands all his energies. He could certainly not have a meeting with a number of people. He feels that if it were with you alone, dear Professor Schlick, he might be able to discuss such matters. It would then become apparent, he thinks, whether he is at present at all capable of being of use to you in this connexion.

Accordingly Schlick was invited to lunch, in order to discuss the matter afterwards.

> Mrs. Stonborough's invitation (Mrs. Schlick recalled) brought with it a great joy and anticipation and this time M.'s expectations and hopes were not thwarted. Again (as on the occasion of the abortive visit to Otterthal) I observed with interest the reverential attitude of the pilgrim. He returned in an ecstatic state, saying little, and I felt I should not ask questions.[6]

6 My account of Schlick's attempts to meet Wittgenstein and his eventual success is based, after the contemporary letters quoted above, on the recollections of the late Mrs. Blanche Schlick as given to Professor F. A. von Hayek and (in much smaller measure) to myself, through the good offices of Professor Kraft.

Wittgenstein's own first reaction to the meeting was not without a certain Socratic irony. 'Each of us thought the other must be mad,' he said next day to his friend Paul Engelmann, with whom he was at the time working as an architect. But the two soon arrived, as Engelmann reports, at a good mutual understanding.

Wittgenstein found Schlick a distinguished and understanding partner in discussion, all the more so because he appreciated Schlick's highly cultured personality.[7]

Apparently Wittgenstein had several conversations with Schlick before he would agree to meet other members of the Circle. Waismann, perhaps the closest to Schlick at the time, was almost always present. Sometimes Rudolf Carnap made the number up to four.[8] Herbert Feigl and Maria Kasper (now Mrs. Feigl) often came as well. Wittgenstein, preoccupied with other things and with his architectural work in particular, was not always prepared to talk about philosophy. Sometimes he preferred to read out poems, especially those of Rabindranath Tagore, usually sitting with his back to the audience. Nevertheless there were many occasions on which he made remarks or gave extensive expositions of his views which were found illuminating and stimulating. During 1927 and 1928 no record of such conversations seems to have been kept. Some but not all their

7 Paul Engelmann, *Letters from Ludwig Wittgenstein with a Memoir* (Oxford, 1967) p. 118.
8 Carnap gives a particularly interesting account of these conversations in his 'Autobiography' in P.A. Schilpp (ed.) *The Philosophy of Rudolph Carnap* (Lasalle, Ill., 1963) pp. 24–30.

discussions concerned the foundations of mathematics, and in particular Ramsey's paper with that title. In summer 1927 a correspondence between Wittgenstein and Ramsey on the topic of identity was evidently carried on through the intermediacy of Schlick and Waismann. The philosophical parts of the letters are given below (p. 189). In his letter of 15 August 1927 giving Ramsey's answer Schlick spoke of his own intended return to Vienna in November and expressed the hope

> that you for your part will be prepared to go on with the small meetings that we started with our Monday evenings. I'm sure you must have felt what unalloyed pleasure discussion with you regularly gave us.

and in October he added, 'I can willingly promise that our talk won't have to be scientific.'

These meetings, however, were not those of the Vienna Circle proper. The latter were held on Thursday evenings and Schlick invited Wittgenstein to one in June 1928, but it is doubtful whether he ever attended any. It seems also that during the years 1927 and 1928 remarks made by Wittgenstein in his conversations were not made the subject of discussion at the Thursday meetings.

The only formal philosophical occasion attended by Wittgenstein seems to have been a lecture (or perhaps a pair of lectures) given by Brouwer in March 1928.[9] Waismann and Feigl at first had difficulty in persuading Wittgenstein to attend, but in the event the lecture stimulated him enormously.

9 See G. Pitcher, *The Philosophy of Wittgenstein*, Englewood Cliffs, N. J. 1964, p. 8.

The year 1929 brought considerable changes for both Wittgenstein's life and the Vienna Circle. The house in the Kundmanngasse was complete by autumn 1928 and, after some delays, Wittgenstein left for Cambridge arriving in January 1929, for a holiday (so at least he had announced to Keynes). But he soon decided—and perhaps had long half-intended—to stay there and work on his philosophy:

> I have decided to remain here in Cambridge for a few terms and work on visual space and other things. . . . Please give my regards to the Round Table and to Mr. Waismann in particular. I hope and look forward to seeing you all again in a month. (Letter to Schlick, 18 February 1929)

There is no record extant of the Easter Vacation conversations anticipated in this letter, but the year as a whole was one of intense and (at the time) satisfying activity. From the area mentioned to Schlick Wittgenstein proceeded to problems connected with arithmetic. He wrote the article 'Some Remarks on Logical Form', which is published in the *Proceedings of the Aristotelian Society Supplementary Volume* IX (1929), but at the meeting at which it should have been presented he in fact gave a lecture on the concept of the infinite in mathematics. At about this time (June–July 1929) he wrote to Waismann:

> I have worked a great deal recently, and with good success, so I should have been glad of an opportunity to explain a number of things to you.

But Waismann, who had just married, was not to meet Wittgenstein during that summer. Nor was Schlick either: he was in America; indeed his absence was indirectly the occasion of Wittgenstein's letter to Waismann. Earlier in the year Schlick had declined a chair at Bonn in order to remain with his circle of friends in Vienna. It was decided, as a mark of gratitude, to present him with a brochure containing an account of the essential common tenets, of the publications, and of the antecedents of the school centred on him. This publication was *Die Wissenschaftliche Weltauffassung. Der Wiener Kreis* (Vienna

1929),[10] first sold at the Prague conference on theory of knowledge in the exact sciences in September 1929. A specially bound copy was sent to Schlick. This may be regarded as the christening of the Vienna Circle, which became a fully fledged philosophical movement in the next year with the acquisition of the periodical *Annalen der Philosophie* (renamed *Erkenntnis*).

This development was not at all to Wittgenstein's taste, When the publication was planned, he wrote to Waismann:

> Just because Schlick is no ordinary man, people owe it to him to take care not to let their 'good intentions' make him and the Vienna school which he leads ridiculous by boastfulness. When I say 'boastfulness' I mean any kind of self-satisfied posturing. 'Renunciation of metaphysics!' As if *that* were something new! What the Vienna school has achieved, it ought to *show* not *say*. . . . The master should be known by his *work*.

Now, so many years later, the brochure seems not to have justified Wittgenstein's worst fears, though we do not know what he himself thought about it when it appeared. Apart from an account of the fundamental tenets of the school, it contains a useful bibliography, a sketch by Waismann of the contents of *TLP*, and an announcement of Waismann's forthcoming work *Logik, Sprache, Philosophie* (see pp. 11f. above), described as an introduction to the ideas of *TLP*. Parts of the 'first draft' of this work are preserved among Waismann's papers. They do not go beyond *TLP* and exhibit no traces of the new ideas expressed in the article 'On Logical Form' or in the conversations reported in the present book.

Perhaps Wittgenstein was repelled by the new role of the Vienna Circle as a philosophical school. At all events his contacts with it were now restricted to meetings with Schlick and Waismann. He no longer attended the Round Table.

Schlick spent the whole summer in Stanford, and Wittgenstein could do no more than report that he was making satisfactory progress in his work and would discuss the results with Schlick as soon as an

10 Now published in English translation as 'The Scientific Conception of the World' in O. Neurath, *Empiricism and Sociology*, Dordrecht, 1973.

opportunity offered. This occurred when Wittgenstein returned to Vienna for the Christmas vacation. He met Schlick and Waismann in the former's house at least six times and during or after these meetings Waismann made the notes translated in the first chapter of the present volume. The atmosphere was more businesslike and formal than earlier. It was even possible (as will be shown) for Waismann to make notes during the conversations. There were two reasons for the formality; first, Wittgenstein now had results to communicate (he was about to give lectures in Cambridge), and secondly (as is apparent from a letter dated 1932) he now saw these conversations as the best way of making his thoughts accessible to the other members of Schlick's circle.

In any case, these are the first transcribed conversations that we have. On the first two days Wittgenstein's contribution only was recorded; but before the end of the vacation the exposition of previously formulated ideas was clearly at an end, since remarks or questions by Schlick or Waismann, and arguments with them, begin to appear, as well as apparently spontaneous discussions of ideas of Husserl's, Heidegger's, and Weyl's.

In the Easter vacation of 1930, when Wittgenstein was next in Vienna, there was only one meeting of which notes survive (Chapter II). This is when Wittgenstein explained his distinction between statements and hypotheses, which was to have a certain influence on the Vienna Circle.

There are notes of two meetings in the summer of 1930 (Chapter III). At the first (19 June) Wittgenstein expounded his views on a number of mathematical topics to Waismann, who was to present them in a lecture at Königsberg during the second conference on theory of knowledge in the exact sciences. Wittgenstein fully supported this plan and was quite disappointed when for a while in the summer it seemed as if Waismann would not be able to attend the conference. This fear, however, proved groundless, and Waismann's lecture 'The Nature of Mathematics: Wittgenstein's Standpoint,' though not announced in the programme, was made the fourth in an outstanding series of lectures along with Carnap on the logistic, Heyting on the intuitionistic, and von Neumann on the formalistic view of the foundations of mathematics. The other three lectures were printed in *Erkenntnis* 2 (1931) 91ff., but Waismann's manuscript never reached the editor.

In the course of the discussion (pp. 138ff. of the same periodical) Hahn and Carnap refer to what Waismann has said. Hahn talks of a polemic by Wittgenstein and the intuitionists 'against the view that the world consists of individuals, properties of individuals, properties of these properties, and so on and the axioms of logic are statements about this world.' The other points mentioned by Hahn and Carnap occur in the (fairly heavily corrected) typescript of the first part of the lecture, which is preserved among Waismann's papers. They are, first, the distinction between operations and functions (see Appendix A) and, second, a methodological principle formulated as follows:

> The meaning of a mathematical concept is the mode of its use and the sense of a mathematical proposition is the method of its verification.

The following topics were intended to be discussed in the lecture:
1. The nature of numbers;
2. The idea of the infinite;
3. The concept of a set;
4. The principle of complete induction;

but only the first part, and perhaps not all of that, is preserved. In Appendix A we give some notes on mathematics that Waismann made about this time and circulated among a number of friends as a transcript of Wittgenstein's views. Mr. Stein saw a copy of these in Vienna before the end of 1930. Some sections of our Appendix give Stein's extracts from Waismann's notes where these are now lost. Engelmann's extracts, which have also been preserved, are inscribed: 'Orally from L. W., taken down before 1930.' Although it is likely that the material in Appendix A was typewritten and copied in late

1930 when Waismann was preparing his Königsberg lecture for publication, it is nonetheless possible that it is derived from conversations or meetings held before December 1929. That would account for the absence of the Appendix A material from the shorthand notebooks that underlie the present volume and also for the small amount of material intended for Königsberg that they contain.

Neither the Appendix A notes nor Waismann's record of summer 1930 nor the *Erkenntnis* report on discussions in Königsberg contain any trace of Wittgenstein's argument against the Frege-Russell definition of number in terms of equinumerousness. It seems, therefore, that that argument was first developed in Cambridge during the Michaelmas Term of 1930. In Waismann's record it appears as an 'addendum' (p. 164) to what was said at Königsberg.

Although it meant interrupting work on another, almost complete manuscript, Waismann was happy to give the lecture at Königsberg. He felt that it was high time that Wittgenstein's ideas should be published and should receive the attention that was their due. They were indeed heard with respect at the conference and were regarded as constituting a fourth position alongside the three most important philosophical schools, but the effect achieved was much reduced by Waismann's failure to publish (which was perhaps itself due to the fact that Wittgenstein was in the process of developing new ideas). The deep impression made by the result of Goedel's announced at Königsberg also tended to overshadow Wittgenstein's contribution.

Waismann wrote to Schlick saying that he would return to Vienna on 10 September and would be seeing Wittgenstein on 20 September. It seems likely, therefore, that at the second recorded conversation of that summer (actually 25 September; see pp. 107ff) Schlick was not present. Like the first conversation, the second seems to have consisted of uninterrupted exposition by Wittgenstein.

IV

Waismann apparently first composed his *Theses* in the course of 1930, but he revised it often in the following year,[11] and more than one version circulated among his friends. The variations are not great. The version printed here as Appendix B seems to be the latest preserved. It may well be that *Theses* was at one time intended to form part of *Logik, Sprache, Philosophie*, perhaps the part dealing with language.

An earlier version of most of *Theses* is preserved among Waismann's papers under the title *Einführung zu Wittgenstein (Introduction to Wittgenstein)*. This deals in addition with philosophy, though in a rather fragmentary way. The third element in the book as planned at this time is represented by Waismann's lecture 'Das Wesen der Logik' ('The Nature of Logic'), given on 8 May 1930, whose text is also preserved. The arrangement envisaged for the book, so far as we can judge from the announcement in *Erkenntnis* 1 (1930–31) 325 and from the account of the lecture with the same title given by Waismann on 15 March 1931 (*Erkenntnis* 2 (1931) 82 and 311) is identical neither with the arrangement of *Theses* nor with that of *Einführung* nor with that of the still earlier first draft mentioned above. Clearly Waismann was experimenting with different arrangements of essentially the same material.

Theses consists of an attempt to interpret some of the main principles of *TLP* with the help of new ideas such as the notion of hypothesis and the definition of sense in terms of verification. Apart from the incorporation of this new material, the aim of the work was to present the results of *TLP* in an easily comprehensible form, not to carry further the discussion begun in that book. As will be seen below, when Wittgenstein discussed this project with Waismann in December 1931, he made clear, in characteristically forceful terms, his opposition to 'a rehash of such theses'—a remark that doubtless affected Waismann's plans for the book.

---

11 Mr. Stein received his copy in Palestine early in 1931, but Schlick wrote about revisions still in progress in October 1931.

V

The meetings recorded in chapter IV took place in the Christmas vacation of 1930–31. The first was held in Neuwaldegg, in one of the houses used by Wittgenstein's family in the spring and autumn. At this season it would have been a quiet retreat for Wittgenstein. Here Waismann visited him, and they discussed Schlick's *Fragen der Ethik* (*Questions of Ethics*), which had reached Wittgenstein in Cambridge during the previous term, and Hilbert's *Neubegründung der Mathematik* (*A New Foundation for Mathematics*).

After Christmas, meetings were once again held in Schlick's house. The last of these Waismann intended to record from memory but failed to. The remaining ones deal with the philosophy of mathematics and (at Schlick's request) with the sense of propositions that permit of two or more distinct methods of verification. The chapter ends with a number of 'Addenda'. Here Wittgenstein discusses in greater detail points already touched on (mere repetitions are omitted here as in the German volume). He also introduces, in part, the above-mentioned criticism of Frege's and Russell's definition of number in terms of equinumerousness. These addenda were probably written after 4 January 1931, certainly before 21 September 1931. In them Wittgenstein refers to a previous exposition of the same criticism in Cambridge lectures. From notes by G. E. Moore, it is clear that this happened in Michaelmas Term 1930.

At Easter 1931 Wittgenstein visited Vienna again, but no conversations were held, perhaps because, as he confessed to Schlick, he was very tired. Summer, as always, was a difficult time for the three to coincide in Vienna. This probably accounts for the fact that only one conversation was recorded (Chapter V), and that on the occasion of a visit to Wittgenstein by Waismann alone. They met in the large house of Wittgenstein's brother and sister in the Argentinierstrasse, probably (again) empty at that time of the year. Here Wittgenstein would occasionally meet his friends in one of the office rooms on the ground floor. He and Waismann continued the conversation on the street. They discussed a manuscript that Wittgenstein had with him and Waismann put a number of questions arising out of earlier conversations on the philosophy of mathematics.

Schlick spent the winter semester of 1931–2 in California. Wittgenstein wrote to him in November, somewhat disturbed about the book being planned by Waismann: 'a lot of things', he thought, 'will be presented quite differently from the way I think right.' He also stressed how far he had moved from the position taken in *TLP*—'There are *many, many* formulations in that book that I am no longer in agreement with.' Both of these sentiments come out quite clearly in the notes that Waismann took at his winter meeting with Wittgenstein, once again held in Neuwaldegg (printed as part of Chapter VI). It begins with a section 'On Dogmatism,' which contains the harsh criticism of *Theses* already mentioned. It was probably at this time that the original conception of *Logik, Sprache, Philosophie* as a presentation of the main theses of *TLP* in an easily comprehensible form was dropped. From then on Waismann worked on a book intended to present Wittgenstein's later ideas.

In March 1932 Wittgenstein again wrote to Schlick: 'Have you received Waismann's notes of what I dictated at Christmas?' The question could refer to the section on dogmatism and the discussion of the philosophy of mathematics that followed (9 December 1931); but the 'Insertion from dictation'[12] which forms the remainder of Chapter VI could also be meant.

12 The German title ('Einfügung aus dem Diktat') could imply a pre-existing document resulting from dictation and partly copied into our notebook. On the other hand, no such document containing all our passage has been found.

In Waismann's notebook there now follows a number of extracts copied from a manuscript or typescript of Wittgenstein's that obviously coincided in part with *PR*, in part with *Ms vol. IV*. These either already have been published, or will be considered for publication, as part of Wittgenstein's work: they are not given here.

Waismann's sixth and seventh notebooks carry the sub-title '(Math.).' The sixth begins with a number of extracts, not given here, from a manuscript or typescript of Wittgenstein's dealing with the philosophy of mathematics, coinciding, again, partly with *PR*, partly with *Ms vol. IV*. The next section is the report of a conversation dated 1 July. It seems that no conversations were held in the Easter vacation, although in his March letter Wittgenstein had expressed his hope of seeing Schlick then.[13]

The summer meeting took place, characteristically, in the empty house in the Argentinierstrasse. This means, probably, that only Waismann was there. The discussion is fairly fragmentary, but seems to be prompted by Carnap's article 'Die physikalische Sprache als Universalsprache der Wissenschaft' ('Physical language as the universal language of science').[14]

The remainder of Notebook 6 and the whole of Notebook 7 (apart from a few extracts from *NL* added in the 1950s) consists of extracts from *GdM*, not given here since the bulk of that work has been published as part of *Philosophical Grammar* (Oxford 1974). It seems consequently that no more recorded conversations were held. In a communication to the present editor, Viktor Kraft confirmed that the old method of contact between Wittgenstein and the Vienna Circle was not continued after 1932. Waismann no longer brought Wittgenstein's latest ideas to their meetings. Wittgenstein seems to have

13 At this period Wittgenstein rarely saw Schlick in Vienna without Waismann. Schlick's wife could remember only one such occasion.
14 Some of the ideas of this article were expounded by Carnap in a lecture in February or March 1931 (*Erkenntnis* 2 (1931) 311). It was printed later in the year (ibid. 432ff.).

felt that this form of disseminating his ideas might lead to publication in a distorted form and without proper acknowledgement.

From then on Wittgenstein met Schlick separately. He spent a holiday with him in Italy in summer 1933, when they engaged in intensive and exhausting discussions. This seems to have happened in other summers also. Occasionally he dictated to Schlick, and the outcome of this (two typescripts made from Schlick's shorthand notes and a few pages of other material) has been deposited with Wittgenstein's papers in the library of Trinity College, Cambridge. He continued to send copies of typescripts he had assembled or dictated to Schlick and Waismann. He also met Waismann fairly frequently in order to discuss the expository work on which Waismann was just then engaged. At length, certainly before Easter 1934, they decided upon a joint work, a general plan for its contents was agreed, and Wittgenstein even gave an impression, orally, of how, in his view, the work should open. But when the two men met again in the summer, Wittgenstein unfortunately declared himself hostile to precisely the draft of this opening. Waismann expressed his misgivings to Schlick.

(Wittgenstein) has the marvellous gift of always seeing everything as if for the first time. But I think it's obvious how difficult any collaboration is, since he always follows the inspiration of the moment and demolishes what he has previously planned.

They agreed, consequently, that Wittgenstein should plan the work and Waismann carry it into execution, though Waismann was in that case not prepared to let his name appear on the title page. It seems that nothing came of this idea, so that eventually the composition of Waismann's *Logik, Sprache, Philosophie* was left to himself alone. It was to appear as his own work, though very strongly influenced by Wittgenstein, who gave him manuscripts for it until at least 1935. But the further history of this book does not concern us here.

Wittgenstein's continued influence on Schlick can be seen not only from articles collected in *Gesammelte Aufsätze* (Vienna 1938) but also from Schlick's notes for seminars and lectures in the last years of his life. Apart from the dictated material and typescripts already mentioned, Schlick's daughter also has a copy of the *Blue Book* and a long letter of July 1935 about Goedel's theorem.

Schlick's assassination in June 1936, a loss deeply felt by Wittgenstein, broke the strongest link that tied the latter to the Vienna Circle. The relation of teacher to disciple that had previously (and fruitfully) bound him to Waismann seemed now to be unsuited to either and was certainly not resumed when Waismann came to England in 1938

VI

Finally, the form in which Waismann's notes of these conversations have been preserved must be reported. He kept them in seven school exercise-books, 16.5×20.5 cm large. The first six consist of 56 unlined pages. For material dictated to him, as for his own notes and drafts, Waismann employed the Gabelsberger system of shorthand.

In establishing the German text, published in 1967, many editorial judgements were necessary: abbreviations had to be expanded, ambiguous signs interpreted (was it 'nur' or 'nun'?). Generally this was done tacitly. But occasionally a footnote is given even in the English, or a supplement is indicated by angle-brackets—'ex⟨istence⟩' for example. These brackets are also used for any heading I have added. All numbers used in headings are mine.

Generally Waismann made his original notes on the recto or right-hand page. The facing verso or left-hand page could then be used for supplementary material or for improving the wording. Where the verso additions were quite clearly nothing more than a filling-out or a more elegant variation on what stood opposite I have omitted them, following a principle I will explain shortly. But the greater part of the verso material seems to me to consist either of later attempts by Waismann to recall and record what Wittgenstein had said when expounding the recto material or else of later remarks by Wittgenstein on the same topics. Sometimes this verso material is entitled 'Addendum' (pp. 59 and 66); sometimes there are contributions by both Waismann and Wittgenstein (p. 172), sometimes remarks that can only have been made by Wittgenstein (p. 196) or that are later ascribed to him (p. 124 cf. p. 131). In view of all this, the greater part of the verso material is reproduced here at the foot of the page with numerical indexes to show which part of the recto material it stood opposite.

Where Waismann used recto and verso indifferently I have of course not distinguished the verso material. Generally this occurs when Waismann is not recording a normal conversation but is copying a manuscript or writing from dictation. Curiously enough, the 'Insertion from Dictation' (pp. 196ff.) is written on recto sides only: on the versos opposite there are remarks by Wittgenstein, further arguments, and paraphrases.

In the shorthand text there are a good number of interlinear improvements and correction. When Waismann deletes a series of words and substitutes others for them I have assumed that he regarded the latter alone as a correct rendering of Wittgenstein's views. When he allows an expression to stand but writes a different formulation above the line or on the opposite page, I have assumed that he meant to use the later version in any writing or exposition of his own, but wished to retain the original as a record of Wittgenstein's actual words. These 'improvements' are often written in an indistinct and cramped hand such as Waismann regularly used for his own notes and drafts, but not when he had to produce a record or a legible copy.

They often serve to refine the style or to assimilate it to that of learned works; or they make it less personal, as when Wittgenstein speaks of 'my brother' (p. 158) and Waismann would substitute 'my friend.' I have omitted them all, my aim in this publication being to give without embellishment the text of what Waismann got from Wittgenstein.

In the present volume (as in the German) Waismann's use of square brackets, '[. . .],' as opposed to parentheses, '(. . .),' has been carefully followed. He used them to indicate remarks, amplifications, and objections of his own. Since they often interrupt the text, they were clearly written down at the time of transcription, whether this was during the actual conversation or subsequently. Even in the former case they were evidently not expressed in the conversation. His own contributions are indicated by Waismann in a quite different way: 'I ask Wi.' (here printed as 'Waismann asks') followed by the question, all without the use of brackets.

At certain points (here indicated in footnotes), Waismann leaves one or two pages free, evidently for the record of some conversation of which he has in fact left us only the title. There are also some blanks, without a heading, which cannot be explained by Waismann's practice of starting each day's notes on a fresh page. From this one can conclude, first, that Waismann sometimes intended to transcribe part of a conversation after the event, but, secondly, that he generally transcribed the conversations as they took place. Only this will explain the blank pages. At the time of the next day's conversation, if he transcribed that simultaneously, he might well leave a gap, hoping to fill it up. But if for that too he relied on memory, he would know when he came to transcribe it that there was no longer any hope of transcribing the earlier conversation and thus no need for a gap. It thus seems probable that the notebooks are for the most part a simultaneous record. Three considerations enhance this probability. First, Waismann's text is not designed to be read aloud; it needed the 'improvements' mentioned above. Second, Waismann on one occasion describes his report as a 'Rough Account' (p. 81), as if this were not always the case. Finally, there are a number of diagrams where Waismann breaks off short, as if the stenography had to catch up with the conversation.

For all that, the notebooks do not give us the direct expression of Wittgenstein's views, but only Waismann's report of them (if we disregard the extracts made from Wittgenstein's manuscripts, which are not printed in the present volume). Sometimes Waismann failed to follow a train of thought; sometimes he omitted what Wittgenstein thought particularly important. Besides, even what Wittgenstein originally said was not, like *PhB*, his considered views more or less prepared for publication. His impromptu utterances have, it is hoped, a certain interest, but as an account of his thought must be treated with caution and regarded, perhaps, as a kind of commentary on his now published works.

VII

The original German publication of the present material was authorized by Waismann's literary executors, Sir Isaiah Berlin, Mr. Stuart Hampshire, and the late Gilbert Ryle. Ryle acted for the others and was particularly helpful with suggestions and encouragement. Wittgenstein's own literary heirs, Professor Elizabeth Anscombe, Mr. Rush Rhees, and Professor G. H. von Wright, consented to the use of Wittgenstein's ideas and the quoting of his letters. Moreover, Mr. Rhees was extremely generous with his time and with his invaluable knowledge of Wittgenstein's papers. Only this enabled me to determine what material was preserved by Waismann alone and might hence be worthy of publication. Twelve years of progress in knowledge of the papers have not invalidated the judgement thus formed.

All these I willingly thank again, as also the following, who supplied me with material and permission to quote it: Dr. T. Stonborough; Major J. J. Stonborough; Mrs. Barbara v.d. Velde-Schlick; Mrs. Lettice Ramsey; Professor F. A. von Hayek; Dr. H. L. Mulder; Professor H. Hänsel; Dr. Josef Schächter; Mr. Shimshon Stein; Mr. J. Hevesi; and Professor H. Motz.

The shorthand was interpreted by the late Miss Mühlfeld (formerly Waismann's secretary), Dr. Hoffman of London, Dr. Karl Pichl of Vienna, and (in much the largest measure) Mr. Heinrich Matzinger of Zürich, with great skill and patience.

The British Academy bore most of the costs of transcription and the Leverhulme Foundation enabled me to stay in Vienna and collect some necessary information. I am extremely grateful to both bodies.

For relevant information on Wittgenstein's life and on the Vienna Circle, I am much indebted to Wittgenstein's lifelong friend Rudolf Koder, and to Bela von Juhos, Viktor Kraft, and Kurt Reidemeister, all four now dead; also to Drs. Heinrich Neider and Walter Hollitzscher of Vienna. My colleague at Queen's College, Oxford, Dr. P. M. Neumann, kindly helped me over some mathematical questions.

For the present English edition I have been fortunate enough to secure the collaboration of Dr. Joachim Schulte and the advice of Dr. Gordon Baker, two further Queen's men.

I

⟨PROOF IN MATHEMATICS⟩

In mathematics there are two different methods of proof.

1. An equation is reduced to another equation which is assumed to be correct, e.g.

$$16 \times 24 = 384$$

or

$$(a+b)^2 = a^2 + 2ab + b^2.$$

2. It is held that the axioms of arithmetic, e.g. the associative law, are proved by means of complete induction. This is not a proof, as can be seen from the fact that the equation to be proved occurs in the actual proof. Induction accomplishes only what it does accomplish and nothing more. E.g.

$$1:3 = 0,333$$
$$10$$
$$10$$
$$10$$

Everything else that is nonetheless *said*, e.g. that infinitely many threes follow, does not belong to mathematics proper but is a private matter. Most people think that complete induction is merely a way of reaching a certain proposition; that the method of induction is supplemented by a particular inference saying, *therefore* this proposition applies to all numbers. Here I ask the question, What about this 'therefore'? There is no 'therefore' here! Complete induction *is* the proposition to be proved, it is the whole thing, not just the path taken by the proof. This method is not a vehicle for getting anywhere. In mathematics there are not, first, propositions that have sense by themselves and, second, a method to determine the truth or falsity of propositions; there is only a method, and what is called a proposition is only an abbreviated name for the method.

Now axioms (e.g. the alphabetical rules of algebra, $a+b = b+a$, etc.) can be laid down, which, though they are, as such, arbitrary, are of course constructed in accordance with complete induction. I can operate by means of these basic rules by reducing every equation to them. But the one thing these rules cannot express is the result of complete induction. This result is subsequently manifested in the applicability of the rules to concrete numbers, but the nature of complete induction is not expressed in the form of a proposition or in the form of an axiomatic system; it is mathematically inexpressible. Complete induction shows itself in the structure of equations. Axioms are laid down to fit mathematical induction as closely as possible, but they do not express mathematical induction. Hence axioms are not provable, but have the logical value of fixed propositions.

WHAT DOES LOOKING FOR SOMETHING MEAN IN MATHEMATICS?[1]

It is not possible to look for a sixth sense. It is not possible to look for something absolutely at random. I can look for an object in space, e.g. in my room. But what can it mean to look for anything in mathematics? There are gaps in space. When I have looked through one room, I

1] What we find in books on mathematics is not a *description of something* but the thing itself. We *make* mathematics. Just as one speaks of 'writing history' and 'making history,' mathematics can in a certain sense only be made.

Mathematics is its own application. This is tremendously important. A lot follows from it. When I say '3 plums + 4 plums = 7 plums,' '3 men + 4 men = 7 men,' etc., I do not apply numbers to different objects; it is always the same application that I have before my eyes. Numbers are not represented by proxies; numbers *are there*.

can go on to the next one. In mathematics *per contra* there are no gaps. A mathematical system, e.g. the system of ordinary multiplication, is completely closed. I can look for something only *within* a given system, not *for* the system. What does 242×897 yield? This is a question within a system. There are indefinitely many such questions and answers. I can look for a certain answer only because there is a method of finding it. Algebra (calculation with letters) is also such a closed system, and the same applies to trigonometry as it is taught at school. I can ask, e.g., Is $\sin^2 x = \tan^2 x$? But I cannot ask, Is

$$\sin x = x - \frac{x^3}{3!} + \frac{x^5}{5!} - + \ldots?$$

This is not for the reason that elementary trigonometry is somehow incomplete, that it has, as it were, gaps that need to be filled up, as though analysis were the completion needed. No, this is not how things are. Rather, we have in fact moved on to a new system that does not contain the old one but contains a part with exactly the same

Only objects are represented by proxies.

The correctness of an arithmetical proposition is never expressed by a proposition's being a tautology. In the Russellian way of expressing it, the proposition $3 + 4 = 7$ for example can be represented in the following manner:

$$(E3x)\varphi x.(E4x)\psi x. \sim (\exists x)\varphi x.\psi x: \supset: (E7x).\varphi x\psi x.$$

Now one might think that the proof of this equation consisted in this: that the proposition written down was a tautology. But in order to be able to write down this proposition, I have to *know* that $3 + 4 = 7$. The whole tautology is an application and not a proof of arithmetic. Arithmetic is used in constructing this proposition. The fact that a tautology is the result is in itself inessential. For I can apply an arithmetical equation both to propositions with sense and to tautologies.

structure as the old system. Simple examples are the natural numbers and the integers. After all, the natural numbers are not identical with the positive integers, as though one could speak of plus two soldiers in the same way that one speaks of two soldiers; no, we are here confronted with something entirely new. It is similar when we take the step from elementary trigonometric functions to analytic functions defined through progressions. In this case we make the discovery that some of these functions have the same properties as the functions $\sin x$, etc. well-known to us from trigonometry, and now we associate these structures with our elementary functions. It must be borne in mind, however, that it is impossible to move from one system to the other by merely extending the former; that a question which has sense in the second system need not therefore have sense in the first system. The new system is not a completion of the old one. The old system has no gaps. What one has not yet got, one has not got at all.

I cannot reach the same point both systematically and unsystematically.

Of a given proposition I cannot declare that it belongs to a certain system.

In the language of the first system I cannot say what is solvable and what is not solvable.

This question does not exist at all.

Example: Trisection of an Angle

Is it possible to look for this in elementary geometry? The impossibility of the construction cannot be understood in terms of the system of elementary geometry, but only in terms of the system of algebraic numbers and equations onto which elementary geometry is projected. This system is much more comprehensive and permits an algebraic characterization of the figures that can be constructed by means of ruler and compasses. In this system the question of trisection has a clear sense. But concurrently with the question the method of answering it is also given. But does the question have a clear sense at all in elementary geometry? At first blush one tends to think, Yes. For the many people who had the ambition to solve this problem must have had something in mind.

Simile: Unravelling a Knot

What if it is not a knot at all but only looks like one? In that case it is not even possible to try to untie it. Certainly one is doing something that has a certain similarity with the unravelling of a knot, but in a strict sense it is in fact impossible to look for a way of untying it. An attempt to untie it would be a *logical* impossibility.

It is equally impossible to look for a solution to the problem of trisecting an angle. The question does not exist in this system. What I do is the following, *I extend my system.*

Weyl[1] puts the problem of decidability in the following way. Can every *relevant* question be decided by means of logical inference? The problem must not be put in this way. Everything depends on the word 'relevant'. For Weyl, a statement is relevant when it is constructed from certain basic formulae with the help of seven principles of combination (among which are 'all' and 'there is').[2] This is where the mistake lies. A statement is relevant if it belongs to a *certain system.*

It is in this sense that it has been maintained that every relevant question is decidable.

What is not visibly relevant, is not relevant at all.

1 H. Weyl, *Philosophy of Mathematics and Natural Science*, Princeton, 1949, p. 24.
2 ibid., p. 5.

Einstein[3] says that geometry is concerned with possible positions of rigid bodies. If I actually describe the positions of rigid bodies by means of language, then it is only the *syntax* of this language that can correspond to *possible* positions.

[There is hence no problem in the fact that we command the entire manifold of space by means of a few axioms (that space is a 'definite manifold' (Husserl)[4]), for it is only the syntax of a language that we lay down.]

CONSISTENCY I[5]

Sunday, 22 December 1929 (at Schlick's house)

'ALL' I

I shall first speak of the ordinary 'all,' e. g. 'All men in this room are wearing trousers.' How do I know this? The sentence means 'Professor Schlick is wearing trousers, Waismann is wearing trousers, Wittgenstein is wearing trousers, and no-one else is present.' Every complete enumeration must end with the words 'and nothing else'. What does this mean? There is a conception here according to which one says: 'Mr. Carnap is not in this room, Mr. . . . , etc.' And the proposition one might expect here, namely 'these are all things,' this proposition does not exist.

---

3 *Geometrie und Erfahrung*, Berlin, 1921, pp. 6–7; *Über die spezielle und die allgemeine Relativitätstheorie*, Brunswick, 1917, p. 2 (E.T. *The Theory of Relativity*, London, 1920, p. 3).

4 "Ideen zu einer reinen Phänomenologie" §72, *Jahrbuch für Philosophie und phänomenologische Forschung*, I, 1913, p. 133 (E.T. *Ideas* London and New York, 1931, §72).

5 There are no notes of this part of Wittgenstein's conversation, but 2$\frac{1}{3}$ pages of the notebook are left blank, see Editor's Preface, p. 29.

Let us suppose I said 'I see a square and in it a circle.' It is clear that this is not an enumeration but something entirely different. I think that here there is a kind of proposition of which I used to have no idea and which corresponds roughly to what I want to call an incomplete picture. I shall explain soon what I mean by this. The point is that in all such cases there is what I now want to call an elementary proposition that is an incomplete picture. Imagine the following case. I have seen two substances of the same colour. Then one might think this meant 'Both were green, or both were blue, or . . .' It is clear to all of us that it cannot mean that. After all, we cannot produce such an enumeration. Whereas the following is the case, 'We saw a substance of the colour x and another one of the colour x.' The point is that the Russellian analysis is not correct, and the difference is this:

$$(\exists x).\varphi x$$

—this symbol permits a twofold negation, namely an outer and an inner one. Our case does not have the character of an apparent variable but that of a real variable. What I am driving at is that the Russellian analysis, which I used to believe to be correct, does not apply in this case. 'There is no man in this room' does not mean 'Professor Schlick is not in this room, nor is Mr. Carnap, nor is . . .' Now I believe that when I realize that nobody is in this room, the process of coming to know this is the same as when I realize that there is no circle in a certain square. 'There *is* a circle in the square.' This does not have the sense of 'Either this circle is in the square, or this circle . . . or . . .' There is no question of there being an enumeration here. It is rather what I call an incomplete picture.

I can describe a state of affairs which consists in there being a circle of a specific size at a specific point of the square. This is a complete picture. For to what follows it does not matter what description I choose, whether I use co-ordinates for example; what matters is only this, that the form of description chosen has the right multiplicity. Thus when numbers occur in the sentence and indicate where the circle is and how large it is, it may happen that I replace the numbers by variables or perhaps only by intervals, e.g. [6–7, 8–9], and then I shall get an incomplete picture. Imagine a portrait in which I have left out the mouth, then this can mean two things; first, the mouth is white like the blank paper; second, the picture is always correct, whatever the mouth is like.

The incompleteness of a picture consists in the occurrence of variables in a proposition. And the question is now, What is the correct way of expressing this proposition? I mean, the right expression does not convey '$(\exists x).\varphi x$', but 'φx'. The difference between these two is the following. The symbol '$(\exists x).\varphi x$' allows a twofold negation, the symbol 'φx' does not. This suffices to show that the symbol '$(\exists x).\varphi x$' does not have the right multiplicity. Further, what will emerge if I carry out the twofold negation?

$$(\exists x).\sim\varphi x = (x).\varphi x$$

This means, 'The two substances agree in all their colours', 'They have all their colours in common'. This is nonsense. Thus the proposition '$(\exists x).\varphi x$' must also be nonsense.

'φx' is hence a proper proposition, not merely preparatory for a proposition. Now I believe that certain data may be left out of an elementary proposition. A proposition is then an incomplete portrait of a state of affairs.

Now, when I have completed a description, does this mean that I have added more incomplete propositions to an incomplete proposition? Is a complete description simply a conjunction of incomplete ones? Suppose I draw the following picture:

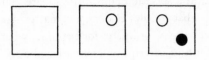

Each proposition is *one* symbol. Such a symbol is not composed of a symbol for a square and a symbol for a circle. If I leave out one symbol, I still get a picture—contrary to the ordinary conception of things according to which I get only a preliminary to a proposition by omitting a part of a proposition.

The proposition 'There is a black circle in the square' does not contain anything but the words 'square,' 'black,' 'circle,' 'in'. That is all. The proposition cannot say more than what it contains, and the fact that we understand it shows that even it its incomplete form it is a proposition.

An incomplete picture must show that it is *incomplete*.[1] It must be possible to gather from a proposition that it is only an incomplete portrait of a state of affairs. Such a proposition must show that everything around it remains open to some extent. It must show its openness. *One* elementary proposition describes all the colours in space.

Perhaps the way things are is that all incomplete descriptions—all incomplete propositions with gaps—link together to form a complete elementary proposition.

Is a complete proposition a conjunction of incomplete propositions?

Objects

This is connected with what conception one has of objects.

When Frege and Russell spoke of objects they always had in mind things that are, in language, represented by nouns, that is, say, bodies like chairs and tables. The whole conception of objects is hence very closely connected with the subject-predicate form of propositions. It is clear that where there is no subject-predicate form it is also impossible to speak of objects in this sense. Now I can describe this room in an entirely different way, e.g. by describing the surface of the room analytically by means of an equation and stating the distribution of colours on this surface. In the case of this form of

---

1] If I describe everything in this room completely, then this is still not a complete picture. For I can ask, What is outside this room? But then I have to be able to see from the proposition concerned that it does not describe everything. The proposition must show its openness.

description, single 'objects', chairs, books, tables, and their spatial positions are not mentioned any more. Here we have no relation, all that does not exist.

Now I think that there is one principle governing the whole domain of elementary propositions, and this principle states that one cannot foresee the form of elementary propositions. It is just ridiculous to think that we could make do with the ordinary structure of our everyday language, with subject-predicate, with dual relations, and so forth. Real numbers or something similar to real numbers can appear in elementary propositions, and this fact alone proves how completely different elementary propositions can be from all other propositions. And what else may appear in them we cannot possibly foresee today. Only when we analyse phenomena logically shall we know what form elementary propositions have. Here is an area where there is no hypothesis. The logical structure of elementary propositions need not have the slightest similarity with the logical structure of propositions.

Just think of the equations of physics—how tremendously complex their structure is. Elementary propositions, too, will have this degree of complexity.

Whatever colour I see, I can represent each of them by mentioning the four elementary colours red, yellow, blue, green, and adding how this particular colour is to be generated from the elementary colours.

Discussion about the form of the colour-body. The elementary colours very pointed:[6]

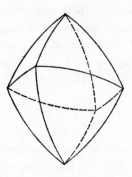

6 The reason for this is explained in *PR*, pp. 278ff.

Sign for a colour:

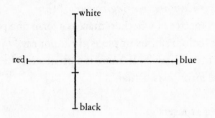

Every statement about colours can be represented by means of such symbols. If we say that four elementary colours would suffice, I call such symbols of equal status *elements of representation*. These elements of representation are the 'objects'.

The following question has now no sense: Are objects something thing-like, something that stands in subject-position, or something property-like,[7] or are they relations, and so forth? It is simply where we have elements of representation of equal status that we speak of objects.

Now you see immediately that the question about the number of objects is without sense. In particular, there cannot be infinitely many objects. 'There are infinitely many chairs' = 'There are infinitely many possibilities for chairs in space.' Whereas it cannot mean this any more if an object is an element of representation.

Logical multiplicity is not depicted by subject and predicate or by relations, but e.g. by physical equations. It is clear that here there is no question of individual objects any more.

7 The shorthand MS. seems to say 'etwas Eigenschaft hat.' 'Eigenschafthaft' ('property-like') occurs in the TS. of *Thesen* (cf. infra, p. 251).

43

1. '*All the men in this room are wearing trousers*' [1]
Here it is first of all a matter of whether 'man' is a form or a predicate.
If 'man' is a form, as 'colour' for example is, I cannot say '*a* is a man',
but the syntax of '*a*' must show it. If 'man' is a predicate, then there is
a proposition of the form '*a* is a man'.

'φx' = '*x* is a man'

'ψx' = '*x* is wearing trousers'

'All men are wearing trousers' = '$(x){:}\varphi x \,.\, \supset .\, \psi x$'

$\qquad\qquad\qquad\qquad\qquad$ or '$(x).\varphi x$'

'All the men in this room'—this must be exactly similar to a circle in a
square. It means that Prof. Schlick is wearing trousers, Waismann, is
wearing trousers, Wittgenstein is wearing trousers. And the proposition supposed to follow now, namely 'Apart from those there is no
one in this room', this proposition is simply to read '$\sim fx$'.

[Assume that 'man' is a form.

$$'\varphi x' = \text{'}x \text{ is in the room'}$$
$$'\varphi x' = \text{'There is someone in the room'}$$
$$'\sim\varphi x' = \text{'There is no one in the room'}$$
$$'(\exists x).\varphi x' = \text{'}\varphi a v \varphi b v \varphi c v \ldots\text{'}$$
$$'\sim(\exists x).\varphi x' = \text{'There is no one who is in the room'}$$
$$'(\exists x).\sim\varphi x' = \text{'There is someone who is not in the room'}$$
$$'\sim(\exists x).\sim\varphi x' = \text{'Everyone is in the room'}$$

Now you may argue again that 'There is someone in the room'
permits only one negation. But '$(\exists x).\varphi x$' permits a twofold negation. Consequently the sense of the proposition 'There is someone in
the room' is not correctly represented by the Russellian symbol.

'All the men in this room are wearing trousers'
$$= \varphi a.\psi a.\varphi b.\psi b.\varphi c.\psi c.\sim\varphi x$$
$$x \neq a, \; x \neq b, \; x \neq c$$

Here the question would be whether '$(\exists x).\varphi x$' is admissible; in what

---

1] Russell: 'I met a man' ('$(\exists x).fx$') is an indefinite statement.

respects does it differ from 'φx'? Or is only 'φx' admissible and '$(\exists x).\varphi x$' not? For which propositional function can the '$(\exists x)$' operator be used and for which not?]

2. *Statements about all colours*

Since there are only four elements of representation, *red, blue, yellow, green*, every such statement can be reduced to a finite conjunction:

red . . . and blue . . . and yellow . . . and green ⟨. . .⟩

In this case 'all' is therefore a logical product, but a *finite* logical product.

3. *'All numbers'*

Here we know that this proposition has been misunderstood and that mathematical induction has nothing to do with the totality of numbers.

SOLIPSISM

I used to believe that there was the everyday language that we all usually spoke and a primary language that expressed what we really knew, namely phenomena.[8] I also spoke of a first system and a second system. Now I wish to explain why I do not adhere to that conception any more.

I think that essentially we have only one language, and that is our everyday language. We need not invent a new language or construct a new symbolism, but our everyday language already is *the* language, provided we rid it of the obscurities that lie hidden in it.

8 In *PR* similar ideas are touched on several times, sometimes as something which has been superseded (e.g. pp. 51 and 84), sometimes with different degrees of agreement (pp. 58, 88, 100, 158, 168, and 267). Here Wittgenstein no doubt refers to earlier manuscript volumes in which some of the *PR* may have occurred for the first time.

Our language is completely in order, as long as we are clear about what it symbolizes. Languages other than the ordinary ones are also valuable in so far as they show us what they have in common. For certain purposes, e.g. for representing inferential relations, an artificial symbolism is very useful. Indeed, in the construction of symbolic logic Frege, Peano, and Russell paid attention solely to its application to mathematics and did not think of the representation of real states of affairs.

These logicians thought, 'If everything else fails, if these logical forms are not applicable to reality, we still have mathematics.' Nowadays we realize that it will not do as regards mathematics either, that no logical propositions occur there.

There is nothing wrong with a symbol like 'φx,' if it is a matter of explaining simple logical relations. This symbol is taken from the case where 'φ' signifies a predicate and 'x' a variable noun. But as soon as you start to examine real states of affairs, you realize that this symbolism is at a great disadvantage compared with our real language. It is of course absolutely false to speak of *one* subject-predicate form. In reality there is not *one*, but very many. For if there were only one, then all nouns and all adjectives would have to be intersubstitutable. For all intersubstitutable words belong to one class.[1] But even ordinary language shows that this is not the case. On the face of it I may say 'This chair is brown' and 'The surface of this chair is brown'. But if I replace 'brown' by 'heavy', I can utter only the first proposition and not the second. This proves that the word 'brown', too, had two different meanings.

At first blush 'right' looks like other adjectives, e.g. 'sweet'. 'Right-left' corresponds to 'sweet-bitter'.

1] Language is already perfectly ordered. The difficulty consists only in rendering syntax simple and perspicuous.

I can say 'farther right', just as I can say 'sweeter'.

But I can only say '. . . is to the right of . . .' and not '. . . is to the sweet of . . .'. Their syntax is thus really different. [1]

If I consider, not only one proposition in which a certain word occurs, but all possible propositions, then they specify its syntax completely, much more completely than the symbol 'φx'.

Now it is remarkable that there is something in our language that I should like to compare to a *wheel turning idly* in a machine. I shall presently explain what I mean by that.

The Sense of a Proposition is its Verification

If I say, for example, 'Up there on the cupboard there is a book', how do I set about verifying it? Is it sufficient if I glance at it, or if I look at it from different sides, or if I take it into my hands, touch it, open it, turn over its leaves, and so forth? There are two conceptions here. One of them says that however I set about it, I shall never be able to verify the proposition completely. A proposition always keeps a back-door open, as it were. Whatever we do, we are never sure that we were not mistaken.

The other conception, the one I want to hold, says, 'No, if I can never verify the sense of a proposition completely, then I cannot have meant anything by the proposition either. Then the proposition signifies nothing whatsoever.'

In order to determine the sense of a proposition, I should have to know a very specific procedure for when to count the proposition as verified. In this respect everyday language oscillates very much, much more so than scientific language. There is a certain latitude here, and this means simply that the symbols of our everyday language are not unambiguously defined.

1] Sweet does not contain a number. I can say that this tea is sweeter than the other one. But in making this statement I have no numbers in mind.

[Words oscillate between different meanings and for this reason it is not certain when a proposition is completely verified. If we lay down the meaning once and for all, we also obtain a reliable criterion for the truth of a statement.]

Sometimes verification is very difficult, for example 'Seitz has been elected mayor.'[9] How should I set about verifying this proposition? Is the correct method to go and make inquiries about it? Or to ask the people who were present? But one was watching from the front and the other one from behind. Or should I read about it in the newspapers?

What appears strangest to a philosopher considering our language is the difference between *being and appearance*.

Wheels Turning Idly

If I turn away, the stove is gone. (Things do not exist during the intervals between perceptions.) If 'existence' is taken in the empirical (not in the metaphysical) sense, this statement is a wheel turning idly. Our language is in order, once we have understood its syntax and recognized the wheels that turn idly.

'I can *merely* remember.' As if there were some other way and memory not the *only* source from which we draw.

Memories have been called pictures.[10] A picture can be compared with its original, but a memory cannot. Experiences of the past are after all not like objects in the next room; although I do not see them now, I can go there. But can I go into the past?

9 Karl Seitz was the Socialist mayor of Vienna from 1925 until 1934.
10 Cf. *PR* pp. 81ff., and infra, p. 53.

What is subject to my will, what are the parts of my body, these are matters of experience. It is e.g. a matter of experience that I have never had two bodies. Now, is it also a matter of experience that I cannot feel your pain? No!

'I cannot feel pain in your tooth.'

'I cannot feel your toothache.'

The first proposition has a sense. It expresses empirical knowledge. In reply to the question 'Where does it hurt?' I would point to your tooth. When your tooth is touched I wince. In short, it is *my* pain and would be my pain even if you too showed symptoms of pain at this point, that is, if when this tooth was pressed you winced just as I do.

The second proposition is sheer nonsense. Such a proposition is prohibited by syntax.

The word 'I' belongs to those words that can be eliminated from language. Now it is very important if there are several languages; in that case it is possible to see what all these languages have in common and that common element is what depicts.[11]

Now it is possible to construct many different languages, each of which has a different man as its centre. Imagine for instance you were a despot in the Orient. All men were compelled to speak the language whose centre you are.[12] If I spoke this language, I should say, 'Wittgenstein has toothache. But Waismann is behaving as Wittgenstein does when he has toothache.' In the language whose centre you are it would be expressed just the other way round, 'Waismann has toothache, Wittgenstein is behaving like Waismann when he has toothache.'

All these languages can be translated into one another. Only what they have in common mirrors anything.

Now it is noteworthy that *one* of these languages has a distinctive

11 Cf. *TLP* 5.512.
12 Cf. *PR* pp. 88f.

status, namely that one in which I can as it were say that I feel *real* pain.

If I am 'A' [1], then I can, to be sure, say 'B is behaving as A does when he feels pain,' but also 'A is behaving as B does when he feels pain.' One of these languages has a distinctive status, namely the language whose centre I am. The distinctiveness of this language lies in its application. It is not expressed.

⟨LANGUAGE AND WORLD⟩

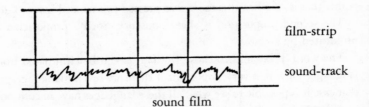

sound film

I want to use an old simile, 'magic lantern'.
It is not the *sound-track* that accompanies the film, but the *music*.
The sound-track accompanies the film-strip.
The music accompanies the film.

film-strip	sound-track	music	film
?	?	language	world

Language accompanies the world.[13]

1] If A has toothache, he can say, 'Now this tooth is hurting', and this is where verification comes to an end. But B would have to say, 'A has toothache,' and this proposition is not the end of a verification. This is the point where the particular status of different languages comes clearly to light.

13 $2^2/_3$ pages are left blank after this remark; cf. editor's Preface, p. 29.

'ALL' II

WAISMANN ASKS: How is the proposition 'All the men in this room are wearing trousers' to be expressed? Perhaps thus:

$$fa.fb.fc. \sim fx.(x \neq a, \neq b, \neq c)$$

WITTGENSTEIN: No.
Let us take this case, 'All the circles in this square have a cross.'

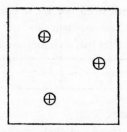

The difficulty of formulating this proposition is connected with naming. Proper names are a confounded business. For example, suppose I wanted to call this chair Jacob. What did I really give the name to? The shape or the chair? If there were several thousand chairs that were absolutely alike, how should I know which one of them was Jacob? If it was the *shape* of the chair that I called Jacob, then I cannot distinguish them. If I meant what can be singled out by pointing, then there is again a difficulty. If two chairs that looked absolutely alike moved towards each other, penetrated each other, and then separated again—how could I know, then, which one of them was Jacob? The possibility of giving names to things presupposes very complicated experiences. (Impenetrability!)

Let us rather move to our circles! There we avoid the difficulty with proper names. We describe their outlines, i.e. *colour-boundaries within the visual field*. Such a description is always complete, and this is why when I say:

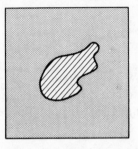

it is *a complete picture* of a state of affairs. It is not possible to add anything later on and continue with 'and'. This space is filled. I can only change the description but not add anything to it. If I describe this room and specify where the chairs and the table and all the other things are, I cannot say after half an hour, 'And then there is also this and that.'

1. *The circle in the square:*
Specification of the square
Specification of the centre of the circle $\left.\rule{0pt}{32pt}\right\}$ complete picture
Specification of the radius of the circle

    Now we want to get a more general picture of this state of affairs.

2. *A circle in the square*: Specification of the square

$$(x-x_0)^2+(y-y_0)^2 = r^2$$
$$0 < x_0 < a$$
$$0 < y_0 < a$$
$$r < \min(\langle x_0, y_0, \rangle$$
$$a-x_0, a-y_0)$$

$\left.\rule{0pt}{60pt}\right\}$ incomplete picture

3. *Three circles in the square:* Same method. Specification of three circles by means of variables.

4. *All the circles in the square:* From such a propositional form I can move to another one. The next proposition does not develop out of the preceding one by means of 'and' but ⟨by means of⟩ op⟨erations⟩ on the form of the proposition. Now I can consider this series of propositions, 1 circle in the square, 2 circles in the square, 3 circles in the

square, . . . *n* circles in the square. *Complete induction* for this series of propositions.

This 'all' is thus the '*all*' of arithmetic, that is, complete induction. 'All the circles in the square are black.' The same.

TIME

The source of all the difficulties of physics is that statements of physics and rules of grammar get mixed up. 'Time' has two different meanings,

a) the time of memory,

b) the time of physics.

Where there are different verifications there are also different meanings. If I can verify a temporal specification—e.g. such and such was earlier than so and so—only by means of memory, 'time' must have a different meaning from the case where I can verify such a specification by other means, e.g. by reading a document, or by asking someone, and so forth. (It is the same with 'images'. Usually an image is called the 'picture' of the object concerned, as if there were another way besides the image to reach the object. But an image has one meaning if I conceive of it as a picture of an object that can also be verified in another way and a different meaning if I consider an object as a logical construction out of images.[14])

Memory as a *source* and memories that can be verified in a different way must equally be kept apart.

We say, 'I have only a *faint* memory.' What does '*only*' mean here? After all, can I compare a memory with its object, as I can compare a

14 Cf. *PR* pp. 81f., and p. 48 above.

photograph with the original? Is there a different way besides memory to reach the state of affairs in question?

Analogy with film: single pictures of different sharpness. We can arrange them according to sharpness. I may *call* the degree to which a picture has grown faint 'time'.

Is time, then, external or internal?

External—Internal

The whole question of external and internal is tremendously confused. This is because I can describe a dissimilar state of affairs in a different way.

A relation that says 'how?' is external. It is expressed by a proposition.

'Internal'—we have two propositions between which a formal relation holds.

Now it seems as if I could express similar states of affairs at one time by means of one proposition and at another time by means of two between which an internal relation holds.

E.g.

$$a \biggl| \quad \biggr| b$$

I can say that *a* is 2m long and that *b* is 1.5m long. Then it makes itself manifest that *a* is longer than *b*.

What I cannot say is that $2 > 1.5$. That is internal.

But I can also say that *a* is 0.5m longer than *b*.

There I obviously have an external relation; for one can just as well imagine that line *a* was shorter than *b*. Yet more clearly expressed, it is of course unthinkable that, of these two definite lines, one rather than the other is longer or shorter than the other. But if I say for example that the line on the left is longer than the one on the right, the relation 'longer than' does tell me something—it is external. This is obviously connected with the fact that now we have only an incomplete picture of the situation. If we describe the state of affairs completely, the external relation disappears. But we must not believe that there is then any relation left. Apart from the internal relation between forms that always obtains, no relation need occur in the description, and this shows that in fact *relational form* is nothing essential; it does not depict anything.

To be sure, I can say that this suit is darker than the other one. But I cannot say that one colour is darker than the other one. For this is of the essence of a colour; without it, after all, a colour cannot be thought.

It is always the same thing, at this or that point of space there is a darker colour than at another point. I have an external relation as soon as I bring in space; but between pure qualities of colour only internal relations can obtain. After all, I have no other means of characterizing colours than by means of their quality.

Application to time. Caesar before Augustus—external. The historical fact can be imagined differently.

But if I can verify what is earlier only by means of memory, then the relation 'earlier than' is internal.

VISUAL SPACE

It is clear to all of us that visual space is connected with Euclidean space. But what does this connection consist in? Visual space is not Euclidean space. They only correspond to each other. Euclidean space is a correlate of visual space. What kind of correspondence is this?[1]

1] Here there occurs a peculiar *indeterminacy-factor* which is absent from Euclidean geometry. The geometry of visual space is compounded of Euclidean geometry, i.e. of a certain syntax, plus the syntax of that indeterminacy-factor.

A striking phenomenon: In visual space I see only boundaries, namely the boundaries between different colours. But then I also see something entirely different, for instance a star and its colour. The star is not extended, it does not have boundaries. It is not possible to ask, 'Is it round or square?' It has no outline. This indicates perhaps that here we are stepping outside Euclidean geometry.

A line is the boundary between two surfaces, and a point is the intersection of two lines.

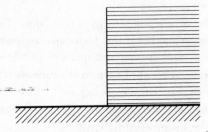

This corner is a point. A star is a point in an entirely different sense.

As what do we see the point of intersection of two pencil-drawn straight lines? + As a rectangle, say? We know that it is a rectangle; but we do not see that. What we see is without an outline.

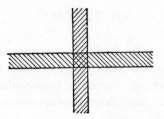

Hjelmslev[15] concluded experiments along these lines, but he did not understand the real significance of the matter. Above all he is not quite clear about where the problem really lies; in the properties of the wooden bodies we use as rulers for drawing, etc., or in the properties

---

15 Cf. J. Hjelmslev's articles in *Abhandlungen aus dem math. Sem. d. Univ. Hamburg*, 2, 1923, pp. 1–36, especially p. 28, and in *Acta Mathematica* 40, 1916, pp. 35–66.

of visual space?[1] The former alternative would be inessential. It would merely be an uninteresting description of the properties of a piece of wood. Obviously something else is meant by our questions, namely, however precise I make the drawing, a circle and its tangent must *appear* to me to have a stretch in common.

Even if in reality they have nothing in common and the straight line is only very *near* the circle, from a distance we get the impression that they coincide for a stretch. The essential thing is this phenomenon of the visual field rather than the properties of drawing instruments.

The point is to reproduce what our language describes by means of the word *'imprecise'*. How would this word have to be rendered in a symbolism and what would its syntactical rules be?

It was F. Klein[16] who brought in the notion of a threshold.[2] But this way of expressing the matter is still not correct. When we say for

1] Hjelmslev has the idea of starting from a *rough geometry*. But precisely this is an error; a rough geometry would still be a geometry, just as much as a precise one. (They have the same multiplicity.) Hjelmslev considers a patch for example rather than a point. But an extended patch has an outline, while a point has none.
2] We come across this threshold for instance when it is said that we can distinguish a regular quadrangle from a regular pentagon, but not a regular 200-sided polygon from a regular 201-sided polygon. When scanning the 4-, 5-, 6-. . .-sided polygons there must accordingly be a point somewhere at which they start shading off into one another. We can also say that we can no longer distinguish the polygons within and outside a circle from the circle itself.

16 *Elementarmathematik von einem höheren Standpunkte*, Vol. III, 3rd edition, Berlin, 1928, pp. 2ff.

example, 'All the figures inside a certain narrow circular band are seen as circles', is this expressed by specifying the lower and the upper

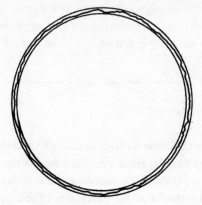

limit of the band, i.e. by specifying the two circles themselves? No! Because this specification does not have the multiplicity of the phenomenon that we are to describe. Because I have to distinguish the two limiting circles themselves.

Imagine the following experiment. We are to ascertain whether two straight lines are parallel. For this purpose a straight line is moved into different positions, and after having made a finite number of experiments we can determine the last of the positions that we call parallel and the first of the positions that we do not call parallel any more. These two positions are different from each other. It is crucial that nothing can change that, however long we continue with the experiment.

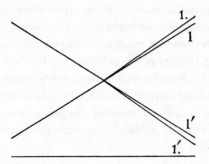

The greater the number of experiments, the smaller the difference between the two positions will be, but it will never be equal to zero. Now there are two possible interpretations here:

a) We see all straight lines within 11′ as parallels and all straight lines outside 11′ as non-parallels.[1]

1] *Addendum, 30 December 1929*

I have to correct my account. The essential thing is that we use two languages, a language of visual space and a language of Euclidean space, giving the language of Euclidean space priority. Language indicates this difference by using 'being' and 'appearing'. Thus we say of two stretches in visual space that they *appear* but *are* not equal. Or of a short arc of a circle that it *appears* straight, although it *is* curved. And so on.

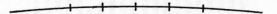

In this the non-Euclidean structure of visual space makes itself manifest. Now the truth about the experiment with parallels is this:

We see a||a′, b||b′ . . . n||n′. From this we can conclude only this one thing: that the word 'parallel' with respect to the visual field means something different (has a different syntax) from what it means with respect to Euclidean space. Similarly with the words 'equal', 'straight', 'curved', 'circle', 'tangent', and so forth. The fact that in the visual field circle and tangent always have a stretch in common just means that the visual circle and tangent have a different syntax from that of the analogous figures in Euclidean space. We need a method of projection for representing in the language of Euclidean geometry this state of affairs in the visual field, and the method of projection consists in our use of the words 'it appears'.

In Euclidean space we thus need a related (but not an identical!)

b) We see all the straight lines outside 1.1.' as non-parallels and all the straight lines within 1.1.' as parallels.[17]

---

relation to render the 'equality' relation of visual space, e.g. the following:

$$a \equiv b \text{ if } b = a + \varepsilon, \ |\varepsilon| < \frac{a}{100}$$

'$a \equiv b$, $b \equiv c \rightarrow a \equiv c$' may be true or not.

For this reason the geometry of visual space has a different multiplicity from the geometry of Euclidean space. We must not replace 'equal' by 'equal', 'parallel' by 'parallel', 'straight' by 'straight'.

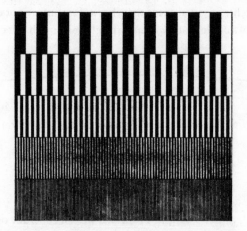

From a certain point on *grey*. Does this demonstrate that the visual field is not infinitely divisible? Or does it not demonstrate that? It does not demonstrate it. It only means that in visual space the phenomenon *grey* corresponds to what is called 'divided' in the geometry of Euclidean space. It may be that a division in visual space corresponds to a division in Euclidean space. But it may also be entirely different. What I do in Euclidean space is in itself of no consequence.

17 In the diagram '1.' evidently means 'first' and '1' 'last'.

One of these two interpretations must be possible. For otherwise the class of parallels and the class of non-parallels would not determine a limit, and that would run counter to the nature of continuity (Dedekindian cut).[18] It is also impossible to say that there are three classes: parallels, non-parallels, and doubtful cases. For we do not see straight lines of the third class.

In any case it is clear that the phenomenon cannot be described by means of specifying two such limits as 1. and 1, but only by means of arbitrarily stipulating one limit as the limit. And this is in effect the crucial point concerning all these things: if the description is to have the right multiplicity for the phenomenon, only *one limit* may occur in it.

Many unsolved questions are implicit in the idea of the visual field. How are we to understand, for example, the fact that the visual field comes to an end? Obviously the visual field does not have limits. There is no point where it borders on other things. Its limits cannot be seen. Thus it is without limits, finite, yet not a sphere. Is it possible e.g. to see anything entering the visual field? No! What could a symbolism describing that look like?

GEOMETRY AS SYNTAX II

The real relation between precise geometry and approximative geometry[19] can be expressed thus. Suppose that on measurement we found different values for the ratio of radius to circumference—should we then say that we had enclosed the number π in different intervals?

---

18 Dedekind proves the following. 'If the system R of all real numbers is divided into two classes A_1 and A_2 of such a kind that any number a_1 of class A_1 is smaller than any number a_2 of class A_2, then there is one and only one number a by means of which that division has been generated.' (*Stetigkeit und irrationale Zahlen*, Brunswick, 1912, p. 18 (E.T. *Essays on Number*, Chicago and London, 1901, p. 20).) Wittgenstein claims in an analogous fashion that there is only *one* line at each end of the fan of parallel lines which separates the parallel ones from the non-parallel ones. That must certainly be true, *if* Dedekind's condition applies here.

19 Expressions used by F. Klein, op. cit.

[Should we assume that we had measured π in the same sense in which a physical constant is measured?] Obviously not. For if all those intervals happened to be too large, we should not suppose that the value of π was greater, but should say that we had made a mistake. But then the real significance of the number π is clear. No measurement can tell us the value of π or between what values it is to be found, the number π is rather the *standard* by which we judge the quality of a measurement.[1] The standard is given to us before we start measuring; this is why I cannot alter the measurement. Thus when we say, π has such and such a value, e.g. $\pi = 3.14159265...$, this cannot mean that we want to say anything about the actual measurements, but only that we are stipulating when a measurement procedure is to be counted as correct and when not. Thus the axioms of geometry have the character of stipulations concerning the language in which we want to describe spatial objects. They are rules of syntax. The rules of syntax are not about anything; they are laid down by us.

We can stipulate only something that we ourselves do.

We can postulate only rules according to which we propose to speak. We cannot postulate states of affairs.

At first blush it seems as though the axioms of geometry did tell us something. Take, for example, the proposition that the sum of the angles of a triangle is 180°; does it not tell us something? Can it not be true or false? How can mere syntax teach us anything of this kind? Suppose a measurement had yielded 190°. What should we say? 'We have made a mistake.' Thus the only value attaching to the proposition that the sum of the angles of a triangle is 180° is this, that it distinguishes erroneous from non-erroneous methods of measuring angles. It can never tell us anything about a state of affairs. And this

---

1] We cannot measure the number π, for it is the number π *by* which we measure the precision of our observations.

shows yet again that in geometry we are never dealing with reality but only with spatial possibilities.

Discoveries about space are discoveries about what there is in space.

In mathematics it is just as impossible to discover anything as it is in grammar.

Geometry plus physics is syntax for the totality.

PHYSICS AND PHENOMENOLOGY

Physics wants to determine regularities; it does not set its sights on what is possible.

For this reason physics does not yield a description of the structure of phenomenological states of affairs. In phenomenology it is always a matter of possibility, i.e. of sense, not of truth and falsity. Physics picks out certain points of the continuum, as it were, and uses them for a law-conforming series. It does not care about the rest.

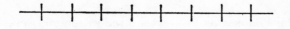

COLOUR-SYSTEM

Once I wrote, 'A proposition is laid against reality like a ruler. Only the end-points of the graduating lines actually *touch* the object that is to be measured.'[20] I now prefer to say that a *system of propositions* is laid against reality like a ruler. What I mean by this is the following. If I

20 *TLP* 2.1512–2.15121. The first sentence has 'It' (i.e. 'the picture') as its subject.

lay a ruler against a spatial object, I lay *all the graduating lines* against it at the same time.

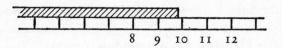

It is not the individual graduating lines that are laid against it, but the entire scale. If I know that the object extends to graduating line 10, I also know immediately that it does not extend to graduating lines 11, 12, and so forth. The statements describing for me the length of an object form a system, a system of propositions. Now it is such an entire system of propositions that is compared with reality, not a single proposition. If I say, for example, that this or that point in the visual field is *blue*, then I know not merely that, but also that this point is not green, nor red, nor yellow, etc. I have laid the entire colour-scale against it at one go. This is also the reason why a point cannot have different colours at the same time. For when I lay a *system* of propositions against reality, this means that in each case there is only *one* state of affairs that can exist, not several—just as in the spatial case.

All this I did not yet know when I was writing my work: at that time I thought that all inference was based on tautological form. At that time I had not yet seen that an inference can also have the form: This man is 2m tall, therefore he is not 3m tall. This is connected with the fact that I believed that elementary propositions must be independent of one another, that you could not infer the non-existence of one state of affairs from the existence of another.[21] But if my present conception of a system of propositions is correct, it will actually be the rule that from the existence of one state of affairs the non-existence of all the other states of affairs described by this system of propositions can be inferred.

21 *TLP* 2.062, 4.211, 5.1314–5.135.

Is Every Proposition Part of a System? I

PROF. SCHLICK RAISES THE QUESTION: How can I *know* that one syntax is right while another is not. Can no profounder reason be given why '*fx*' can be true for only one value of '*x*'? How do we know that? In what relation does empirical knowledge stand to syntax?

WITTGENSTEIN REPLIES that there is experience of *that* and experience of *how*.

SCHLICK: What about the so-called *law of relativity* in psychology (Hamilton),[22] for example, that it is only by means of a contrast that we become aware of a sensation? We do not hear the music of the spheres, because we hear it without interruption.

WITTGENSTEIN: Here again we have to discriminate. What does it mean to say that we *hear* the music of the spheres? If it means anything that can also be verified in a way other than by listening, then the proposition does not have a phenomenological meaning, but another, perhaps a physical, meaning (vibration in the air). But if something is meant that can be verified *only* by means of *listening*, then what is being said is that we ought to hear something but do not hear it—and in this form the proposition cannot be verified in any way, and therefore has no sense. A wheel turning idly.[23]

⟨*The World is Red I*⟩

SCHLICK: You say that colours form a system. Does that mean something logical or something empirical? How would it be, for example, if a person was locked in a red room for his whole life and

---

22 It is A. Bain who must really be meant here. As an example of his fundamental law of relativity he gives the following, 'If we had never been affected by any colour except red, colour would never have been recognized by us' (*The Senses and the Intellect*, 2nd edition, London, 1864). (Cf. infra.) Hamilton's law of relativity has another sense which does not fit here.

23 Cf. pp. 47 and 48, above.

could not see any colour but red? Or if a person's entire visual field contained only a uniform red? Could he then say to himself, 'I see only red; but there must also be other colours'?

WITTGENSTEIN: If a person never leaves his room, he nevertheless knows that there is space beyond it, i.e. that there is the possibility of being outside the room (even if its walls were made of adamant). This is therefore not a matter of experience. It is *a priori* part of the syntax of space.

Does it, then, make sense to ask, How many colours must a person have experienced, in order to come to know the *system* of colours? No! (By the way, to think of a colour does not mean to hallucinate it.) Here there are two possibilities:

a) Either his syntax is the same as ours: red, redder, bright red, yellowish red, etc. In this case he has our complete system of colours.

b) Or his syntax is not the same. In that case he does not know a colour in our sense at all. For if a sign has the same meaning, it must also have the same syntax.[1]

1] *Addendum, Monday, 30 December 1929*

I was wrong when I presented the matter in this way. It is not possible to say anything, either in the case where a man knows only one red or in the case where he knows several shades of red. I want to give a simple counter-example that is very old. What about the number of strokes that I can *see*? I could also draw the following inference. If I can see 1, 2, 3, 4, 5 strokes and seen strokes have the same syntax as counted ones, then I must be able to *see* any number of strokes. This, however, is not the case.

| | || ||| |||| |||||

||||||||||||| |||||||||||||

I can, to be sure, distinguish 2 strokes from 3 *by looking at them*, but

The crucial point is not how many colours one has seen, but the syntax. (Just as the 'amount of space' does not matter.)

ANTI-HUSSERL

SCHLICK: What answer can one give to a philosopher who believes that the statements of phenomenology are synthetic *a priori* judgements?[24]

WITTGENSTEIN: If I say 'I have not got stomach-ache,' then this presupposes the possibility of a state of stomach-ache. My present state and the state of stomach-ache are in the same logical space as it were. (Just as when I say 'I have no money.' This statement presupposes the possibility that I do have money. It indicates the zero point of money-space.) The negative proposition presupposes the positive one and *vice versa*.

Now let us take the statement, 'An object is not red and green at the same time.' Is all I want to say by this that I have not yet seen such an object? Obviously not. What I mean is, 'I *cannot* see such an object,' 'Red and green *cannot* be in the same place.' Here I would ask, What does the word '*can*' mean here? The word 'can' is obviously a grammatical (logical) concept, not a material one.

Now suppose the statement 'An object cannot be both red and green' were a synthetic judgement and the words 'cannot' meant logical impossibility. Since a proposition is the negation of its negation, there must also exist the proposition 'An object can be red and green.' This proposition would also be synthetic. As a synthetic proposition it has sense, and this means that the state of things

---

not 100 strokes from 101. Here there are two different verifications, one by looking, the other one by counting. One system has a different multiplicity from the other. The visual system says: *1, 2, 3, 4, 5, many*.

24 Schlick quotes Husserl's *Logische Untersuchúngen* II, 2, 3rd edition, Halle, 1922, p. 203, on this point in his 'Gibt es ein materiales Apriori?' (1930/1), reprinted in his *Gesammelte Aufsätze*, The Hague, 1938 (E.T. 'Is there a factual a priori?' in *Readings in Philosophical Analysis* (H. Feigl and W. Sellars edd., New York, 1959)).

represented by it *can obtain*. If 'cannot' means *logical* impossibility, we therefore reach the consequence that the impossible *is* possible.

Here there remained only one way out for Husserl—to declare that there was a third possibility. To that I would reply that it is indeed possible to make up words, but I cannot associate a thought with them.

Monday, 30 December 1929 (at Schlick's house)

APROPOS OF HEIDEGGER

To be sure, I can imagine what Heidegger means by being and anxiety.[25] Man feels the urge to run up against the limits of language. Think for example of the astonishment that anything at all exists. This astonishment cannot be expressed in the form of a question, and there is also no answer whatsoever. Anything we might say is *a priori* bound to be mere nonsense. Nevertheless we do run up against the limits of language.[1] Kierkegaard too saw that there is this running up against something and he referred to it in a fairly similar way (as running up against paradox).[28] This running up against the limits of language is *ethics*. I think it is definitely important to put an end to all

---

1] Feeling the world as a limited whole—it is this that is mystical.[26] 'Nothing can happen to me,' that is, whatever may happen, for me it is without significance.[27]

25 M. Heidegger, *Being and Time*, Oxford, 1962, pp. 230–231, *'That in the face of which one has anxiety is Being-in-the-world as such*. What is the difference phenomenally between that in the face of which anxiety is anxious and that in the face of which fear is afraid? That in the face of which one has anxiety is not an entity within-the-world . . . *the world as such is that in the face of which one has anxiety.*'
26 Cf. *TLP* 6.45.
27 Cf. *LE*, p. 8.
28 Cf. e.g. Kierkegaard, *Philosophical Fragments*, Princeton, 1962, pp. 49 and 55, 'But what is this unknown something with which the Reason collides when inspired by its paradoxical passion . . .? It is the Unknown . . . It is the limit to which the Reason repeatedly comes.'

the claptrap about ethics—whether intuitive knowledge exists, whether values exist, whether the good is definable. In ethics we are always making the attempt to say something that cannot be said, something that does not and never will touch the essence of the matter. It is *a priori* certain that whatever definition of the good may be given—it will always be merely a misunderstanding to say that the essential thing, that what is really meant, corresponds to what is expressed (Moore).[29] But the inclination, the running up against something, *indicates something*. St. Augustine knew that already when he said:[30] What, you swine, you want not to talk nonsense! Go ahead and talk nonsense, it does not matter!

DEDEKINDIAN DEFINITION

The mistake Russell makes is the following.[31] He believes that he can describe a logical form and that he can do so in an incomplete way.

When you describe a logical form, everything must be described. Nothing must remain incomplete. I can, to be sure, describe a man by saying what the colour of his eyes is. What I mean by this is that I say nothing for the time being; things will turn out one way or the other.

---

29 Waismann's shorthand is particularly difficult ro read in this sentence, although its general sense is beyond doubt. The word before 'good' is completely illegible ('reinen', 'int⟨rinsischen⟩'?). 'das Eigentlich' may of course be 'daß eigentlich' ('the essential thing'—'that essentially'). The reference is no doubt to Moore's discussion of the undefinability of the good in his *Principia Ethica*, Cambridge, 1903, §§5–14.

30 Waismann seems to have added the quotation later. It appears to be a paraphrase of Confess. I. iv, 'et vae tacentibus de te, quoniam loquaces muti sunt'. This was a favourite quotation of Wittgenstein's, see M. O'C. Drury in *Acta Philosophica Fennica*, Vol. 28 (1976) p. 34.

31 R. Dedekind, *Was sind und was sollen die Zahlen?*, Brunswick, 1923, p. 17 (E.T. *Essays on Number*, Chicago and London, 1901, p. 63), 'A system *S* is called *infinite* if it is similar to a real part of itself; in the opposite case *S* called a *finite* system.' In *Principia Mathematica*, II, Cambridge, 1912, pp. 190 and 278ff. Whitehead and Russell use that definition as the definition of a 'reflexive class.'

We await the development of things, as it were, and describe them more and more precisely. You cannot describe a logical form in this way, at first roughly and imprecisely and then more and more precisely. For example, I describe a class. I do not yet say if it is finite or infinite. Afterwards I notice that there is still this unexpected difference, finite and infinite. So I complete my description of a class by saying 'A class is finite if etc.' This looks as if at first I had a noun (class) to which I can later on add an adjective (finite, infinite). Just as when I talk about shoes and then say that they are white or green. But in reality I *cannot* at all describe the noun without the adjective or the adjective without the noun. The two are inseparable. An infinite class is from the start something entirely different from a finite class. The word 'class' has different senses in these two cases; for the verification of the statements concerned is different.

'*There are infinitely many fixed stars.*' What does that mean? Let us imagine the following case. I describe the movement of a pendulum, and the more fixed stars I assume, the more precisely I can explain the movement. If we say for instance that if I assume one fixed star, the error is 1, if I assume 2, the error is $1/2$, with 3 fixed stars it is $1/4$, . . . with n fixed stars the error is $1/2^{n-1}$ (altogether the observed magnitude is 2), then I have the right to assume that there are infinitely many fixed stars. But here also 'infinitely' is only a means of representation. After all, it means only that I have a sequence of descriptions, each of which is more precise than the previous one, and this sequence can be continued indefinitely.[32] Here too 'infinitely' is the adverb of a possibility, namely of the possibility of going on to a more precise description.[1]

_____

1] If I speak for example of 'all propositions', e.g. (p) . . . , then this can mean two things:

32 'Unbegrenzt' ('indefinitely')—it is unclear what follows after the prefix 'un–'. As far as this kind of shorthand is concerned, 'unbegrenzt' is possible, although Waismann does not usually write it that way; 'unendlich' ('infinitely') is impossible.

Or let us imagine the following case. Throughout my life I see a band pass by, white-red, white-red, and all my ancestors have seen this band. Then I can describe this too by means of the assumption that there is an infinitely long band passing by.

But now we encounter something very odd, for I wish to claim that here the words 'white-red' have a meaning different from what they usually have when I speak of white-red in the visual field. For in the visual field there is no possibility to speak of infinitely many white and red patches. But as regards this band, such a possibility does exist. If syntax is different, meaning must be different too. I wish to claim (strange as it may sound) that white and red here signify concepts of geometry. (This is presumably what Einstein meant when he took geometry to be a branch of physics.[33])

REAL NUMBERS I

$$\pi = 3.14159265.\ .\ .\ .\ .$$

The extension of such a number can only be an induction.

There can be no such question as, Do the figures 0, 1, 2 . . . 9 occur in π? I can only ask if they occur at *one* particular point, or if they occur among the first 10,000 figures. No expansion, however far it may go, can refute the statement 'They do occur'—therefore this statement cannot be verified either. What is verified is an entirely different assertion, namely that this sequence occurs at *this or that point*. Hence you cannot affirm or deny such a statement, and therefore you cannot apply the law of the excluded middle to it.

---

1) I specify the form of the propositions p, e.g. all propositions of the form xRy.

2) By all propositions I also mean propositions of the form $xRy \lor uRv$. In this case I have to know the law according to which these propositions are constructed. I have to know how I arrive at these propositions.

33 See the continuation of the passage quoted on p. 38 above.

Induction is analogous to a spiral. If I know the first coil, I know the *whole* spiral. The whole one? How is that? Here there is an analogy that will tempt you very easily into speaking of 'whole'. For if I know one coil, then I do not know a whole spiral, although I do know the law of a spiral and therefore also the first ten coils. In this latter case it makes good sense to say, 'I know one coil, therefore I know the whole (finite!) spiral. Similarly with the expansion of a decimal. What I

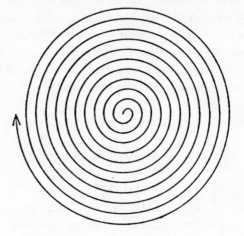

know is the induction in question, thus the *law* of its expansion. Here too I can now consider the relation between a shorter and a longer expansion.

I construct a decimal fraction according to the following instruction. I shall write 0 at the nth position, if my attempts with the first 100 numbers for x, y, z will not yield a value of n satisfying Fermat's equation $(x^n + y^n = z^n)$; I shall write 1 when I find such an n. Thus the beginning of the decimal number looks like this:

$$0,110000 \ldots \ldots$$

Let us compare it with the number 0,11. Is it larger or is it equal to that? Whal I think is that the decimal fraction we have just constructed is not a real number, since it is not comparable with rational numbers. The decisive thing about the construction of real numbers consists precisely in their comparability. It is only in virtue of this that the real numbers can be interpreted as points on a straight line.

If, now, there are constructions that cannot be compared with rational numbers, then we have no right to find them a place among the rational numbers. Thus they simply are not on the number lines. (In Brouwer it appears as if they were real numbers about which we merely did not *know* whether they were larger than, or smaller than, or equal to another rational number.)[34]

There is an analogy between the relation of one coil of a spiral to 10 coils and the relation between one coil and the whole spiral. But this is merely an analogy and it has tempted people into introducing infinite classes or sets.

Thursday, 2 January 1930 (at Schlick's house)

⟨ELEMENTARY PROPOSITIONS⟩

I want to explain my views on elementary propositions and first I want to say what I used to believe and what part of that seems right to me now.

I used to have two conceptions of an elementary proposition, one of which seems correct to me, while I was completely wrong in holding

---

34 Probably a reference to Brouwer's lecture 'Mathematik, Wissenschaft, Sprache', which had stimulated Wittgenstein very much when it had been given in Vienna in March 1928 (see G. Pitcher, *The Philosophy of Wittgenstein*, Englewood Cliffs, N.J., 1964, p. 8). The lecture was printed in *Monatshefte für Mathematik und Physik*, 36, 1929, pp. 153–164. On p. 163 Brouwer e.g. defines a pendulum number, 'which is not rational although its irrationality is absurd, and not comparable with zero, although its incomparability with zero is absurd'.

the other. My first assumption was this: that in analysing propositions we must eventually reach propositions that are immediate connections of objects without any help from logical constants, for 'not', 'and', 'or', and 'if' do not connect objects.[35] And I still adhere to that. Secondly I had the idea that elementary propositions must be independent of one another.[36] A complete description of the world would be a product of elementary propositions, as it were, these being partly positive and partly negative.[37] In holding this I was wrong, and the following is what is wrong with it.

I laid down rules for the syntactical use of logical constants, for example '$p.q$', and did not think that these rules might have something to do with the inner structure of propositions. What was wrong about my conception was that I believed that the syntax of logical constants could be laid down without paying attention to the inner connection of propositions. That is not how things actually are. I cannot, for example, say that red and blue are at one point simultaneously. Here no logical product can be constructed. Rather, the rules for the logical constants form only a part of a more comprehensive syntax about which I did not yet know anything at that time.

A good example of this is a description of a surface, e.g. of this sheet of paper here. (I want to mention at once that this is not a mere analogy, but that it really is the same as this everywhere.) There will be a propositional form describing the distribution of the colours on this sheet of paper, and I want to assume that there are sharp border-lines and no continuous transitions between the colours. What we shall be describing then will be the colour-boundaries. This will be done by means of equations of analytic geometry for instance. Further, we shall have to describe the colours. This will be done by

35 There is surely something wrong with the original German sentence which has 'sind' ('are') instead of 'nicht' ('not'). None of the normal possibilities in shorthand ('deren' for 'denen', 'verbindende' for 'verbinden die') seems to help at all.
36 See footnote on p. 64, above.
37 Presumably 'a product of elementary propositions and negations of elementary propositions' is meant here.

means of an arbitrary system of colour-description, for instance by means of indices. (We can devise different such systems.)

Thus the description will contain equations for lines and indices for colours. These elements of description are necessary, i.e. every possible description must have this multiplicity. The description may also be incomplete. I say for example, 'The inside of a certain patch is blue, outside it the paper is partly white, partly black.'[38]

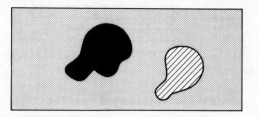

Now I shall simplify the example a bit further and assume that the colour patches that I have to describe are exclusively rectangles and squares set parallel to the edges of the sheet of paper.

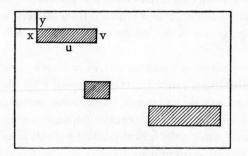

I can describe any rectangle by supplying four numerical specifications, that is, the co-ordinates of its upper left corner, its length, and its width, say by means of $(x,y; u,v)$. The specification of these four co-ordinates is incompatible with any other specification, I can describe the colour of the rectangle in the same way by laying the

38 In the note-book the following illustration is over the page and was surely supposed to be a general illustration of what follows *it*.

colour-scale against it, as it were. (Naturally, colours do not have the multiplicity of lengths, thus they cannot be measured by means of *one* yardstick.) Instead of describing colours by means of propositions I could also do it by means of a system of yardsticks, by taking as many yardsticks as there are co-ordinates occurring in my description and *adjusting these yardsticks*:

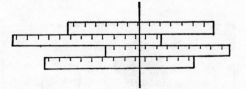

A complete description of such a surface would be given by a group of yardstick-systems so adjusted. Things are everywhere the same as in this case. We ascribe a certain co-ordinate to reality—a certain colour, a certain brightness, a certain hardness, and so forth. Description must always proceed in such a way that the same co-ordinate is not determined twice over. In order to prevent this, we need a syntax. We can even make do without syntax if from the very beginning we use a descriptive system that cannot ascribe two different co-ordinate values to reality.

Every proposition is part of a system of propositions that is laid against reality like a yardstick. (Logical space.)[39]

What I at first paid no attention to was that the syntax of logical constants forms only part of a more comprehensive syntax. Thus I can, for example, construct the logical product $p.q$ only if p and q do not determine the same co-ordinate twice.

But in cases where propositions are independent everything remains valid—the whole theory of inference and so forth.

SCHLICK: Is there nothing that can be said in reply to the question, How do I know that such-and-such rules of syntax are valid? How do I

39 Cf. *TLP* 2.1512 and 3.42.

know that red and blue cannot be in one place simultaneously? Have we not in this case a kind of empirical knowledge?

WITTGENSTEIN: Yes and no. It depends on what you mean by empirical. If what you mean by empirical knowledge is not such that it can be expressed by means of a proposition, then this is not empirical knowledge. If it is something different you mean by empirical thinking, then syntax too is empirical. At one point in my *Tractatus* I said: Logic is prior to the question 'How?', not prior to the question 'What?'.[40] Logic depends on this: that something exists (in the sense that there is something), that there are facts. It is independent of the characteristics of facts, of anything's being-so. No proposition can describe that there are facts. If you wish, I could just as well say, logic is empirical—if *that* is what you call empirical.

[What we mean by saying of something that it is empirical is this: that we can imagine it to be different. (In this sense every proposition with sense is accidental.) The existence of the world is not empirical in this sense, for it is something that we cannot imagine to be otherwise. We cannot imagine a world that exists at one time and does not exist at another. Remark after Wittgenstein's lecture on ethics; roughly.[41]]

SCHLICK: But how do I know that precisely these rules are valid and no others? Can I not be wrong?

WITTGENSTEIN: In this matter it is always as follows. Everything we do consists in trying to find the liberating word. In grammar you cannot discover anything. There are no surprises. When formulating a rule we always have the feeling: That is something you have known all along. We can do only one thing—clearly articulate the rule we have been applying unawares. If, then, I understand what the specification of a length means, I also know that, if a man is 1.6m tall, he is

40 *TLP* 5.552.
41 *LE*, p. 9. The lecture was given to the Heretics Club in Cambridge in November 1930.

not 2m tall. I know that a measurement determines only *one* value on a scale and not several values. If you ask me, How do I know that? I shall simply answer, Because I understand the sense of the statement. It is impossible to understand the sense of such a statement without knowing the rule. [I may know the rule in terms of applying it without having formulated it explicitly.]

If I understand the sense of a statement about colours, I also know that two colours cannot be at the same place, and so forth. Let us take the following case. You say, There is a circle. Its length is 3cm and its width is 2cm.

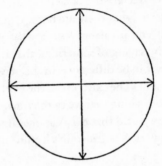

In this case I would say, wouldn't I?: Indeed! What do you mean by a circle then? If you understand the word 'circle' in the same meaning as us, the rules of syntax prohibit you from determining the co-ordinates of a circle (its radius) twice. It is simply the definition of a circle that yields the rule of syntax, and this definition tells us, then, what sense statements about a circle have. Thus if I understand the sense of a proposition at all, I must also understand the syntax of an expression occurring in it. You cannot discover anything in grammar, you can only elucidate.

SCHLICK: But how does it come about that this is easy to understand with specifications of length but not with colours? Because Husserl thinks he has discovered a series of synthetic *a priori* judgements here.[42] Where does the psychological difference lie in this case, that it

42 See above, footnote on p. 67.

is so easily understood in one case and not in the other—after all, in order to be consistent Husserl would also have to assume that the syntax of specifications of lengths was a set of synthetic *a priori* judgements.

WITTGENSTEIN: There may be several reasons for that. For example, when laying a yardstick against anything you see after all that, if it is 2m long, it is not 3m long; for one metre will stick out. As a matter of fact, we do not have a yardstick for colours.

WAISMANN: Some psychologists believed so firmly that this was a matter of empirical states of affairs that they even performed empirical investigations whether two colours could not be at the same place.

WITTGENSTEIN: That too might be possible—you would have to tell me what methods these psychologists employed, that is, what counted as verification for them. Only then can I say what sense such an assumption has. It is thinkable, after all, that such an investigation makes good sense—but it is only the method of answering a question that tells you what the question was really about. Only when I have answered a question can I know what it was aimed at. (The sense of a proposition is the method of its verification.)

SCHLICK: I am not yet quite satisfied with that. Ought we not to construct such a language that the rules of syntax are immediately self-evident?

WAISMANN: That is the case, is it not?, if we take a system of yardsticks as a description. If a symbolic system has the right multiplicity, the rules of syntax become superfluous. Thus our use of the words 'to the north of' is subject to certain syntactic rules. I must not say, 'A is to the north of B and B is to the north of A.' But a map cannot represent this nonsense, since it has the right multiplicity.

WITTGENSTEIN: The case is thus: syntax and symbols always operate in opposite directions. Results achieved by symbols are achieved at the expense of syntax, and results achieved by syntax are achieved at the expense of symbols. I could say that a symbolic system with the right multiplicity will render syntax superfluous. But I could just as well say that syntax will render such a symbolic system superfluous. And I can indeed use an incomplete symbolic system and add rules of syntax. Together the two of them achieve exactly the same result, thus it is exactly the same system of representation.

My notation for the logical constants,[43] for example, is neither better nor worse than the Russellian one. The Russellian symbols and syntax accomplish exactly the same as my notation. It may be that mine has just the advantage of rendering some things more clearly recognizable. It shows for example what all propositions of logic have in common, what it is really needed for. But in itself the Russellian notation is just as legitimate. The multiplicity of my symbolic system is correct from the beginning, and for that reason I do not need Russell's syntactic rules.

As a summary you could say that the truth-functional connection of propositions forms only one part of syntax. The rules I laid down at that time are now restricted by the rules that originate from the inner syntax of propositions and prohibit propositions from ascribing different co-ordinates to reality. All truth-functions that are not forbidden by these rules are permitted.

SCHLICK: Is there not a feeling that the logical constants (the truth-functions) are something more essential than the particular rules of syntax, that for instance the possibility of constructing a logical product '$p.q$' is more general, more comprehensive as it were, than the rules of syntax according to which red and blue cannot be in the same place? For the former rule does not contain anything about colour and place.

WITTGENSTEIN: I do not think that there is a difference here. The

43 E.g. '(TTFT) (p. 9)' means 'If p, then q'; cf. *TLP* 4.442, 5.101.

rules for logical products, etc., cannot be severed from other rules of syntax. Both belong to the method of depicting the world.

⟨'THE PRESENT STATE OF KNOWLEDGE IN MATHEMATICS'⟩

Wittgenstein reads Weyl (article in Symposium)[44] and makes various remarks about it.

Rough account

WEYL HOLDS: Either a mathematical judgement refers to all numbers—in that case it cannot be negated. Or a mathematical judgement refers to a concrete number. That means existence. Or neither of these things is the case. The first case and the second case do not stand in the same relation as a proposition and its negation.

WITTGENSTEIN REMARKS UPON THAT: In the second case we have a mathematical statement—I can affirm it or deny it. This has nothing at all to do with existence. [1] When I say that a sequence occurs at the

---

1] Weyl pretends there may indeed be universal statements but they do not have negations, on the ground that an existential statement is a 'judgement-abstraction' and that only construction (finding a number) tells us anything. But in reality these are two completely different things—a universal statement is correctly expressed by means of induction and as such it naturally cannot be negated. The claim that a number occurs at a certain place is of course an assertion and can as such be in turn negated. Such a negation simply says that at the place in question that number does not occur. The error arises from regarding an extension as a totality. For it makes good sense to say: If 7 occurs at the 25th place, then 7 occurs between the 20th and

44 'Die heutige Erkenntnislage in der Mathematik', in *Symposion* I (1927), pp. 1–32.

800th place of π—then by saying it I have told you exactly that and nothing else. And also by denying it I say only that no sequence occurs at the 800th place, not that there is no sequence.

A statement about *all* numbers is not represented by means of a proposition, but by means of induction. Induction, however, cannot be denied, nor can you affirm it, for it does not assert anything. Therefore, where there is a statement it can be negated; and where a certain structure cannot be negated, there is no statement either. The law of excluded middle however does not apply—simply because we are not dealing with propositions here.

Generality does not make itself manifest in letters. These have nothing at all to do with generality. Generality makes itself manifest in the fact that something *goes so on*. (This is manifest from a single turn of the spiral.)

---

the 30th place. But it does not make sense to say: 7 occurs, full-stop. This is not a statement at all.

Thus Weyl lumps several different things together. The proposition '7 does not occur between the 20th and the 30th place' is verified in a different way from the proposition '7 does not occur, though.'[45] But if it is verified in a different way, then *it is a different proposition*.

If you answer the question whether the figure 7 occurs in the expansion of π by saying: Yes, it occurs at the 25th place, you have answered only the question whether 7 occurs at the 25th place but not the question whether 7 occurs at all. If the question has a sense, then the answer has a sense too, no matter if it turns out positive or negative.

45 The word 'though' ('zwar') is uncertain; it is surely not 'überhaupt' ('at all').

A freely developing sequence is in the first place something empirical. It is nothing but the numbers that I write down on paper. If Weyl believes that it is a mathematical structure because I can derive a freely developing sequence from another one by means of a general law, e.g.,

$$m_1, m_2, m_3, \ldots$$
$$m_1, m_1 + m_2, m_1 + m_3, \ldots$$

then the following is to be said against it: No, this shows only that I can add numbers, but not that a freely developing sequence is an admissible mathematical concept.

What is the meaning of the statement that there is a prime number at the fourth place of a freely proceeding sequence? What does it mean when I arrange plums in little heaps and say, 'That little heap over there contains a prime number of plums'?

Suppose that statement was rendered by the following translation. Draw equidistant strokes (as many as there are plums), draw a semicircle every time, and see whether a semicircle ends at the last stroke.

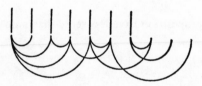

Curiously enough this would *not* mean that the number of strokes is prime. While the representation involves this, it would not express it. The representation presupposes a mathematical statement. I have not spoken of mathematics, only of pencil and paper, of compasses and turns, and so forth. But I have not spoken of prime numbers. If a demon always conjured away one stroke—would 7 not be a prime number because of that? All this is not enough to express the matter clearly. What is meant is roughly that arithmetic is always contained in a description; but the description *is* not arithmetic.

To be sure I can say that the number of plums is prime, without having counted them. I can make such a statement without paying my respects to the number concerned. But I cannot say: The number of plums is 7, *and 7 is a prime number*.

⟨*Miscellanous*⟩

Criticism of Weyl's conception of time in arithmetic.[46] Rejection of the question whether cardinal or ordinal numbers are primary. Rejection of Kaufmann's view that a number is what remains invariant when things are counted in a different order.[47]

Schopenhauer: Every number presupposes all preceding ones as grounds for its existence.[48] Wittgenstein: but also those that succeed it.[49]

Sunday, 5 January 1930 (at Schlick's house)

POSITIVE AND NEGATIVE PROPOSITIONS [1]

Does a negative proposition have less sense than a positive one? Yes and no.

1] A very good method of illustrating the representational character of language consists in understanding the propositions of our language as *instructions* for doing something. I lead you around my room

46 Here the reference does not seem to be to the *Symposion* article but to *Philosophy of Mathematics* (see footnote p. 37 above), p. 34.

47 F. Kaufmann, *Das Unendliche in der Mathematik und seine Ausschaltung*, Leipzig and Vienna, 1930, pp. 78–79 (E.T. *The Infinite in Mathematics*, Dordrecht and Boston Mass., 1978, p. 69).

48 *On the Fourfold Root of the Principle of Sufficient Reason*, § 38, quoted by Weyl in *Philosophy of Mathematics,* loc. cit.

49 In the note-book there follows a gap of $1\frac{1}{4}$ pages.

Yes, if the following is meant: If I can infer q from p but not p from q, then q has less sense than p. If, then, I say 'This azalea is red' and 'This azalea is not blue', I can infer the second proposition from the first one, but not conversely. To this extent you may say that a negative proposition has less sense than a positive one.

No, if it is a matter of the following (which is what I really chiefly have on my mind): A negative proposition confers the same multiplicity upon reality as a positive one. If I say, 'I have no stomach-ache', then I have conferred the same multiplicity upon reality as when I say, 'I have stomach-ache'. For if I say, 'I have stomach-ache', then just by means of this proposition I presuppose the existence of a positive proposition, I presuppose the possibility of stomach-ache, and my proposition determines a position in the space of stomach-aches. It is not as if my present state had not the least connection with stomach-aches. [If I say, 'It is zero centigrade,' then by means of this I have

_____

by means of my words, 'Now you go three steps straight ahead, now three to the left, now you stretch out your right arm, a bit higher up, no! that is too high, and so on.' Here it is completely clear that language must have the same multiplicity as the movements that I direct by my propositions. All you do must already be contained in what I say. (If I am to make a machine work at three different speeds, I cannot possibly achieve this by moving a lever that has only two positions.) Similarly I can control somebody's mixing of colours by means of words. Thus I say, 'Take blue, some white, more white, now a wee bit more blue,' and so forth. If now I pronounce a negative proposition, such as 'Do not take blue,' then this does not tell you that you ought to raise your hands or to dance; the proposition prohibits you only from taking blue and permits every other colour. Thus a negative proposition too ascribes the same multiplicity to reality as a positive one, and this is all I have on my mind when I say that a negative proposition has just as much sense as a positive one.

characterized the zero-point of temperature-space.] If I say, 'I have no stomach-ache', I say as it were, 'I am at the zero-point of the stomach-ache space.' But my proposition presupposes the entire logical space.

[Similarly, 'There is no distance between these two bodies' is of the same kind as the proposition, 'These two bodies stand at such-and-such a distance from one another.' In both cases the same multiplicity.]

I mean the latter when I say that a positive proposition does not have more sense than a negative one. Both confer the same multiplicity upon reality.

WAISMANN: A negative proposition gives reality more leeway than a positive one. If I say, for example, 'This azalea is not blue,' I do not know yet what colour it has.

WITTGENSTEIN: Certainly. In this sense a negative proposition says less than a positive one. I once wrote, 'I understand the sense of a proposition if I know what is the case if it is true and if it is false.'[50][1] By this I meant that if I know when it is true, then *by the same token* I know when it is false. If I say 'This azalea is not blue,' I also know when it is blue. In order to recognize that it is not blue I have to compare it with reality.

WAISMANN: You use the word *'compare'*. But when I compare a proposition with reality I know that the azalea is red and from this I

1] In order to understand the sense of the proposition 'This azalea is not blue' I need not be able to imagine the other colours. And if I do imagine something, this means something less than that I understand the sense of a proposition.

In order to understand the words 'blue', 'red', . . . I need not hallucinate colours. [Thinking has nothing to do with the generation of experiences.] I need only understand the sense of the propositions in which those words occur.

50 *NL* p. 93–94; cf. *TLP* 4.024, 2.223.

infer that it is not blue, nor green, nor yellow. What I see is nothing less than a state of affairs. But I never see that the azalea is not blue. WITTGENSTEIN: I do not see red: rather, I see *that the azalea is red*. In this sense I also see that it is not blue. It is not that a conclusion is drawn consequential upon what is seen: no—the conclusion is known immediately as part of the seeing.

Positive and negative propositions are on the same level. When I lay a yardstick against something, I know not only how long a certain thing is, but also how long it is not. In verifying a positive proposition I also falsify its negation. At the very moment when I know that the azalea is red I also know that it is not blue. These two things are inseparable. The truth-conditions of a proposition presuppose its falsity-conditions and *vice versa*.

THE COLOUR BLUE IN MEMORY

The nature of our memory is very odd. Usually it is thought that we carry a kind of memory-picture of a seen colour around in ourselves and that this memory-picture is *compared* with a colour that I see at this moment. It is thought that this is a matter of comparison. That is not quite how things are. Imagine the following. You have seen a particular blue—say, sky-blue—and presently I show different patterns of blue to you. Then you say, 'No, no, it was not this one, nor that, nor that.—Now, that is the one!' Is it as if you had various push-buttons in your head and I was trying them out until I pushed a particular one and then the bell rang? Does the recognition of a colour come about in the same way? Does a bell ring in me, as it were, does something click when I see the right colour? No! Rather, not only do I know that a particular blue is not the right one but I also know in which direction I have to alter the colour in order to reach the right one.[1] This means, I *know a way of looking for this colour*. If you have to mix that colour I can give you hints by saying, 'More white, still more white, no, that is too much, some blue, and so forth.' That is, this colour presupposes the whole *colour-system*. Recognizing a colour is not simply a matter of comparison, although in some respects it is similar to a comparison. Recognizing appears to be like comparing, but to recognize is not to compare.[2]

By the way, if, in playing a parlour-game, you look for a hidden pin, it is not really in space that you are looking for it—for you have no method whatsoever of looking—but in the logical space that I generate by means of the words 'cold,' 'warm.' 'hot.' You can look for something only where there is a *method of looking for it*.

'THE WORLD IS RED' II [3]

I come back again to Prof. Schlick's question what it would be like if I knew only the colour red.[51] About that the following should be said: if everything I saw were red and I could describe it, then I should also

---

1] For if I press a button and the bell does not ring, I have no idea in which direction I have to continue in order to reach the right button. Whereas it is not as if I had no idea where the right colour is. There is something I know about it—the way to reach it.

2] The meaning of a word does not reside in the fact that my being able to visualize (imagine vividly, hallucinate) its content, but in my knowing the way of reaching the object.

3] 'The world is red.' If I can express this by means of a proposition, then this proposition can also be denied and belongs to a space. If it cannot be described by means of a statement, then I cannot even *ask* whether red presupposes the system of colours.

51 Cf. pp. 65f., above

have to be able to construct the proposition that it was not red. This presupposes the possibility of other colours. Or else red is something that I cannot describe—then I have no proposition either and there is nothing I can deny. Nor would there be statements of the form 'Everything is red,' or, 'Everything I see is red,' in a world where red played the same rôle, as it were, as time does in our world.

Therefore, if there is a state of affairs, then it can be described and the colour red presupposes a system of colours. Or red means something entirely different and then no sense attaches to calling it a colour. In that case you cannot even speak of it.

IS EVERY PROPOSITION PART OF A SYSTEM? II

First of all this depends on what you mean by a 'system'. Every specification of length is part of a system. For if I understand that a certain thing is 3m long, then I also understand what it means to say that it is 5m long. This specification belongs to a space of possible lengths. Equally the thing is surrounded by colour-space, hardness-space, and so forth.[52] When I wrote this I had not yet seen that the number of positions in this space form the graduating marks of a yardstick as it were and that we always lay the entire system of propositions against reality like a yardstick. The general question should be asked in the form, Does the proposition 'φa' presuppose other propositions of this kind, e.g. 'φb'?

———————

[Everything that is can also be otherwise. Conversely, only what can be otherwise is.]

A symbol (word) has meaning only in a proposition. If I cannot construct the statement 'Everything I see is red', then the word 'red' has no meaning either.

If the word 'red' has any meaning at all, then it presupposes a *system* of colours. [Our system?]

52 Cf. *TLP* 2.0131.

WAISMANN: That this is the case can be seen from the mere fact that in every proposition a constant can be replaced by a variable. The very possibility of concept-formation shows that every proposition belongs to a logical space which is nothing but the system.

WITTGENSTEIN: It is not as certain as all that. Can I always replace a constant by a variable? Obviously the case is thus: if 'φa' is possible, then '$\sim\varphi a$' is possible too.

WAISMANN: But how can I know that '$\sim\varphi a$' is true? Surely only by finding out that a state of affairs of the form 'φb' exists? So the possibility of negation already presupposes a logical space.

WITTGENSTEIN: It all depends on whether the symbol 'a' is a *necessary symbol*. If there were only the proposition 'φa' but not '$\varphi\beta$,' it would be superfluous to mention 'a'. It would suffice to write just 'φ'. The proposition would thus not be composite. But it is the essential feature of a proposition that it is *a picture* and has compositeness. If 'φa' is supposed to be a proposition, then there must also be a proposition 'φb,' that is, the arguments of '$\varphi()$' form a system. What I admittedly do not know is how large the domain of arguments is. And there might, for example, be only two. (Telephone dialling: free, in use—here we know that only these two values exist and they depict reality. An intermediate position does not signify anything. No transition.)

But does 'φa' presuppose 'ψa' too? Decidedly yes. For the same consideration tells us: if there were only a single function 'φ' for 'a,' then it would be superfluous; you could leave it out. The propositional sign would be simple and not composite. It[53] does not depict.

Symbols that are dispensable have no meaning. Superfluous symbols signify nothing.[54]

---

53 Probably 'The proposition'.
54 Cf. *TLP* 3.328; 5.47321.

Result: a proposition can be varied in as many dimensions as there are constants occurring in it. The space to which the proposition belongs has just as many dimensions.

A proposition reaches through the whole of logical space.[55] Otherwise negation would be unintelligible.

INFERENCE

WAISMANN: An incomplete proposition can be inferred from a complete one.[56] If I know for example that a certain circle lies in a square, then I know also that there is some circle or other in this square. What does the inference look like in this case? Is it a tautology? Or are there forms of inference that are not of the form of tautologies?

WITTGENSTEIN: Tautology is indeed quite irrelevant. It is only in a particular notation that an inference comes out as a tautology. Only the rules of syntax are essential and they have always been applied, a long time before anybody knew what a tautology was.

A definite description looks like this: A certain length is 25m. And the following would be an indefinite description: A certain length is between 20 and 30m. Now these two descriptions become 'p' and 'q'. Then it is determined by consideration of the syntax of the words 'length'[57] that the first cannot possibly be true while the second is false; i.e. '$p.\sim q$' is disallowed. Let us now construct the truth-function '$p \supset q$' (or, rather, a truth-function that is *analogous* or *similar* to implication) and allow for the requirements of syntax, then a tautology will result.

Frege, Peano, and Russell believed that in inference 'if' plays a very special rôle, and Russell even believed that inference is represented by

55 Cf. *TLP* 3.42.
56 See pp. 39f. above.
57 Sic.

means of implication ' ⊃ '.[58]

p	q	p⊃q
W	W	W
~~W~~	~~F~~	~~F~~
F	W	W
F	F	W

In reality inference has nothing to do with 'if'. In my notation[59] the correctness of the inference makes itself *manifest* in the fact that '$p \supset q$' becomes a tautology. But it is absolutely unnecessary to show the correctness of this inference in exactly this way. The correctness of an inference manifests itself just as well by means of the usual rules of inference. This is only one of various possible notations and perhaps it has only the advantage of making it possible to see the matter more clearly. But basically the Russellian symbols together with the rules of their syntactic employment achieve the same result.

That inference is *a priori* means only that syntax decides whether an inference is correct or not. Tautologies are only one way of showing what is syntactical.

LECTURE ON ETHICS[60]

In ethics our expressions have a double meaning: a psychological one of which you can speak and a non-psychological one: 'good tennis-player,' 'good'. We are constantly using different expressions to

58 Peano really calls every proposition containing this logical constant 'une déduction' (*Notations de logique mathématique*, Turin, 1894, p. 10). Frege's 'only mode of inference' involves this constant (*Grundgesetze* I, Jena, 1893, p. 26). Whitehead and Russell (*Principia Mathematica* I, Cambridge, 1910, pp. 21ff.) think that formal implications, which of course involve this constant, are useful for deductions; together with two assertion signs this constant is used in order to express an inference (op. cit., p. 96).
59 Probably the notation illustrated in the immediately preceding diagram.
60 This schematic report, including small changes, of the lecture mentioned on 2 January 1930 (see p. 77 above and footnote) is probably based on a German text now lost.

indicate the same thing.

Astonishment at the fact of the world. Every attempt to express it leads to nonsense.

Man has an inclination to run against the limits of language. This running against them signalizes ethics. Everything I describe is within the world. An ethical proposition never occurs in the complete description of the world, not even when I am describing a murderer. What is ethical is not a state of affairs.

PROBABILITY I

The first question is this, When I toss a coin and say that tossing heads or tails is equally probable—is this a prophecy?

If it were a prophecy, then it should be possible to confirm or refute it by means of experience. But it is clear that there is no possibility of verifying a statement about probability. Whatever happens, I can always maintain a statement of equiprobability. But what, then, does a probability statement mean?

When I say that tossing heads or tails with a coin is equally probable I mean that I do not know if the outcome will be heads or tails; but all the circumstances I know about (all I know about the coin, all I know about the procedure of tossing a coin, the laws of falling bodies, and so forth) give no better reason for heads than for tails.

Probability is a form of description. There is a form of describing reality, namely probability, just as there are, say, natural laws of minimum form.

My conception of probability must be a different one now, since my conception of elementary propositions has fundamentally changed. Probability is an internal relation between propositions.

What I verify by means of experiment is never the correctness of a *probability calculation*, but the presuppositions that I took as my basis.

Just as a physicist does not test the correctness of his logical deductions by means of his experiments but rather the truth of his hypotheses, so too experience cannot confirm or refute the correctness of the probability calculus.

[Probability deals only with the form of statements. There is no object called 'probability'.

Statements of probability do not describe probability but use the form of probability to describe reality. Probability is needed when our description of states of affairs is incomplete. Probability is connected with the nature of incomplete description.]

An entirely different case is that of insurance cases. This is a matter of *a posteriori* probability. This has nothing at all to do with probability. [?]

What is really stated when it is said that there is such-and-such a probability that a person of 40 will become 60? Here we have a statement of statistics: Of such-and-such a number of people of 40 such-and-such a number has become 60. Does this mean that in the future also the same percentage will become 60? That is not what it means. But the insurance company relies on the calculation's applying to the future too. But this is simply *induction*, just as in the case of a natural law. No probability can be specified for this induction, nor would it make sense.

Insurance companies prophesy, and what they say, if it is to have any sense at all, must be verifiable in a *definite way*. It must say: So and so many people will die during the next 70 years, or during the next 10 years. If the period is not specified, the statement loses all its sense.

When a deviation occurs people say: Here our statistics do not apply. In this year there was a war, in that there was pestilence, and so forth. But if there were a deviation without its being possible to specify such a factor, you could still hold time itself responsible for it.

(For example by saying that every 1930 years after a great founder of a religion the rate of mortality shows such-and-such a deviation. Everything you can describe you can also regard as the cause of a deviation.)

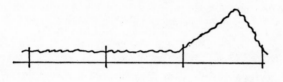

Dice

What does it mean to say that systematic deviations from the probability 1/6 occur?

We must first make it clear to ourselves that in connexion with dice we presuppose a tremendous system of experience, namely that the numbers written on their surfaces have no effect on the outcome. Let us make, for example, the following experiment: on both sides of a coin we glue signs that have been weighed in advance and found to have the same weight. Then we can find out that it makes no difference to the fall of the coin which signs we glue on. (Had our experiences been different, we should also have to approach probability in an entirely different way.)

Which of its six surfaces a die falls on does not depend on the number written on it. If the relative frequency deviates systematically from the probability that was calculated, we as it were lay down the *postulate* that there must be further causes to be found and their number must be such that their addition to the system of propositions known to us generates exactly this probability. Our minds are at rest only when the relative frequency coincides with the *a priori* probability.

The other circumstances that we introduce must not have the character of assumptions contrived *ad hoc*. Though we do need a stipulation regarding equiprobability.[61]

You may speak of 'all propositions' only if you have a *method* of constructing those propositions.

---

61 There follows a diagram about light rays and half a blank page. See editor's Preface, p. 29.

II

22 March 1930 (at Schlick's house)

⟨VERIFICATION AND THE IMMEDIATELY GIVEN⟩

How do I verify the proposition 'This is yellow'?

First of all it is clear that I must be able to recognize 'this,' which is yellow, even when it is red. (If 'this' and 'yellow' formed a unit, then they could be represented by means of *one* symbol and we should not have a proposition.)

An image of 'yellow' is not a picture of a yellow that I have seen in the sense in which I carry a picture of my friend, for instance, in my wallet. An image is a picture in an entirely different, formal sense. I may say, 'Imagine a certain yellow; now make it become whitish until it is completely white, and now make it turn green.' By means of this I can guide your images, and they change in the same way as real colour impressions. All operations that correspond to reality I can perform on images. *An image of a colour has the same multiplicity as the colour*. That is what its connection with reality consists in.

If, then, I say, 'This is yellow,' I can verify it in entirely different ways. The sentence has completely different sense, according to what method I allow as a verification. If, for example, I admit a chemical reaction as a means of verification, then it makes sense to say, 'This looks *grey*, but in reality it is *yellow*.' But if I regard what I see as a valid verification, then it makes no sense any more to say, 'This looks yellow, but it is not yellow.' In that case I can no longer look for a symptom of its being yellow, I have arrived at the fact itself; I have reached the ultimate point beyond which you cannot advance. I must not produce any *hypotheses* concerning what is immediately given.

It is the same with time as with colour. The word 'time' too means entirely different things: the time of my memories, the time of another person's statements, the time of physics.

My memories are ordered. *Time is the way memories are ordered.* Thus time is given in immediate connection with memories. Time is, as it were, the form in which I have memories.

An ordering can also be achieved in a different way, for example by means of statements made by me or another person. If I say, e.g., 'This event occurred earlier, that one later,' then this is an entirely different ordering. Both kinds of ordering can combine, as for example when I talk about the great fire I heard stories about in my childhood. Here the time of memory and the time of statements are, as it were, superimposed on one another. It is even more complicated with respect to historical statements or the time of geology. Here the sense of a temporal specification depends entirely on what is admitted as a verification.

PROBABILITY II

'Probability' can have two completely different meanings:
1. the probability of an event;
2. the probability of an induction.
In the latter sense it means the inconvenience I should feel, if I gave up a certain induction.

It is a fact of experience that if I throw a die 100 times, a 1 will occur. After throwing it 99 times without throwing a 1 I will say, 'It is high time for a 1; I bet there will be a 1 now.' The calculus of probabilities says that this inference is not justified. I think, though, that it is justified; for it is very 'probable' that there will be a 1 now, although not probable in the sense of the calculus of probabilities, but in the sense of the probability of an induction. The confusion of these two concepts of probability gives rise to a whole series of misunderstandings. (A time will come, just as differences in temperatures will come about of their own accord, and so forth.)

We should be highly astonished, if a deviation from the usual distribution occurred. Machines for mixing chocolate, almonds, and raisins. Everybody expects to find almonds and raisins in his piece, and if this were not the case, the producers would soon have the machine overhauled.

In everyday life probability means the probability of induction. this cannot be measured, at least not in the same sense in which the probability of the probability calculus can be measured. [1] [Perhaps not at all by means of numbers in the ordinary sense?]

HYPOTHESES I

Distinctions between 'statements' and 'hypotheses': An hypothesis is not a statement, but a law for constructing statements.

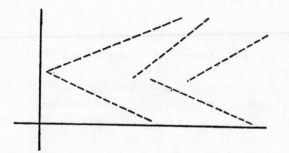

points of light

1] We can indeed say that a natural law that has frequently stood the test is probably more plausible than another one; but we have no means of measuring to express this difference numerically.

What we observe are always merely 'sections' through the connected structure of the law.

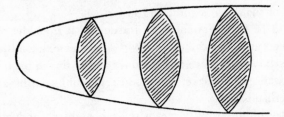

A natural law cannot be verified or falsified. Of a natural law you can say that it is neither true nor false but 'probable,' and here 'probable' means: simple, convenient. A statement is true or false, never probable. Anything that is probable is not a statement.

Sense of physical statements [1]—they refer to the future *ad infinitum*. They never count as proved; we always reserve the right to drop or alter them, in contrast with a real statement, whose truth is not subject to alteration.

Double Meaning of Geometry

The geometry of the visual field is the grammar of statements about objects in the visual field. You cannot say that this geometry is plausible.

The geometry of physical space is an entirely different matter. It can be rendered plausible (probable). It stands on the same level as the laws of nature. It is part of the description given by physics and can be altered.

'This surface is a cylinder' is an hypothesis.

1] The sense of a physical statement is not exhausted by observation.

If I find a brownish egg and say, 'This egg comes from a lark,' then this statement is not verif⟨iable⟩. Rather, I construct a hypothesis about this bird laying eggs.

It is *mathematical* induction that occurs in an hypothesis. Connection with the system of space-time, with mathematics.

Logic of an hypothesis [1]: What does it mean, two hypotheses contradict one another? A contradiction between two propositions is due to a contradiction between statements that result from these propositions.

You know a physical equation only when you know the method of projection that correlates propositions with the numbers. The equations are set in relation to a system of propositions in which numbers appear.

$S=2W$; S refers to a proposition, so does W.

Physics constructs a system of hypotheses represented as a system of equations. The equations of physics can neither be true nor false. It is only the findings in the course of a verification, i.e. phen⟨omenological⟩ statements, that are true and false. *Physics is not history*. It prophesies. If you tried to conceive of physics as a mere report on the facts observed to date, it would be lacking its most essential element, its relation to the future. It would be like the narration of a dream.

The statements of physics are never completed. Nonsense to think of them as completed.

I step out of the house and see that I am standing in the Ringstraβe.[62] What would I do?

Hypothesis as postulate. Convention.

Mr. Waismann and his brother.[63] I would say for example, 'This is certainly not Mr. Waismann; it is only his brother who looks very similar to him.'

1] [If geometry is contradictory, this means that it leads us to make statements that are contradictions.]

62 At the time of this conversation neither Schlick's flat nor the house of Wittgenstein's family were on the Ringstraβe.
63 Waismann had no brother.

III

⟨WHAT TO SAY AT KÖNIGSBERG⟩

WITTGENSTEIN SETS OUT WHAT OUGHT TO BE SAID AT KÖNIGS-BERG:[64] In logic there are no concepts. What looks like a concept is the title of a chapter in grammar. In speaking of different kinds of number, for example, you are not dealing with different concepts. We do not have *one* concept of number that splits up into different sub-concepts. Numbers do not fall into sub-classes: instead we have different kinds of word before us in a sense similar to that in which grammar distinguishes between nouns, adjectives, verbs, etc. There are certain similarities between the syntax of different kinds of number, and this is why we call them all numbers.

A class cannot be finite or infinite. The words 'finite' and 'infinite' do not signify a supplementary determination regarding 'class'. They are not adjectives.

In logic we do not have an object and the description of that object. You will say for example, 'To be sure, we cannot enumerate all the numbers of a set, but we can give a description.' That is nonsense. You cannot give a description instead of an enumeration. The one is not a substitute for the other. What we can give, we can give. We cannot reach the same target from behind.

Set theory starts from Dirichlet's concept of a function.[65] Here a

---

64 See editor's Preface, p. 19.

65 The first formulation of the general concept of a function of real variables is usually ascribed to P. Lejeune-Dirichlet; see his *Werke*, Vol. I, Berlin, 1899, pp. 132 and 135. H. Hankel's formulation of Dirichlet's concept runs, '*y* is called a function of *x* if within a definite interval there is a definite value of *y* for every value of the variable magnitude *x*, no matter whether *y* is dependent on *x* according to the same law within the whole interval or not and no matter whether the dependence can be expressed by means of mathematical operations or not.'

function is conceived of as a correlation. The ordinary man thinks that a correlation is a kind of list. Suddenly the list comes to an end and a law is supplied. A law is not another method of giving what a list gives. The list *cannot* give what the law gives. No list is imaginable any more. We are actually dealing with two absolutely different things. People always pretend that the one is an indirect method of doing the other. I could supply a list; but as that is too complicated or beyond my powers, I will supply a law. This sounds like saying, Up to now I have been talking to you; when I am in England I shall have to write to you.

Nothing is more suspect than too great generality. In giving his definition of the infinite Dedekind pretends he has no idea that afterwards he will be dealing with *numbers*.[66] Perhaps the definition will fit lions! All this is nonsense. We must make clear to ourselves that we cannot prepare ourselves for a logical form. We cannot study the properties of a logical form and think that when we encounter such a form, we shall be prepared.

Formalism

Part of formalism is right and part wrong.

The truth in formalism is that every syntax can be conceived of as a system of rules of a game. I have been thinking about what Weyl may mean when he says that a formalist conceives of the axioms of mathematics as like chess-rules.[67] I want to say that not only the axioms of mathematics but all syntax is arbitrary.

In Cambridge I have been asked whether I believe that mathema-

66 See footnote p. 69 above.
67 *Symposion* I (1927), p. 25.

tics is about strokes of ink on paper.[68] To this I reply that it is so in just the sense in which chess is about wooden figures. For chess does not consist in pushing wooden figures on wood. If I say, 'Now I shall get a queen with very terrible eyes and she will drive everything from the field,' you will laugh. It does not matter what a pawn looks like. It is rather the totality of rules of a game that yields the logical position of a pawn. A pawn is a variable, just like 'x' in logic.

It is clear that in chess it is not the actual movements that matter. The moves on a chess-board are not the movements of physics. If I say, 'The knight *can* move only by means of a triple jump, the bishop can move only diagonally, the castle only straight ahead,' then the word 'can' means grammatical possibility. What is against the rules is a violation of syntax.

If I am asked, then, what it is that distinguishes the syntax of a language from the game of chess, I answer: It is its application and nothing else. We can lay down the syntax of a language without knowing if this syntax can ever be applied. (Hypercomplex numbers.) All you can say is that syntax can be applied only to what it can be applied to. If on Mars there were human beings and they waged war against each other in the way chessmen do on a board, then their headquarters would use the rules of chess for prophesying. Then it would be a scientific question whether checkmate can be reached in a certain constellation of the game, whether mate can be reached in three moves, and so forth.

The essential thing is that syntax cannot be justified by means of language. When I am painting a *portrait of you* and I paint a black moustache, then I can answer to your question as to why I am doing it:

68 This was in the Lent term 1930, according to G. E. Moore's lecture notes, which Mr. C. Lewy and the late Mrs. Dorothy Moore kindly allowed me to look at.

Have a look! There you see a black moustache.[69] But if you ask me *why* I use a syntax, I cannot point at anything as a justification. You cannot give reasons for syntax. Hence it is arbitrary. Detached from its applications and considered by itself it is a game, just like chess.

This is where formalism is right. *Frege* was right in objecting to the conception that the numbers of arithmetic are signs.[70] The sign '0', after all, does not have the property of yielding the sign '1' when it is added to the sign '1'. Frege was right in this criticism. Only he did not see the other, justified side of formalism, that the symbols of mathematics, although they are not signs, lack a meaning. For Frege the alternative was this: either we deal with strokes of ink on paper or these strokes of ink are signs *of something* and their meaning is what they go proxy for. The game of chess itself shows that these alternatives are wrongly conceived—although it is not the wooden chessmen we are dealing with, these figures do not go proxy for anything, they have no meaning in Frege's sense. There is still a third possibility, the signs can be used the way they are in the game. If here (in chess) you wanted to talk of 'meaning', the most natural thing to say would be that the meaning of chess is what all games of chess have in common.

If we construct a figure in geometry, once again we are not dealing with lines on paper. The pencil-strokes are the same thing as the signs in arithmetic and the chessmen in chess. The essential thing is the rules that hold of those structures—or, better, they are not the 'essential thing' but they are what interests me about those structures.

Equation and Tautology I

I believe that mathematics, once the conflict about its foundations has come to an end, will look just as it does in elementary school where

---

69 Waismann in fact had a dark moustache.
70 *Grundgesetze der Arithmetik* II, Jena, 1903, §§88–137.

the abacus[71] is used. The way of doing mathematics in elementary school is absolutely strict and exact. It need not be improved upon in any way. Mathematics is always a machine, a calculus. The calculus does not describe anything. It can be applied to everything that allows of its application. You can count only what admits of being counted and that is also what the results of our calculus hold good for.

You can easily come to believe that the expression of an equation is a tautology. That e.g. $28+16 = 44$ might be expressed in the following way:

$$(E28x) \; \varphi x . \; (E16x) \; \psi x . \text{Ind.}: \; \supset : (E44x) \; \varphi x \lor \psi x$$

This expression is a tautology. But in order to find the number on the right-hand side that turns this expression into a tautology, you have to use a calculus, and this calculus is entirely independent of tautology. Tautology is an application of the calculus, not its expression. A calculus is an abacus, a calculator, a calculating machine; it works by means of strokes, numerals, etc. Subsequently a calculus may be used to construct a tautology; but this does not at all connect a calculus with propositions or with tautology.

As a fact, everyone at school calculates by means of numbers, and they do it quite strictly without having any idea what tautology is. In that case, however, the essence of our calculus cannot have anything to do with tautology.

Incidentally, two conceptions are possible here. In *Principia Mathematica* Russell believed that his logical propositions said something, that they described something. If this is your conception, then it is understandable that you think that a tautology expresses the sense of the equation $28+16 = 44$. But once you have moved on to the other conception, according to which the propositions of logic are tautologies and say nothing, it would not be consistent at all to cling to the claim that a tautology expresses that $28+16 = 44$.

A mathematical equation is in a certain sense more like an empiri-

---

71 When Wittgenstein was a teacher he himself thought very highly of the abacus, although the 'Schulreform', which was then in its early stages, looked at it somewhat askance.

cal proposition than like a tautology. For it is similar to what a tautology *shows*.

25 September 1930[72]

⟨MISCELLANEA⟩

It seems as if you can say that only the present has reality. Here you must ask, In contrast with what? Is this supposed to mean that my mother did not exist, or that I did not get up this morning? That cannot be what we mean. Is it supposed to mean that the events I cannot now recall did not exist? It does not mean that either.

The present moment that we are here talking about must mean something that is not *within* a space but itself is a space.

There seems to be something that is not generality but a *symptom* of generality, thus, e.g., when I say, 'When you see the window lit up this is a sign of my being at home'. The window that is lit up does not have the multiplicity of generality.

I do not believe that it is correct to say that every proposition must be composite in a literal sense.[73] What would it be like if 'ambulo' consisted only of its root syllable? What is correct in this is that every proposition is a special case of a general rule for constructing signs.

To be sure I can ask the question, Was that thunder or a shot? but not, Was that a noise? I can say, 'Check if this is a circle or an ellipse.'

72 No place is mentioned. Down to the next title the entries are written on both pages; at the end there is a gap of half a page. See editor's Preface, pp. 28–29.
73 *TLP* 4.032, 'Even the proposition 'Ambulo', is composite, etc.'

Here you might raise the objection that the word 'this' means something different according as the proposition is true or false.

It is clear that word 'this' must have a fixed meaning, whether the proposition turns out true or false. If I may say, 'This is a circle,' then it must also make sense to say, 'This is an ellipse.'

To be sure I can say, 'Wipe the table.' But not, 'Wipe all the points!'

If I say, 'The table is brown', then it makes sense to relate the property 'brown' to a bearer—the table. If I can imagine the table to be brown, then I can imagine it to have any other colour. What does this mean—I can imagine *the same* circle to be red or green? What has remained the same? The form of the circle. But this is something I cannot imagine by itself.

'This proposition has a sense' is an unfortunate phrase.
'This proposition has a sense' sounds like 'This man has a hat'.
'These signs mean a proposition' means that we trace the form of a proposition in the signs.

In a proposition we trace the form of reality, as it were. [F.W.]

If I know that these signs mean a proposition, then I cannot ask, What proposition?

VARIABLES[74]

Euler's[75] proof is immediately in error, as soon as prime numbers are written down in the form $p_1, p_2, \ldots p_n$. For if the index n is to mean

74 Here Waismann goes back to his habit of writing the main entry on the recto.
75 Cf. L. Euler, *Variae Observationes circa series infinities*, 1744, Theorema VII, and H. Hasse, *Vorlesungen über Zahlentheorie*, 2nd edition, Berlin, 1964, pp. 192–3.

an *arbitrary* number, then this already presupposes a law of progression, and this law can be given only in terms of an induction. Thus the proof presupposes what it is supposed to prove.

What is the meaning of a variable? By what means can I distinguish a variable from the sign of an unknown quantity?

It is only in virtue of the existence of rules for the substitution of numbers for a sign that a sign of a variable can mean a variable. That a variable can take the place of all the natural numbers is expressed by the fact that the rules for substitution have the form of induction.

PROOF

A proof is not a vehicle for getting anywhere, but is the thing itself. I can say, 'Up to such-and-such a place I go by train; then I walk until I reach X.' In this case we have two vehicles for the same thing, namely for a distance in space.

In contrast with that two different proofs cannot lead to the same thing. Two proofs can either meet, like two paths leading to the same destination, or they prove different things: a difference between proofs corresponds to a difference between things proved. [1]

REAL NUMBERS II

You can speak of a real number only when you have got it.

If you think that a set of decimal fractions will be dropped if you restrict yourself to constructing decimal fractions in accordance with

---

1] A transformation of two proofs into one another is the proof of their proving the same thing.

the rules, then that raises the question, Which ones are dropped? Specify one of them! A proof for 'all real numbers' means something entirely different from a proof for all natural numbers.

In the first place you cannot originally prove a proposition about the natural numbers and subsequently discover that it also holds for a larger domain: no, you are then faced with a completely new proposition.

If we prove a proposition for all real numbers, then this means that we prove the proposition by means of induction for all rational numbers, and then add something else, namely, that if the variable in question means e.g. $\sqrt{2}$, then the proposition is to be interpreted to mean: Such-and-such is true of the limiting case.

A proof for all real numbers is not analogous to a proof for all rational numbers so that you could say that what has been proved for all rational numbers—by means, of course, of induction—can in *the same way*, by means of an extension of this proof-procedure, be proved for all real numbers. [1]

1] Thus it is not as though I first proved a proposition for rational numbers and then extended it in an *analogous way* to real numbers. A proof for real numbers is not analogous to a proof for rational numbers but means something entirely different.

A proof for real numbers is not a continuation of a proof for rational numbers but an entirely different thing.

If any real number is given, then such-and-such holds for this number too, not because of an induction but because of the rules that I have laid down when calculating with real numbers.

Thus such a formula does not mean that such-and-such holds good for all real numbers, but that if a real number is given, then I interpret this formula in such a way that it means that such-and-such is true of the limiting case, and I prove this on the basis of the rules that have been laid down for calculating with real numbers.

Accordingly, things are as follows: I think of a *particular* real number as given and hold that unchanged throughout my proof. This is an entirely different matter from the case of rational numbers; for in

A proof for real numbers must be understood in an entirely different way from a proof for rational numbers. Only in this latter case can the proof be conducted by means of induction, and this makes it appear as if the proof indicated something outside itself.

This is of course wrong. A proof must contain everything that it means.

A proof for all real numbers is not an abbreviation of something that could also be proved at length. The extra that is added to a proof for rational numbers is not analogous to induction. A proof for real numbers is in no way deficient.

Suppose for example that I have, by induction, proved the formula

the case of rational numbers the question was precisely whether a certain formula remains correct if the rational numbers vary and it was *because of this* that our proof had the form of an induction. But here the question whether the formula holds for 'all real' numbers is not raised at all and it is not raised for the reason that we do not vary our real number at all.

For we do not prove that *however* you choose the sequence r_1, r_2, . . . r_n . . . , it will always be the case that such-and-such.

We do not make a variable real number assume all values—i.e. all laws.

We simply rely on the rules for calculation and nothing else.

If a formula holds good for a certain natural number, that is not enough to tell me whether it holds for another number, and this is why I have to prove it.

Variable for natural numbers: n

$$F(n) \xrightarrow{\text{proof}} \text{basic formula} \longrightarrow \text{induction}$$

Variable for real numbers: ρ

$$F(\rho) \xrightarrow{\text{proof}} \text{basic formula} \longrightarrow \text{rules for calculating with real numbers}$$

$a^m.a^n = a^{m+n}$ for rational values of m, n, and that I now want to prove it for values that are real numbers. How can I manage to do this? Obviously it is no longer possible to conduct the proof by means of induction.

The idea that this proposition holds for 'all real numbers,' whether I know them or not, is completely void. In fact, I can talk about a real number only if I have got it. In fact, I can give the proposition a meaning only *if* I already know the real number.

You must not think, This proposition holds for all rational numbers, and now we will show that it holds for all real numbers too. This additional element is not a collateral proof.

What is additionally contained in this proof is not, say, a second part comparable to induction; this second part has an entirely different character—it is an interpretation.

Thus if a formula is asserted for real numbers, then this comprises a proof and an interpretation.

If I prove that my formula holds for the real numbers, then I infer everything from the rules that are laid down for calculating with real numbers. *I prove by means of induction that the formula holds for rational numbers and then I show that it carries over to the real numbers, simply on the basis of the rules that I have laid down for calculating with real numbers.* But I do not prove that the formula holds for 'all real' numbers, for the reason that the rules for calculating with real numbers do not have the form of an induction.

'Therefore this proposition holds for all numbers.' Once again we must say, In this case there is no 'therefore'. The proof is all there is, it is not a mere vehicle. The proof proves only what it does prove and everything else is incidental.

Now it might be thought that this proposition should really be proved for all real numbers, while what we have given is nothing but a hint. This is false. Our proof for real numbers is all that is required. The proof is not an abbreviation of something that could be proved at greater length. The proof simply follows from the rules that we have laid down for calculating with real numbers.

The formula is to be understood in this way: If I am given a real number, then such-and-such holds.

A formula that has been proved for real numbers does not say: It is true of all real numbers that . . . , but it says that if a real number is given, then it is true that . . . .

And this not because of a proof, but because of an interpretation.

Can this not be asserted of formulas for natural numbers too? No, it cannot. The difference is that there the proof consists in an induction.

IDEALIZATION

What does idealization mean? Does anything become different by my idealization? Do I change anything by idealization?

In logic an object and its description do not co-exist. If I speak of 9^{99} objects I have already represented this number, precisely by means of the structure of the operations.

I need not worry about whether there actually is a set that contains 9^{99} individuals. Indeed, raising such a question presupposes the previous existence of this number.

If it were suggested that mathematics rested on our idealization of reality, its properties, relations, and the like—then the first question would be this: And what becomes different in virtue of my idealization?

INTERPRETATION

What does interpretation mean? Either an interpretation is something inessential, something that depends on my mood for example; in which case you may say that every interpretation is superfluous, that an interpretation can neither be true nor false. Or an interpretation is essentially connected with mathematics. What, then, does it consist in? An interpretation cannot consist in propositions, but again only in rules: the rules of a calculus are fitted into a certain setting, as it were, into a wider syntactical context.

If we wished to interpret the Russellian calculus, for example, then it would become apparent that the sign 'infinite' or ' $\aleph_0$ ' does not fit into the context it was really intended for, since it would produce nonsense there.[76] That is, the syntax of the sign 'infinite' is an entirely different one from the syntax of the Russellian sign for the infinite.

Thus this calculus *qua* calculus is all right. Only it does not accomplish what Russell believed it did when he set it up. Of course, when Russell was constructing his calculus he did not intend to develop merely a game of chess, but meant to reproduce with his calculus what the word 'infinite' really means when it is applied. But in this he was wrong.

The calculus can be applied to anything that admits of such application. (And you cannot say anything that goes beyond this.)

By this interpretation, however, the calculus is pushed into an entirely different context, namely into a context of syntactical rules that is completely inappropriate.

The statement 'If you go on looking for a sufficiently long time, you will certainly find a number' is totally meaningless. You cannot look for anything *ad infinitum*.

In logic there are no general and no special cases.[77]

76 Cantor's number was introduced by Whitehead and Russell in *Principia Mathematica* II, Cambridge, 1912, pp. 268ff.
77 Cf. *TLP* 5.454.

IV

Wednesday, 17 December 1930 (Neuwaldegg)[78]

ON SCHLICK'S ETHICS

Schlick says that in theological ethics there used to be two conceptions of the essence of the good: according to the shallower interpretation the good is good because it is what God wants; according to the profounder interpretation God wants the good because it is good.[79] I think that the first interpretation is the profounder one: what God commands, that is good. For it cuts off the way to any explanation 'why' it is good, while the second interpretation is the shallow, rationalist one, which proceeds 'as if' you could give reasons for what is good.

The first conception says clearly that the essence of the good has nothing to do with facts and hence cannot be explained by any proposition. If there is any proposition expressing precisely what I think, it is the proposition 'What God commands, that is good.'

VALUE[80]

In describing reality I describe what I come upon among men. Similarly, sociology must describe our conduct and our valuations

---

78 A suburb of Vienna where the Wittgenstein family owned two mid-season houses. See editor's preface, p. 23.

79 *Fragen der Ethik*, Vienna, 1930, p. 9. '*That* is the profound interpretation' Wittgenstein wrote at the corresponding point on the margin of his copy of the book. In the English translation, which was partly revised by Schlick, 'die flachere Deutung . . . die tiefere Deutung' (translated above as 'the shallower . . . the profounder interpretation') becomes 'one interpretation . . . another, perhaps profounder, interpretation' (*Problems of Ethics*, New York, 1939, p. 11).

80 This section too probably originated in a discussion about Schlick's book, cf. §9

just like those of the Negroes. It can only report what occurs. But the proposition, 'Such-and-such means progress,' must never occur in a sociologist's description.

What I can describe is that preferences are stated. Suppose I discovered by experience that of two pictures you always prefer the one containing more green, or a greenish tinge, etc. In this case I have described only *that* but not that the picture in question is more valuable.

What is valuable in a Beethoven sonata? The sequence of notes? No, it is only one sequence among many, after all. Indeed, I would go so far as to say that even the feelings Beethoven had when he was composing this sonata were not more valuable than any other feelings. And the fact of being preferred has equally little claim to be something valuable in itself.

Is value a particular state of mind? Or a form attaching to some data or other of consciousness? I would reply that whatever I was told, I would reject, and that not because the explanation was false but because it was an *explanation*.

If I were told anything that was a *theory*, I would say, No, no! That does not interest me. Even if this theory were true, it would not interest me—it would not be the exact thing I was looking for.

'Ethics as Factual Science', p. 20 (p. 14 of the original), 'Such norms as are recognized as the ultimate norms or highest values, must be derived from human nature and life as facts. Therefore, no result of ethics can stand in contradiction to life; . . . Where such opposition occurs it is a sure sign that the philosopher has misunderstood his problem, and has failed to solve it; [Wittgenstein comments in the margin, 'But how curious that such a misunderstanding arises!'] that he has unwittingly become a moralist, that he feels uncomfortable in the role of a knower and would prefer to be a creator of moral values.' [Wittgenstein, 'But how can one be such a creator? And wasn't it said earlier that a creator in this sense was only affirming something?']
81 Schlick, *Problems of Ethics*, p. 21 (German p. 15), 'The ultimate valuations are facts existing in human consciousness, and even if ethics were a normative science it would not cease because of this to be a science of facts.'

What is ethical cannot be taught. If I could explain the essence of the ethical only by means of a theory, then what is ethical would be of no value whatsoever.[82]

At the end of my lecture on ethics I spoke in the first person:[83] I think that this is something very essential. Here there is nothing to be stated any more; all I can do is to step forth as an individual and speak in the first person.

For me a theory is without value. A theory gives me nothing.

RELIGION

Is talking essential to religion? I can well imagine a religion in which there are no doctrinal propositions, in which there is thus no talking. Obviously the essence of religion cannot have anything to do with the fact that there is talking, or rather: when people talk, then this itself is part of a religious act and not a theory. Thus it also does not matter at all if the words used are true or false or nonsense.

In religion talking is not *metaphorical* either; for otherwise it would have to be possible to say the same things in prose. Running against the limits of language? Language is, after all, not a cage.[84]

---

82 Wittgenstein wrote into *Ms. vol.* III (no. 107 in the catalogue of G. H. von Wright (henceforth V.W.); see *Philosophical Review* 78 (1969) pp. 483–503), 15 November, 1929, 'You cannot lead people to the good; you can only lead them somewhere. The good lies outside the space of facts.'

83 Perhaps Wittgenstein does not refer to his report on his own 'ethical' experiences (*LE*, pp. 7ff.) but rather to his concluding remarks (op. cit., pp. 11f.) where he rejects the view that a correct logical analysis of ethical and religious assertions—which would explain them as factual statements—could ever be found. 'Now when this is urged against me I at once see clearly, as it were in a flash of light, not only that no description that I can think of would do to describe what I mean by absolute value, but that I would reject every significant description that anybody could possible suggest, *ab initio*, on the ground of its significance. &c.'

84 *LE* p. 12.

All I can say is this: I do not scoff at this tendency in man; I hold it in reverence. And here it is essential that this is not a description of sociology but that I am speaking *about myself*.

The facts of the matter are of no importance for me. But what men mean when they say that *'the world is there'* is something I have at heart.[85]

WAISMANN ASKS: Is the existence of the world connected with what is ethical?

WITTGENSTEIN: Men have felt that here there is a connection and they have expressed it thus: God the Father created the world, the Son of God (or the Word that comes from God) is that which is ethical. That the Godhead is thought of as divided and, again, as one being indicates that there is a connection here.

OUGHT

What does the word 'ought' mean? A child ought to do such-and-such means that if he does not do it, something umpleasant will happen. Reward and punishment. The essential thing about this is that the other person is brought to do something. 'Ought' makes sense only if there is something lending support and force to it—a power that punishes and rewards. Ought in itself is nonsensical. [86]

'To moralize is difficult, to establish morality impossible.'[87]

---

85 *LE* p. 8.
86 Cf, *TLP* 6.422. Schlick too rejected the concept 'the absolute ought' for similar reasons (op. cit. pp. 110ff.).
87 'To moralize is easy, to establish morality difficult.' Schopenhauer, *Über den Willen in der Natur*, Frauenstädt edition, p. 140.

CONSISTENCY II

I have been reading a work by Hilbert on consistency.[88] I have the impression that the whole question has been put wrongly. I would like to ask, Is it even *possible* for mathematics to be inconsistent?

I would like to ask these people, What are you really up to? Do you really believe that there are contradictions hidden in mathematics?

Axioms have two meanings, as Frege saw:[89]

1. The rules *according to* which you play.
2. The opening positions of a game.

If you take the axioms in the second meaning, I can attach no sense to the claim that they contradict each other. It would be very odd to say, This configuration of the pieces ('0 ≠ 0,' for example, in Hilbert's game with formulas) is a contradiction. And if I call an arbitrary configuration a contradiction, then this has no essential significance, at least not for the game *qua* game. If I arrange the rules in such a way that this configuration of pieces cannot come about, I have merely made up another game. But the game is a game, and I cannot understand in any way why people want to attach so great a significance to the occurrence of this configuration; they behave as if just this configuration was 'tabu'. In contrast to this I ask, And what is there to get excited about if this configuration turns up? [1]

The situation is entirely different if the axioms are taken as rules *according to* which the game is played. The rules are—in a certain

---

1] Why should a certain configuration of signs not be allowed to arise? Why this dread? Why the tabu?

88 '0 ≠0' occurs as a symbol for a contradiction in 'Über das Unendliche' (1925) and in 'Grundlagen der Mathematik' (1927), *Grundlagen der Geometrie*, 7th edition, 1930, appendix VIII and IX. This reference, however, is probably to 'Neubegründung der Mathematik' (1922) where Hilbert talks about 'a metamathematics which serves to secure mathematics' (*Gesammelte Abhandlungen*, III, Berlin, 1935, especially p. 175). There, however, his typical contradiction is 'a ≠ a'.
89 Cf. e.g. *Grundgesetze der Arithmetik* II, Jena, 1903, § 109.

sense—statements. They say, 'You may do this and this, but not that.' Two rules can contradict one another. Suppose in chess, for example, a rule ran, 'Under such-and-such conditions the piece in question must be taken.' But another rule said: 'A knight must never be taken.' Now if the piece concerned *is* a knight, then the rules contradict one another; I do not know what to do. What do we do in such a case? Very simple—we introduce a new rule and the conflict is resolved.

I think, then, if contradictions arose between the rules of the game of mathematics, it would be the easiest thing in the world to find a remedy. All we have to do is lay down a new stipulation concerning the case in which the rules conflict, and the matter is dealt with.

Here, however, I must make an important observation. A contradiction is a contradiction only *if it is there*. People have the notion that a contradiction that nobody has seen might be hidden in the axioms from the very beginning, like tuberculosis. You do not have the faintest idea, and then some day or other you are dead. Similarly people think that some day or other the hidden contradiction might break out and then disaster would be upon us.

I think that as long as no procedure for finding a contradiction is given, there is no sense in wondering if our inferences might not *eventually* lead to a contradiction.

As long as I can play the game, I can play it, and everything is all right.

The truth of the matter is this—our calculus *qua* calculus is all right. It does not make sense to speak of contradictions. What is called a contradiction springs into existence as soon as you step outside the calculus and say in everyday prose, *Therefore* this property is true of all numbers, but the number 17 does not have this property.

In the calculus a contradiction cannot manifest itself at all.

I can play with chessmen according to certain rules. But I could also invent a game in which I play with the rules themselves: Now the rules of chess are the pieces of my game and the laws of logic for instance are the rules of the game. *In this case I have yet another game and not a metagame.*

What Hilbert does is mathematics and not metamathematics. It is another calculus, just like any other one.

Friday, 26 December 1930 (at Schlick's house)

STYLE OF THINKING[90]

Sunday, 28 December 1930 (at Schlick's house)

CONSISTENCY III

The problem of the consistency of mathematics stems from two sources: 1 From the ideas of non-Euclidean geometry where it was a matter of proving the axiom of parallels after the established model of *reductio ad absurdum*. 2 From the Burali-Forti and Russellian antinomies.

It was chiefly the antinomies that initiated the present preoccupation with consistency. If nowadays you asked the mathematicians, 'Tell me, why are you so interested in this question? Have you ever encountered a contradiction *in* mathematics?,' they would appeal to the antinomies in the first place, and this is what they do actually say.

Now it has to be said that these antinomies have nothing whatsoever to do with the consistency of mathematics; there is no connec-

90 Three pages (recto) were left blank for notes of this conversation. See editor's Preface, p. 29.

tion here at all. For the antinomies did not arise in the calculus but in our ordinary language, precisely because we use words ambiguously. Hence the resolution of the antinomies consists in replacing the hazy way of expressing ourselves by a precise one (by recalling the real meanings of our words). Thus the antinomies vanish by means of an *analysis*, not by means of a *proof*.

If the contradictions in mathematics arise through an unclarity, then I can *never dispel this unclarity by a proof*. A proof proves only what it does prove. But it cannot lift the fog. What is needed is an analysis, not a proof. A proof cannot dispel the fog.

This is enough to show that there can be no such thing as a proof of consistency (if you imagine the contradictions of mathematics as being of the same kind as the contradictions of set theory), that this proof cannot accomplish what it is expected to do.

If I am unclear about the nature of mathematics, no proof can help me. And if I am clear about the nature of mathematics, then the question about its consistency cannot arise at all. [?]

Sheffer's Discovery[91]

In what sense was it really a discovery that you can make do in logic with a single logical constant? What is the nature of Sheffer's discovery?

Suppose Frege happened to write down all his basic laws of logic in this form:

$$\sim (. . .) .v. \sim (. . .)$$

while thinking that he needed two constants. Now suppose another

91 *Transactions of the American Mathematical Society*, 14 (1913) pp. 481–488. Of the two possible interpretations of the one logical constant, Wittgenstein here chooses the OR form preferred by J. Nicod (*Proceedings of the Cambridge Philosophical Society*, 19, 1917–20, pp. 32–41), although he himself had used the AND form in *TLP*.

man *saw* what Frege had not noticed and said, We can make do with a single constant! What is it that this man has really discovered? He has seen the new system in the old one. Here *seeing* matters essentially: as long as you do not see the new system, you have not got it. Frege would not have got it, even if by chance he had written everything in terms of the multiplicity of the new system. From the point of view of the old system you cannot look for the new system. This is why it *cannot be proved* by means of transformation.

It seems possible to say: In logic we can make do with three constants, and also with two; can we also make do with *one* constant? This sounds like a legitimate question, but it is not, since I have no method of looking for this system. By the way, you cannot count the logical constants like three apples, either; for the apples constitute objects that fall under a concept, whereas the logical constants are a structure. What I here call one logical constant has a structure that is entirely different from that of two logical constants. What I can count is the signs and they do not matter here.

There cannot be a proof which says that I can make do with one logical constant.

Thus if you wanted to ask, 'Can we make do with a single logical constant?,' or to prove that we can make do with a single logical constant, it would all be without sense.

This example elucidates what I mean by my claim that there cannot be a proof of the consistency of mathematics and that, if one existed, it would not be an object of fundamental interest.

⟨*Rules and Configurations of a Game*⟩

Russell was of the opinion that his five 'primitive propositions'[92] were at the same time the basic configurations and the rules of progression.

---

92 For the five true 'primitive propositions' see *Principia Mathematica* I, Cambridge, 1910, pp. 96–7, 1.2– 1.6.

But in this he was wrong, and this was shown by the fact that he himself had to add further rules (in words!).

Thus we must distinguish: the basic configurations of the calculus (the opening positions of the game) and the rules that specify how we have to move from one configuration to another.

This was already explained by Frege in his criticism of the theories of Heine and Thomae: 'This is a surprise. What would somebody say if, on asking for the rules of chess, he received no answer—being shown instead a group of chessmen on the chess-board? He would probably say he could find no rules there, since he associates no sense with the chessmen and their positions.' (*Grundgesetze der Arithmetik* II, § 106, p. 113.)

Now if I take the calculus *qua* calculus, then the configurations of the game cannot represent a contradiction (unless I arbitrarily call a configuration that occurs in the game a 'contradiction' and exclude it; this serves only to declare that I am playing a *different* game.) [1]

The idea of a contradiction—and this is something I hold fast to—is that of a logical contradiction, and this can occur only in the *true-false game*, that is, only where we make statements.

This means that a contradiction can occur only among the *rules of a game*. I can, for example, have a rule of a game that says: A white piece has to move by jumping over a black one.

If a black piece, then, is at the edge of the board, the rule fails. Thus it may be the case that I do not know what to do. The rule tells me nothing further. What would I do in such a case? Nothing is easier

---

1] It is always only *a game* that I can define by means of permission and prohibition, but never a *game* as such.[93] What Hilbert wants to show by means of his proof is that the axioms of arithmetic have the properties of a game as such, and this is impossible.

It is as if Hilbert wished to prove that a contradiction is *inadmissible*.

93 See p. 131 infra.

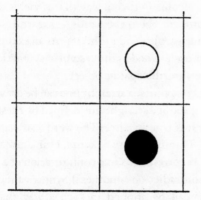

than removing the contradiction—I must make a decision, i.e. *introduce another rule*.

By the way, suppose among the rules there were two that contradicted each other, but I had such a bad memory that I never noticed this and always forgot one of these two rules or obeyed alternately the one and then the other. Even then I would say, Everything is all right. After all, the rules are instructions for playing the game, and as long as I can play, they must be all right. It is only when I *notice* that they contradict each other that they cease to be all right, and that manifests itself only in this: that I cannot apply them any more. For the logical product of the two rules is a contradiction, and a contradiction no longer tells me what to do. Thus the conflict appears only when I notice it. There was no problem as long as I was able to play the game.

In arithmetic, too, we reach the 'edge of the chess-board,' for example when we have the problem 0/0. (If I wanted to say that 0/0 = 1, then I could prove that 3 = 5, and thus I would come into conflict with the other rules of the game.)

Thus we see that as long as we take the calculus as a calculus, the question of consistency cannot seriously come to the fore at all. Is consistency thus perhaps connected with the *application* of a calculus? For this purpose we must ask ourselves:

What Does it Mean to Apply a Calculus?

This can mean two things:

1. You apply a calculus in such a way that it yields the *grammar* of a language. In grammar, then, the words 'sense' and 'senseless' correspond to what a rule permits and prohibits. As an example we may take *Euclidean geometry* understood as the system of syntactical rules according to which we describe spatial objects.

'Through any two points, a straight line can be drawn' means that a statement talking about a straight line defined by these two points has a sense, whether it is true or false. [The word 'can' has two meanings: 'I can lift 10kg,' 'Through any two points, I can draw a straight line.']

A rule of syntax corresponds to a configuration of a game. [Can the rules of syntax contradict one another?] Syntax cannot be justified.

2. A calculus can be applied in such a way that *true* and *false propositions* correspond to the configurations of the calculus. In this case the calculus yields a theory that describes something.

Newton's three laws have an entirely different meaning from geometry. There is a verification for them, namely by means of physical experiments. For a game, however, there is no justification. This is very important. Geometry too can be understood in this way by taking it as a description of the results of actual measurements. (?)

Then it is statements that we have before us, and statements can indeed contradict each other.

Whether a theory *can* describe anything depends on whether the logical product of its axioms is a contradiction. Either I see immediately that they produce a contradiction, and then the matter is clear. But how is it when I do not see this directly? In this case we have got a *hidden* contradiction.

For instance, Euclid's axioms plus the axiom 'The sum of the angles of a triangle = 181°.' Here I do not see the contradiction at once, for I do not at once see that a sum of 180° follows from the axioms.

As long as we move within the calculus, we do not have any

contradiction, for $s = 180°$, $s = 181°$ do not contradict each other at all. We can simply make two different stipulations. Now we can say that the calculus can be applied to everything to which it is applicable. We could even imagine another application in this case, supposing that the sum of the angles of a triangle amounts to $180°$ when measured according to one method, and $181°$ according to another. The point is only to find a domain whose description requires the multiplicity that the axioms possess.

Observation: Here the contradiction must be *logical contradiction* not *contrariety*.

'This patch is green' and 'This patch is red,' for example, do not contradict each other as long as we do not add another rule that has the effect of making their logical product a contradiction.

If, then, a contradiction occurs within a theory, this would mean that the propositions of the theory could no longer be translated into statements about the deflection of a galvanometer needle, etc. The results might for example be that the needle remains still or is deflected, and therefore this theory could not be verified. [1]

Unlike the equations of geometry, Maxwell's equations do not represent a calculus; they are a fragment, a part of a calculus.

What does it mean, mathematics must be 'made secure'?[94] What would happen if mathematics were secured? Is it a statement at all to say that the axioms are consistent?

Can you look for a contradiction? Only if there is a method of looking for it. There can be no such question as whether you will some day reach a contradiction by progressing in accordance with the rules.

1] There could be such a result as 'The needle is deflected to the left' without its being said from which side the needle is to be looked at.

94 See footnote, p. 119, above.

I believe that this is the essential thing on which everything to do with the question of consistency depends.

In a certain sense rules are statements, 'You may do such-and-such.' Where there are rules, you can always take the step to descriptions of the same multiplicity; in chess for example by describing how human beings play the game. Hence rules can contradict each other if the corresponding statements contradict each other.

⟨*Independence I*⟩

WAISMANN ASKS: Does it not make sense to ask oneself questions regarding an axiom system? Consider, for instance, the propositional calculus which Russell derives from five axioms. Bernays has shown that one of these axioms is redundant and that four are sufficient. He has further shown that these axioms form a 'complete system', i.e. that the addition of another axiom which cannot be derived from these four makes it possible to derive any proposition you might write down.[95] For this amounts to saying that any proposition follows from a contradiction. Is this, then, not a *material insight* into the Russellian calculus? Or let me take another case: I choose three axioms. I cannot derive the same class of propositions from them as I can from all five together. Is this not a material insight? Is it thus not possible to regard the demonstration of consistency too as a material insight?

WITTGENSTEIN: If I first take three propositions and then five, I can in no way compare the classes of consequences unless I construct a *new system* in which both groups occur.

---

95 *Mathematische Zeitschrift* 25, 1926, pp. 305–20.

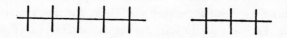

It is hence not as if I had both systems—the system with three axioms as well as that with five axioms—in front of me and compared them from outside. I cannot do that any more than I can compare, say, the integers and the rational numbers as long as I have not accommodated them in *one* system. Thus I do not gain a material insight, either: what I am really doing is, again, constructing a new calculus. And in this calculus the proposition, 'The one class is more comprehensive than the other one', does not occur at all. This is the everyday prose that accompanies the calculus.

You cannot gain a fundamental understanding of mathematics by waiting for the result of a theory.

Ramsey, for example, wrote that there is a leading problem of mathematical logic, the problem of decidability.[96] You do not know if the calculus is in order, he says, until this problem is solved. To that I would reply: Such *'leading problems' cannot exist!* the question whether what I am doing here is legitimate or not must not turn on what somebody or other will work out in the calculus.

Is it possible to ask, When did I apply the calculus? Is it possible that I do not know whether I have applied the calculus and that I have to wait for a demonstration of consistency?

The following is a question I constantly discuss with Moore: Can only logical analysis explain what we mean by the propositions of ordinary

96 In 'On a Problem of Formal Logic,' 1928; see *Foundations of Mathematics*, London, 1930, p. 82.

language? Moore is inclined to think so. Are people therefore ignorant of what they mean when they say 'Today the sky is clearer than yesterday'? Do we have to wait for logical analysis here? What a hellish idea! Only philosophy is supposed to explain to me what I mean by my propositions and whether I mean anything by them. I must, of course, be able to understand a proposition without knowing its analysis.

Tuesday, 30 December 1930 (at Schlick's house)

⟨CONSISTENCY IV⟩

⟨*Frege and Wittgenstein I*⟩

WAISMANN READS OUT FREGE:
Grundgesetze der Arithmetik II, §117: '. . . to obtain the group '0:0 = 3'; similarly we could construct '0:0 = 4'. From these two we could then go on to derive the group '3 = 4'. And this may be the reason for Thomae's assertion that division cannot always be performed uniquely; i.e. (?)[97] consistently. But here, in formal arithmetic, there is no immediate contradiction. Why should a group such as '3 = 4' not be permitted? . . . Till now . . . no prohibition has been issued against writing a figure group like '3 = 4'. Only when such a prohibition is issued will there arise a contradiction or, better, disagreement among the rules, some of which permit, and some of which prohibit.'

ibid. §118: 'Furthermore, it is remarkable that consistency is predicated of a figure. It would sound strange if someone suspected a chessman of harbouring a contradiction . . . we see that a contradic-

97 The question mark is Waismann's way of expressing what Frege says in the following note. 'The words "i.e." are remarkable here, since the extraction of a square root cannot in general be performed uniquely, though no contradiction results.' (*Translations from the Philosophical Writings of Gottlob Frege*, edited by P. Geach and M. Black, Oxford, 1952, p. 212.)

tion prevailing among the rules of chess would appear to be transferred to the interior of a chessman. To reach any understanding we will have to transfer the contradiction back again to the rules.'

WITTGENSTEIN: What must appear striking in this to an ordinary person is that mathematicians are always afraid of only *one* thing, which is a kind of nightmare to them, of a contradiction. They are not the least bit afraid e.g. of the possibility that a proposition might turn out to be a tautology, although a contradiction is no worse than a tautology. In logic a contradiction has exactly the same significance as a tautology, and I could study logic just as well by means of contradictions. A contradiction and a tautology do not *say* anything, do they?, they only provide a method for demonstrating the logical connections between statements.

People always speak of 'the law of contradiction.' I actually think that the fear of contradictions is connected with taking a contradiction to be a *proposition*:
$$'\sim(p.\sim p)'$$
I can easily take the law of contradiction to be a rule, for I prohibit the construction of the logical product '$p.\sim p$'. The tautology[98] '$\sim(p.\sim p)$', however, in no way expresses this prohibition. How could it? It does not say anything, after all, whereas a rule does say something.

WAISMANN REPEATS HIS QUESTION: You said that by permission and prohibition I can define only a particular game, never a game as such. Is this really true?[99] Imagine, for instance, the case where I permit any move in chess and do not prohibit anything—would this still be a game? Thus, must not the rules of a game have certain characteristics in order to define a game at all? Could the requirement of consistency

---

98 Waismann here wrote 'Kontradiktion', no doubt a slip of the pen.
99 See p. 124, above.

not be understood in such a way that it serves to exclude the 'tautological' game, the game in which everything is permitted? For if the formula '$0 \neq 0$' can be derived by a legitimate proof and if we, furthermore, in accordance with Hilbert, add the axiom '$0 \neq 0 \rightarrow A$', where 'A' means an arbitrary formula, then we can infer the formula 'A' from the deductive pattern.

$$\frac{\begin{array}{c} 0 \neq 0 \\ 0 \neq 0 \rightarrow A \end{array}}{A}$$

and write it down too.[100] This means, however, that in this case *any* formula can be derived, and thus the game loses its character and its interest.

WITTGENSTEIN: Absolutely not! This is a mistake, a confusion of 'rule of the game' and 'configuration of the pieces of the game'. The fact of the matter is that the game is tautological if the *rules of the game* are tautological (if they no longer permit or prohibit anything), but this is not the case here. This game, too, has its particular rules; it is one game among many, and the fact that the configuration '$0 \neq 0$' arises in it is of no consequence whatsoever.

It is just a configuration which arises in *this* game, and if I exclude it, I shall be faced with a *different* game. It is not true that in the first case I have no game but do have one before me in the second case. For it is clear that one class of rules and prohibitions borders on another class of rules and prohibitions; but *a game does not border on a non-game*. The 'tautological' game must turn out as the limiting case of games, as the natural border of games. The system of games must be limited from within, and the limit consists precisely in this, that the *rules of the game vanish*. I cannot get this limiting case by myself issuing certain rules and prohibitions; for precisely by doing this I again define one game among many. Thus if I say, The configuration '$0 \neq 0$' is to be permitted, I once more specify a rule, I define a game, but a different one from the one where I exclude this configuration.

100 Op. cit. (see footnote p. 119, above), p. 175.

Therefore: I can never define a game as such by means of rules, but always only a particular game.

WAISMAN ASKS: Is there a theory of chess? Yes, there is. So we can use this theory to help us to learn about the possibilities of the game—e.g. whether in a certain position I can checkmate the king in eight moves, and the like. If, then, there is a theory of chess, I do not see why there should not be a theory of the game of arithmetic, either, and why we should not use the propositions of this theory to learn something substantial about the possibilities of this game. This theory is Hilbert's metamathematics.

WITTGENSTEIN: What is called the 'theory of chess' is not a theory describing anything, but rather a kind of geometry. Of course, it is again a calculus and not a theory.

In order to make this clear, I shall ask you whether in your opinion there is a difference between the following two propositions: 'I can get there in eight moves' and 'By means of the theory I have proved that I can get there in eight moves'? No, for if in the theory instead of using a chess-board and chessmen I use a symbolism, then the demonstration that I can get there in eight moves consists in my actually getting there in the symbolism, hence in doing with signs what, on a chess-board, I do with chessmen. If I make the moves and prove their possibility—then I will have done the same thing over again in the proof. I shall, then, have made the moves symbolically. What is missing is in fact only real movement, and we agree, don't we?, that pushing little pieces of wood across a board is something inessential.

In the proof I do the same thing that I do in the game, just as if I said: Mr. Waismann, you are doing a sum, but I will predict what digits will be your result. In this case I do the same sum a second time, though possibly using different signs, (or using the same signs, differently conceived). I can *compute* over again the result of doing a sum; I cannot get this result in some entirely different way. It is not as if you were the one who is doing sums while I am coming to know the results of your computations by dint of a *theory*. And this is just as it is with the *'theory of chess'*.

If I thus establish in the 'theory' that such-and-such possibilities exist, then I am again making moves in the game, not in a metagame. To every move in the calculus there corresponds a move in the game, and all the difference there is consists only in physical movements of a little piece of wood.

It is, incidentally, very important that by merely looking at the little pieces of wood I cannot see whether they are pawns, bishops, castles, etc. I cannot say, 'This is a pawn *and* such-and-such rules hold for this piece.' Rather, it is only the rules of the game that *define* this piece. A pawn *is* the sum of the rules according to which it moves (a square is a piece too), just as in language the rules of syntax define the logical element of a word.

WAISMANN NOW RAISES THE FOLLOWING OBJECTION: Right, all this seems plausible to me. So far, however, we have only been dealing with the case where the theory says that such-and-such a configuration is possible. But what is the situation like if the theory proves that a particular configuration—e.g. the four castles standing next to each other in a row—*cannot* arise? And this is precisely Hilbert's case. In this case, surely, the theory cannot reproduce the game. The moves of the game no longer correspond to the steps of the calculus.

WITTGENSTEIN: Certainly, they do not. But in this case too the theory must turn out to be a calculus, only a different one from the game. Here we are faced with a *new* calculus, a calculus with a different multiplicity.

In the first place: *If I prove that I cannot do such-and-such, I do not prove a proposition, I supply an induction.*

Induction, too, can be *seen on a chess-board*. I shall presently explain what I mean by this. What I prove is that, however long I continue playing the game, I cannot reach a certain position. The only way of giving such a proof is by induction. Now it is crucial that we get clear about the nature of a proof by induction.

In mathematics there are *two kinds of proof*:

1. A proof proving a particular formula. This formula occurs in the proof itself, as its last step. [1]

2. Proof by induction. Here it is first of all striking that the proposition to be proved does not occur in the proof itself at all. Thus the proof does not actually prove the proposition. That is to say, induction is not a procedure leading to a proposition. Rather, induction allows us to see an infinite possibility, and in this alone does the nature of proof by induction consist.

Afterwards we articulate what we have been shown by the inductive proof as a proposition, and here we use the word 'all'. But this proposition adds something to the proof, or better, the proposition is related to the proof as a sign is to the thing signified. The proposition is a name for the induction. The former goes proxy for the latter; it does not follow from it. [2]

It is also possible to render induction visible on a chess-board, e.g. by means of saying that I can move to and fro, to and fro, etc. But what corresponds to the induction is no longer a chess-move.

Accordingly, if I prove in the 'theory' that such-and-such a position can never occur, then I have provided an induction that shows something but does not expressly say anything. Thus there is also no such thing as the proposition 'This and that is impossible' in the 'theory'. But now you will say that surely there must be a connection between the actual game and the induction. And such a connection does exist; it consists in this, that, once the proof by induction is given, I shall no longer try to bring about this configuration in the

1] $(a+b)^2 \ = \ (a+b) \ (a+b) \ = \ a(a+b)+b(a+b) \ = \ a^2+ab+ba+b^2$
$\qquad \qquad = a^2+2ab+b^2$

2] $1{:}3 = 0.33$ $\qquad\qquad\qquad\qquad\qquad$ $1{:}3 = 0.\underline{3}$
$\qquad 1$ $\qquad\qquad\qquad\qquad\qquad\qquad\quad \underline{1}$
$\qquad\quad 1$

game. Before the proof was given I might have tried to do so and eventually given up. Now I do not try to do so any more. The situation is precisely the same as in the case where I prove by induction that there are infinitely many prime numbers or that $\sqrt{2}$ is irrational. The effect of these proofs on actual computation consists simply in this, that human beings no longer look for a 'greatest prime number' or a fraction that is equal to $\sqrt{2}$, respectively. But here it is necessary to express oneself more exactly. *Could* you previously look for these things at all? Although what you were previously doing was externally similar to looking for a thing, it was of an entirely different kind: you were doing one thing and expecting that in virtue of it another thing would come about. But that was not looking for anything, any more than I can look for a way of waggling my ears. The only thing I can do is move my eyebrows, my forehead, and certain parts of my face in the hope that my ears will move too. But I cannot *know* whether they will do so; thus I cannot *look for* it, either.

Within *that* system in which I come to know that a certain number is prime I cannot even ask what the number of primes is. This question only arises through using the substantival form. And once you have discovered the induction, this is again a different matter from computing a certain number.

What corresponds to inductions are the formulae of algebra (calculations with letters), for the internal relations between inductions are the same as the internal relations between those formulae.

The system of calculating with letters is a new calculus; but it does not relate to ordinary calculation with numbers as a metacalculus does to a calculus. *Calculation with letters is not a theory*. This is the essential point. In so far as the 'theory' of chess studies the impossibility of certain positions it resembles algebra in its relation to calculation with numbers. Similarly, Hilbert's 'metamathematics' must turn out to be mathematics in disguise.

Hilbert's Proof

('Neubegründung der Mathematik', 1922)[101]

'If formalism is to offer a substitute for the previous, real theory, which consisted in derivations and assertions, then material contradiction, too, must find its formal equivalent.' '$a = b$' and '$a \neq b$' are to be formulae that cannot both be proved at the same time.'

The demonstration of consistency in fact proceeds inductively in Hilbert's simple model: the proof shows us, by means of an induction, the possibility that $\rightarrow$ signs must go on occurring for ever.

The proof lets us see something. What it shows, however, cannot be expressed by means of a proposition. Thus it is also impossible to say, 'The axioms are consistent.' (Any more than you can say, 'There are infinitely many numbers.' That is everyday prose.)

To prove consistency can, I think, mean only one thing: to check through the rules. There is nothing else I can do. Imagine that I give somebody a long list of errands he is to run in the city. The list is so long that I may have forgotten one errand and given a different one, or I may have put different people's errands on the same list. What can I do to convince myself that the errands can be carried out? I have to go through the list. But I cannot 'prove' anything. (We must not forget that here we are only dealing with *rules* and not with configurations of a game. Regarding geometry it would be perfectly conceivable that I go through the axioms and fail to notice the contradiction.) Saying that I want to see whether a logical product is a contradiction amounts to the same thing. Writing things down in the form of a logical

101 See footnote p. 119, above. The quotation that follows occurs on p. 170 and the consistency proof on pp. 172–3 of the work cited there.

contradiction merely *facilitates* the matter. If you wish to call this a 'proof', you may do so—it is then merely a method for facilitating checks. It must be said, however: strictly speaking, even such a 'proof' cannot save me from overlooking anything.

No calculation can achieve what checking does.

But how is it if I look through the rules of a game 'systematically'? As soon as I make moves within a system, I again have a calculus; but in this way the question of consistency arises anew. So I can actually do nothing but scrutinize one rule after another.

If a calculus yielded the result '$0 \neq 0$,' what would that mean? It is clear that then we should not be dealing with a modified kind of arithmetic, but with a totally different kind of arithmetic, which would not have the slightest similarity to 'cardinal arithmetic'. Here you could not say that in this or that feature it still agrees with our arithmetic (as non-Euclidean geometry does with Euclidean geometry—there the alteration of an axiom is not such a far-reaching matter); here there would no longer be the slightest trace of similarity. Whether I can apply such a calculus is a different question.

There are, by the way, various difficulties here. First of all, there is something I am not clear about: '$a = b$' of course expresses just the substitutability of b for a. Thus an equation is a rule about signs, a rule of our game. [1] How, then can it become an axiom, i.e. a configuration of the game? From this point of view a formula such as

---

1] Frege, *Grundgesetze der Arithmetik* II, § 107: 'So, if we regard formal arithmetic as a game, the formula '$a + a' = a' + a$,' as expression of a rule of the game, is one of the foundations of the theory of the game, upon which inferences belonging to that theory can be based; but it is not anything which is changed in the course of the game, not an object of the game, not comparable with a configuration of chessmen, but rather with the verbal expression of a rule of chess.' (*Translations from the Philosophical Writings of Gottlob Frege*, op. cit., p. 203.)

'$0 \neq 0$' is not intelligible at all. For it would mean—would it not—0 cannot be substituted for 0—am I to look, then, whether one 0 perhaps has a flourish which the other one does not? What on earth does such a prohibition mean? It comes to the same thing as saying '$a = a$.' That, too, is rubbish, however you write it down. In school a teacher is perfectly right to teach the children that $2 + 2 = 4$, but not that $2 = 2$. The way children learn calculating in school is perfectly all right, and there is no need to wish it to be any stricter. That '$a = a$' does not mean anything whatsoever can also be seen from the fact that this formula is never employed.

WITTGENSTEIN: What do you think, if I arrived in a calculus at the formula '$0 \neq 0$' would the calculus be uninteresting because of that?

SCHLICK: Yes, a mathematician would say that such a thing does not interest him.

WITTGENSTEIN: But excuse me! It would be tremendously interesting that just that was the result! In a calculus you are surely always interested in results! How strange! Here this is the result—and there that! Who would have thought so! How interesting it would be, especially if a contradiction were the result! Indeed I am prepared to predict that there will be mathematical investigations of calculi containing contradictions, and people will pride themselves on having emancipated themselves from consistency too.

[One could e.g. use such a calculus as a model onto which other ones are mapped and thereby see that these, too, contain a contradiction.]

What would it be like if I wished to apply such a calculus? Would I have no clear conscience as long as I had not proved consistency? But can I put the question this way? If I can apply the calculus, I have applied it; there are to be no subsequent corrections. What I can do, I can do. I cannot undo the application by saying: strictly speaking that was not an application. (?)

Do I have to wait for the proof of consistency before I can apply the calculus? Have all previous calculations really—*sub specie aeterni*—been made on credit? And is it conceivable that one day all this will turn out to be illegitimate? Am I ignorant of what I am doing? It actually amounts to a wish to prove that certain propositions are not nonsense.

Accordingly the question is this: I have a series of propositions, e.g. '$p, q, r, \ldots$' and a series of instructions for operations, e.g. '. , v, $\sim$' and now it is asked whether we may at some point arrive at a piece of nonsense by applying these instructions for operations to the given propositions. This question would be legitimate if by 'nonsense' I meant contradiction and tautology. In this case I would have to formulate the rules for the construction of statements in such a way that these forms do not appear.

What would it be like, really, if a physicist had been using a calculus subsequently found to be inconsistent by mathematicians?

SCHLICK: That would do absolutely no harm.

WITTGENSTEIN: The only thing that matters is the interpretation. Even an inconsistent calculus could be applied, it would only need to be re-interpreted. What would Aristotle have said if anybody had told him about three-valued logic? He would have said, Nonsense! A statement can only be true or false, there is no third possibility. Now Tarski joins in and says, 'Why do you think so? A three-valued logic is equally possible.' Absolutely all right! We have only to call a tautology 'true,' a contradiction 'false,' and the third value 'possible'.[102]

Think of Newton's three laws. It can surely not depend on the

---

102 The idea of a many-valued system, which was introduced by Łukasiewicz and Tarski in 1930, is entirely due to Łukasiewicz. See A. Tarski, *Logic, Semantics, Metamathematics,* Oxford, 1956, pp. 25ff., where the original article is reprinted. That the idea is ascribed to Tarski at this point is presumably due to the fact that he had expounded it at a public discussion in Vienna a short time before this conversation took place (21 February, 1930). See *Monatshefte für Math. u. Phys.,* 38, 1931, pp. 24–5.

properties of the calculus whether these equations express anything, whether they have sense.

It is always the same thing I want to get across. *For mathematics* the demonstration of consistency cannot be *a question of life and death*.

This, I think, is essentially connected with the fact that I must not ask, Can I *ever* arrive at a contradiction? Only where I have a procedure for looking for an answer can I ask a question. I cannot look for anything *ad infinitum*.[103]

Applying an inconsistent calculus would be just like a situation in which a physicist had made a mistake in his calculation—arithmetic would nonetheless be applicable. And a proof does not save us from making mistakes in our calculations.

WAISMANN ASKS: What if a hundred years ago a physicist had constructed a theory like the general theory of relativity, i.e. a system of both physical and geometrical axioms? At that time, when the matter was not yet clearly understood, would it not have been right to ask, But is such a theory even thinkable without inconsistency?

Furthermore, the problem of consistency only becomes acute in analysis, i.e. in the theory of real numbers. For it is here that impredicative concept formations emerge (upper bound of a restricted set) that are of the same kind as those to which the antinomies are due, and it is here that people suspect the possibility of contradictions. Similarly with set theory (axiom of choice and axiom of infinity) where you cannot see if you will not arrive at a contradiction.

WITTGENSTEIN: Right. This is connected with the fact that analysis and set theory are always taken to be theories describing something, not calculi.

---

103 See pp. 34f.

America.[104] *The Institution of Colleges.*

WITTGENSTEIN: What should be given to the Americans? Surely not our half-rotten culture. The Americans have no culture yet. From us, however, they have nothing to learn.

Russell's 'What I Believe'.[105] Absolutely not a 'harmless thing'.

Russia. The passion is promising. Our waffle, on the other hand, is powerless.

⟨CONSISTENCY V⟩

Is it *legitimate* to ask questions about consistency? Here the odd thing is that we are looking for something without knowing what the object that we are looking for really is. How, for instance, can I ask whether Euclidean geometry is consistent if I cannot imagine what it would be for it to contain a contradiction? What would it be like if it contained a contradiction? This question is surely to be answered before investigating such questions.

[It is thus not certain what object we are looking for.]

One thing is clear: I can understand a contradiction only if it is a logical contradiction. So I assume that I have a series of propositions, *p, q, r, . . .*, say, and I construct their logical product. Now I can check whether the logical product is a logical contradiction. Is *that*, then, our question about consistency? It would not take more than five minutes to decide that question. To be sure, in this sense no one can doubt that the Euclidean axioms are consistent.

1] The only resolution you can make is to be a decent person: anything else is not matter for a resolution.

104 Perhaps this remark was caused by Schlick's intention to visit America later in the year.
105 *Forum*, 82, 1929, pp. 129–134, reprinted in *Living Philosophies*, New York, 1931, pp. 9–19 (*not* identical with the article which appeared under the same title in *Nation* 132, 1931, and 150, 1940). Russell claims that no obedience to moral rules could replace love and that love, where it is genuine, united with intelligence suffices to generate all necessary moral rules.

But what else can our question mean? Perhaps the following: if we continue to draw inferences, then at some point a contradiction will occur? The reply to this will be, Have we a method for finding the contradiction? If not, then there is no question here. For you cannot look for anything *ad infinitum*.[106]

WAISMANN: But perhaps there is something you can imagine here, namely the schema for indirect proof. By analogy this is transferred to an axiom system. We must distinguish two things: a problem that can be formulated within mathematics and for whose solution, for this very reason, a method already exists, and, on the other hand, a guiding idea which precedes the construction of mathematics. And mathematicians do have such guiding ideas, e.g. in the case of Fermat's Last Theorem. I should think, then, that the question of consistency belongs to this group of questions that are preliminary to mathematics.

WITTGENSTEIN: What is meant by analogy? E.g. analogy with indirect proof? This case is just like that of the trisection of an angle. What is really going on when a mathematician is occupied with this question? Two things may be going on.
1. He imagines the angle trisected:

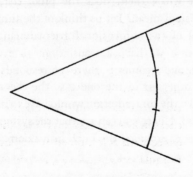

106 See pp. 34f., above

2. He thinks of the construction for dividing angles into two, four, . . . parts. And this is where the mistake comes from: It is thought that, because we can speak of dividing an angle into two and four parts, it is also possible to speak of trisection, just as we can count two, three, and four apples. But trisection—if it existed—would surely belong to a completely different category, a completely different system from the division into two and four parts. In the system in which I can talk of division into two and four parts I cannot talk of trisection. These are structures that are *logically* completely different.

I cannot reconcile division into two, three, and four parts, since they are completely different forms. Forms cannot be counted in the same way as real things can. You cannot bring them under one concept.

It is just as with ear-waggling. A mathematician is of course guided by associations, by certain analogies with the previous system. After all, I do not claim that it is wrong or illegitimate if anyone concerns himself with Fermat's Last Theorem. Not at all! If e.g. I have a method for looking integers that satisfy the equation $x^2 + y^2 = z^2$, then the formula $x^n + y^n = z^n$ may stimulate me. I may let a formula stimulate me. Thus I shall say, Here there is a *stimulus*—but not a *question*. Mathematical 'problems' are always such stimuli.

These stimuli are in no way a preliminary to a calculus.

WAISMANN: But what, then, does the proof that non-Euclidean geometry is consistent mean? Let us think of the simplest case where we give a model of two-dimensional Riemannian geometry on a sphere. In this case we have a translation: to every concept, or theorem, of the one geometry there corresponds a concept, or theorem, of the other. If in the one case the theorems included a contradiction, then the contradiction would have to reveal itself in the other geometry too. Hence you can say that the system of Riemannian axioms is consistent, provided the Euclidean axioms are. In this case consistency has been demonstrated relative to Euclidean geometry.

WITTGENSTEIN: Consistency 'relative to Euclidean geometry' is complete nonsense. What is going on here is the following. One rule corresponds to another rule (one configuration of a game to another configuration of the game). Here we have a mapping. That's all! Whatever else is said is everyday prose. People say, 'Therefore the system is consistent.' But there is no 'therefore' here, any more than in the case of induction.[107] This is again connected with the fact that people have a false understanding of proof. The proof is the proof.

The rules (configurations) of the one group stand in internal relations to one another similar to those of the rules (configurations) of the other group. This is what is shown by the proof and nothing else.

Independence II

Let us suppose we have five axioms. Now we make the discovery that one of these axioms can be derived from the other four and was hence redundant.[108] Now I ask, *What does such a discovery mean?*

I believe that here the situation is just the same as with Sheffer's discovery that we can make do with one logical constant.[109]

Above all, 'let us get clear about the following: The axioms—together with the rules of progression in the calculus—define a group of propositions. This domain of propositions is not given to us in any other way, but *only* by the five axioms. Accordingly we cannot ask, Can *the same* domain be defined by only

107 See p. 33 above.
108 See p. 128 above.
109 See p. 122 above.

four axioms? This is because the domain is not anything independent of these five axioms. These five axioms and what is generated by them is, so to speak, my entire world. I cannot step outside this world.

Now what about the following question. Are these five axioms independent of one another? To this I would reply, Is there a method for deciding this question? Here various cases are possible:

1. *There is no such method.* In this case the matter is as I have described it—all I have are the five axioms and the rules of progression. In this case I cannot look to see whether one of these axioms will *some day* be derived as a conclusion from the others. Hence I cannot ask myself the question about independence at all.

But now suppose that one of the axioms is derived as the result of a proof; in this case we have *in no way* proved that only four axioms suffice, that one of them is redundant; the only thing I have proved is that this axiom follows as a consequence from such-and-such assumptions. Now you will say, Right, but then I can further *infer* from that that this axiom is redundant. No! I cannot arrive at this insight by a logical inference; I must *see* it, just as Sheffer saw that he could make do with one constant.

I must see the new system in the system in which I make my moves and conduct my proof.

The point is seeing, not proving. No proposition corresponds to what I see—to the possibility of the system. Nothing is being asserted, thus I cannot prove anything, either.

It is a stroke of luck, as it were, that I come to see the new system. To be sure, I can go over to the new system; but I cannot look for it, I cannot reach it by means of a transformation, and I cannot come to see its possibility by means of a proof.

2a. *There is a method* for establishing independence, and that in the sense that the one axiom is, say, '$p \lor q$', while the other one is 'p'. I intend to represent different axioms by different letters and, moreover, express the truth-functions. Then it must be easy to see if one axiom follows from another one or not. If *that* is what is meant by independence, then there is no serious problem here at all.

Suppose I was making a list of the people present in this room and I wrote down Prof. Schlick's name twice over. Then I add the rule, If one mention is already contained in another one, it is to be left out. I think it is then no problem to check the independence of a certain mention. You would be right to say, So write down the list correctly from the very beginning. For that you do not need an investigation into independence, and this is the situation here too.

Now you will reply, 'But this is surely not how it was meant!' This leads us to another case.

2b. *There is another, non-trivial method* for establishing independence. In that case the word 'independence' means something else.

Such a method could for instance consist in this: I take four axioms, add the negation of the fifth axiom, and show that the axiom system thus altered admits of an application (the method of models). Accordingly, if in this case I specify five axioms where four of them are enough, I have simply been guilty of an oversight. For I might surely have known from the very beginning that one of these axioms was redundant, and if I have nonetheless written it down, that was a mistake, was it not? In this case it is of course not enough merely to give axioms; we must also prove that they really possess the characteristic of independence.

Now, in geometry, Hilbert seems to pursue this last course.[110] Here, however, an important point is left unclear: is the method of models a *method*? Can I methodically look for a model or am I

110 *Grundlagen der Geometrie*, Leipzig, 1899, pp. 22ff. (E.T. *The Foundation of Geometry*, Chicago, 1921). The method here applied (namely that of finding an interpretation of non-Euclidean geometry within Euclidean geometry) is an absolutely normal one, and it is not clear why Wittgenstein says that Hilbert 'seems' to apply it.

dependent on a happy accident? What if I cannot find a model that fits?

Summary

The question whether an axiom system is independent only makes sense if there is a procedure for deciding the question. Otherwise the question cannot be raised at all, and if you discover that e.g. an axiom is redundant, you have not proved a proposition; you have read a new system into the old one.

And the same holds for consistency.

Hilbert's Axioms I.1 and I.2[111]

'Two distinct points A, B always define a straight line a.'
'Any two distinct points on a straight line define that line.'
I am straight away at a loss to know how these axioms are to be construed, what their logical form is.

WAISMANN: You can of course write them down as truth-functions by saying, e.g., 'For all x, if x is a point, then. . . .' but I believe that by so doing you miss the real point of the axioms. We must not introduce points one after another. It seems to me much more correct to introduce points, straight lines, planes by means of co-ordinates, as it were, at one go.

WITTGENSTEIN: I think so too. But there is one thing I do not understand: What would it mean to say that these axioms form a contradiction? The point is that as they stand they cannot yield a contradiction unless I lay down by means of a rule that their logical

111 Op. cit., p. 5. Later editions have a small change here.

product is a contradiction. With this contradiction the case is the same as with the contradiction between the propositions, 'This patch is green', and 'This patch is red.' As they stand they do not contradict one another at all. They only contradict each other when we introduce a further rule of syntax which forbids us to regard both of them as true. Only then does a contradiction arise.

I think, then, every contradiction must be a logical contradiction, not a case of contrariety. If e.g. in geometry I conclude from one proof that the sum of the angles of a triangle is equal to 180° and from another proof that the sum of the angles is greater than 180°, then this is in no way a contradiction. Both conclusions might hold at the same time and I can even imagine a case where we would even apply such an axiom system: if the sum of angles of a triangle were by *one* method of measuring equal to one value and by a different method equal to a different value.

I have got a contradiction only if I postulate by means of a rule of syntax that the product is a contradiction. (Cf. above.)[112]

⟨*Calculus and Everyday Prose*⟩

It is a strange mistake of some mathematicians to believe that something *inside* mathematics might be dropped because of a critique of the foundations. Some mathematicians have the right instinct: once we have calculated something it cannot drop out and disappear! And in fact, what is caused to disappear by such a critique are names and allusions that occur in the calculus, hence what I wish to call *prose*. It is very important to distinguish as strictly as possible between the calculus and this kind of prose. Once people have become clear about this distinction, all these questions, such as those about consistency, independence, etc., will be removed.

112 Evidently a reference to p. 127 above.

Frege and Wittgenstein II

WAISMANN STATES THE DIFFERENCE BETWEEN FREGE AND WITTGENSTEIN: For Frege, the alternative is this: either a sign has a meaning, i.e. it goes proxy for an object—a logical sign for a logical object, an arithmetical sign for an arithmetical object—or it is only a figure, drawn on paper in ink.

But this is not a legitimate alternative. As the game of chess shows, there is a third possibility: in chess a pawn neither has a meaning in the sense of going proxy for anything, of being a sign *for* anything, nor is it merely a piece carved in wood and pushed about on a wooden board. It is only the rules of the game of chess that define what a pawn is.

This example shows that we must not say that a sign is either a sign for something or only a structure perceivable by our senses. Thus there is a legitimate element in formalism, a true core that Frege failed to see.[113]

The 'meaning' of a pawn is, if you like, the totality of rules holding for it. And thus you can also say that the meaning of a numeral is the totality of rules holding for it.

WITTGENSTEIN AGREES

WAISMANN READS OUT FREGE, *Grundgesetze der Arithmetik* II, §107: 'Let us remember that the theory of the game must be distinguished from the game itself. It is true that the moves of the game are made in accordance with the rules; yet the rules are not objects of the game, but the foundation of the theory of the game. It is true that the moves of chess are made in accordance with rules; but no position of the chessmen and no move expresses a rule; for it is not at all the job of chessmen to express anything; they are rather to be moved in accordance with rules. So, if we regard formal arithmetic as a game, the formula '$a + a' = a' + a$', as expression of a rule of the game, is one of the foundations of the theory of the game, upon which inferences

---

113 See p. 105 above, and footnote.

belonging to that theory can be based; but it is not anything which is changed in the course of the game, not an object of the game, not comparable with a configuration of chessmen, but rather with the verbal expression of a rule of chess.'

§108: 'We . . . notice that equations play a double role here; first, in the game itself, where, like configurations in a chess game, they express nothing; and secondly, in the theory of the game, where they must express the rules and also . . . deductions from these rules. Let us try to imagine the corresponding situation in the game of chess. In such a case the rules of the game would be expressed by means of groupings of chessmen which might also occur in the game itself. In other words, some language would have to be given whose means of expression would be the chessmen and their positions on the chessboard. It might then happen that a position would need to be regarded in two ways: first, in the game itself, where it would express nothing . . . ; secondly, in the theory of the game, where it would be a theorem, and so have a sense.'[114]

It thus comes out clearly here that the identity-sign is a rule permitting the substitution of one sign for another one but is at the same time a configuration *within* arithmetic.

WITTGENSTEIN COMMENTS: The problem can be put in the following form:

If from the equations:
$$4 = 2+2$$
$$2 = 1+1$$
I proceed to the equation
$$4 = (1+1)+(1+1)$$
you may ask, Was it *from* the first two equations or from the first equation *by means of* the second that we arrived at the third?

That is to say, are the first two equations the configuration from which by means of an inference we arrived at e.g. the third equation, or is the second equation the *rule in accordance with which* we transformed the first equation into the third one?

114 *Translations from the Philosophical Writings of Gottlob Frege*, op. cit., pp. 203f.

It seems to me that in both cases we mean precisely the same thing.

(I know that, for the foundations of arithmetic, the whole question is not a crucial problem.)

I could say that I construct the logical product

$$(4 = 2+2).(2 = 1+1)$$

and now need a rule that allows me to write down the equation

$$4 = (1+1)+(1+1).$$

The equation $2 = 1+1$ cannot be the expression of this rule, any more than the connection '$p \supset q$' is the expression of the rule of inference in *modus ponens*:

$$\frac{\begin{array}{c} p \\ p \supset q \end{array}}{q}$$

The rule of inference cannot be expressed by a proposition at all. Now I think that the rule of substitution too cannot be expressed by the equation $2 = 1+1$. But we can say, on the other hand, that the rule and the equation have something in common, their logical multiplicity, and *for this reason*, we can as it were *project* the rule onto the equation. For if I ask how I got from the equation $4 = 2+2$ to the equation $4 = (1+1)+(1+1)$ I can say, By means of a rule that allows me to substitute $1+1$ for 2. The rule thus expressed in words and the equation $2 = 1+1$ correspond to one another, but they are not identical.

Sunday, 4 January 1931 (at Schlick's house)

⟨EQUATION AND SUBSTITUTION-RULE I⟩

$$\begin{array}{c} 2+2 = 4 \\ 1+1 = 2 \end{array}$$

$$\overline{(1+1)+(1+1) = 4}$$

Can I say, I have transformed the first equation by means of the second one—construed as a rule—and thus got the third equation? If I say that, it will look as if the one equation was *given preference* over the other one. It seems to me that such a conception does not make sense. To make this clear: imagine that I have written down the first two equations and then ask a person, How will you proceed? According to the first equation *or* according to the second equation? Now you see immediately that that is not a possible way of putting the question. I need *both* equations—one of them by itself is not enough.

I want to put it more clearly still. If it is held that one of the two equations *by itself* is the rule, you must ask, By itself—in contrast with what? I can say, I proceeded in accordance with the rule $1+1 = 2$ in contrast with the rule $1+1 = 3$, or, I proceeded in accordance with the rule $2+2 = 4$ in contrast with the rule $2+2 = 5$. But I cannot say, I proceeded in accordance with the rule $1+1 = 2$ in contrast with the rule $2+2 = 4$, for these two rules do not stand in contrast with one another! That is why I also cannot say, I proceeded in accordance with the rule $1+1 = 2$ *only*, and this is enough to show that both equations have the same status and that, consequently, neither of them singly is the expression of the transformation-rule.

In considering all of this another circumstance which makes the whole business unclear must be taken into account, and that is the following: suppose I write down the following numbers, one under the other,

$$1 \quad 2 \quad 3 \quad 4 \quad 5$$
$$1 \quad 4 \quad 9 \quad 16 \quad 25$$

and now ask you, Do you understand the rule already? Can you go on from here? 'Yes, I can.' Can you apply the rule from here on? 'Yes, I can.' Can you now apply the rule in such a way that you prompt yourself every time by the expression of the rule? When you are playing chess, for instance, do you prompt yourself with the rule in question before making every single move? 'No, I don't.'

It is very important that you understand the rule and apply it without rehearsing it to yourself. For it might be thought that writing the numbers one under the other was not yet the expression of the rule; that I had to express it in the following way, for instance:

$$x \qquad\qquad\qquad (\ )$$

or in this way:

$$x^2 \qquad\qquad\qquad (\ )^2$$

For one might say that the rule consists in constructing the sequence of natural numbers and *always* writing the square underneath. That is to say, the rule is *general* and this generality is not expressed by its original formulation. This, however, is a mistake. For the letters are not at all the expression of generality, since generality in no way finds its expression in symbols; it shows itself in induction. A formula of algebra corresponds to an induction, but it does not express the induction for the reason that the latter is inexpressible.

Thus if I wrote down:

$$x$$
$$x^2$$

I should not yet know how to apply this rule; I have not as it were expressed the *general* rule, I have once again only formed a certain configuration of letters; for x is just as much an individual sign as 1, 2, 3. The rule cannot be expressed by a single, concrete configuration and hence not by the one written down above; the essential thing about it, its generality, is inexpressible. Generality shows itself in application. I have to *read* this generality *into* the configuration. But it is neither easier nor more difficult to recognize the general rule in the expression

$$x$$
$$x^2$$

than it was previously in the case where I recognized it from the individual numbers. I have to read the rule into the expression with letters in the same way as into the expression with numbers, and if I do not do it, the letters do not help me at all.

I did not 'apply' the rule

$$x$$
$$x^2$$

to the single numbers, for otherwise I should have needed a further rule which told me how to infer the construction of the sequence of numbers from the expression with letters. And if I had wished to formulate such a rule, in letters, I should again not have got any further—I should have needed a further rule that told me how to apply it, etc.

A rule is not like the mortar between two bricks.

We cannot lay down a rule for the application of another rule. We cannot apply one rule 'by means of' another rule.

Here we hit on a strange mistake which consists in the opinion that in logic you can connect two things by means of a third one [that things are brought about by mediation]. Here people imagine two things connected by a rope. But this image is misleading. For how is the rope connected with the thing? [Things must connect directly, without a rope, i.e. they must already stand in a connection with one another, like the links of a chain.[115]]

From this false conception there arises a difficulty you encounter when considering the question, How *can* a rule be applied? The answer seems to be, By means of another rule—and in this way you would never get off the ground.

There is no rule that interposes itself between the expression

$$x$$
$$x^2$$

and its application to numbers, like the mortar between bricks; I have already to read a certain kind of application into the expression.—Now we return to our question.

$$2+2 = 4$$
$$1+1 = 2$$

$$(1+1)+(1+1) = 4$$

Neither of the first two equations is given precedence over the other. So neither can be the expression of the rule. For the rule is surely the general instruction, 'Wherever there is an expression in which 2 occurs, you may substitute $1+1$ for 2.'

$$f(2)$$
$$1+1 = 2$$

$$f(1+1)$$

We now see what the rule really is. It relates to this whole pattern; it is not a part, an isolated element of it. I have already to read this whole

115 Cf. *TLP* 2.03.

pattern into the equation '$1+1 = 2$'—only then shall I have the rule in front of me. The isolated equation is not yet the rule.

An analogy with a syllogism can make this clearer.

$$p$$
$$p \supset q$$
$$\overline{}$$
$$q$$

Here too people have, illegitimately of course, taken one part of the syllogism, '$p \supset q$', to be the expression of a rule of inference. In isolation '$p \supset q$' in no way expresses the rule of inference, whereas it does do so when seen in relation to this set pattern, which is given once and for all. Accordingly I always have to think of '$p \supset q$' in terms of the completed pattern. '$p \supset q$' has the same multiplicity as the pattern (I can infer the pattern from it) and this is why it is after all in a certain sense legitimate to project the rule of inference onto the expression '$p \supset q$'.

Now I can similarly project the substitution-rule

$$f(2)$$
$$1+1 = 2$$
$$\overline{}$$
$$f(1+1)$$

onto the part '$1+1 = 2$'. This equation of course does not itself express the rule, but it does so when seen in relation to the complete pattern. (For this purpose I must read something different into the equation.)

An equation is a substitution-rule, which is applied outside arithmetic, in the propositions of ordinary language. I can say: 2 apples plus 2 apples equals 4 apples. But it is clear that when I am talking *about* equations a substitution-rule (a transformation-rule) must mean something entirely different from the substitution-rules that the equations actually are.

That I can project a rule onto an equation is due to the fact that an equation has the same character as a rule. A rule of the game of chess, on the other hand, has a different character from a configuration in a game. (Unless we expressed a rule of chess by means of this configuration.)

Strictly speaking, we ought to use different languages. We ought, on the other hand, to write the equation of arithmetic as '1+1 = 2' and the rule, on the other hand, we ought to pronounce in words 'For "2," wherever it occurs, "1+1" may be substituted.' And here the words 'may be substituted' function in the same way as the equality sign in arithmetic. They fulfil the same task. It is like calculating by means of figures on paper instead of doing it by means of an abacus. I shall then have done the same thing by different means—I shall have repeated the calculation.

It is for this reason that '1+1 = 2' is also a picture of the rule about the transformation of equations.

Basically the rule is the internal relation which obtains between the equations:

$$2+2 = 4$$
$$1+1 = 2$$

and the equation

$$(1+1)+(1+1) = 4.$$

As an internal relation it cannot be expressed by means of a configuration of the game.

WAISMANN ASKS: Let us try to apply what has been said to the game of chess. Here too we must say that a rule of the game of chess is not a transition from one configuration to another. Here too we must read the rule into the transition. But here we are not tempted to construe the same structure at one time as a configuration and at another as a rule of the game. There must of course be a reason for this and I believe that this reason is connected with the way arithmetic is applied, namely with the fact that the application of arithmetic consists in substitution-rules.

WITTGENSTEIN: And so it does. We could, however, also express the rules concerning the moves of the white pieces by means of possible configurations of the black ones. (?)

If equations were tautologies, they could never serve as substitution-rules.

An equation is a substitution-rule, just like a definition.

⟨VERIFICATION OF THE PROPOSITIONS OF PHYSICS⟩

SCHLICK RAISES A 'SIMPLE QUESTION': It is surely possible in a certain sense to verify the propositions of physics. Now there are different ways of verifying a proposition of physics. Thus there are twelve or fourteen independent ways of determining the mass and the charge of an electron. How, then, is this to be understood if the sense of a proposition is the method of its verification? How is it at all possible to say that *one* proposition is verified in different ways? I believe that here the laws of nature are what connect the different kinds of verification. That is, on the basis of the connections given by the laws of nature I can verify one proposition in different ways. We can take a very simple example: at one time I measure a length by laying a measuring-rod against it, at another time by means of gauging-instruments. In and of itself it would not be necessary that the two results coincide. But if they do, then this is the manifestation of a natural law. (?) In what way have I established 'the same thing' in both cases?

WITTGENSTEIN: Just a minute! That does not occur only in science, does it?, but also in everyday life. For instance, I hear piano-playing in the next room and say, 'My brother is in that room.'[116] If I were now asked how I knew, I would answer, 'He told me that he would be in the next room at that time.' Or, 'I hear the piano being played and I recognize his way of playing.' or, 'Just now I heard steps that sounded just like his,' etc. Now it seems as if I had verified the same sentence

116 Wittgenstein is thinking of his brother who actually was a pianist.

in ways that were different every time. But this is not so. What I have verified are different 'symptoms' of something else (I have called them 'symptoms' in my manuscript[117]). The playing of the piano, the steps, etc. are symptoms of my brother's presence.

Hypotheses II

It is very important, I think, and will soon clarify the matter to remind you of the fact that the equations of physics are not propositions but *hypotheses*. What we observe are, as it were, individual 'cross-sections' though hypotheses, and in fact essentially different cross-sections, i.e. not merely cross-sections at different places and times, but cross-sections of different logical forms, thus completely different facts. What we can verify is always only *one* such cross-section. A hypothesis is what connects all these different cross-sections (as a curve connects different points). Now in cases where we appear to have verified the same proposition in different ways, we have in reality verified different cross-sections of the same hypothesis.

A hypothesis always has different sides or different cross-sections, like a three-dimensional body, which can be projected in different ways. Now it is very crucial for answering your question that in all these examples we are dealing with *hypotheses*.

I will elucidate the matter by means of an example. Imagine a creature having a sense with which it can gauge angles as we do by eye [it can furthermore measure distances] and, in addition, possessing two feelers for touching things.

Now suppose this organism collects certain experiential data, obtains certain numerical results, say, notes down propositions, and at home accommodates them in a CS ⟨co-ordinate system⟩. Now it

117 This doctrine is alluded to in *PR*; see pp. 200 and 283.

would be able to describe these experiences in such a way that it may say, '*A sphere has moved towards me.*'

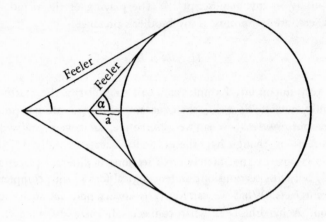

Let us imagine that there were no experiences through feelers, then we could also describe the whole matter two-dimensionally: a circle in the visual field coming nearer. Now even where the experiences with feelers are missing we might prefer to represent the experience by means of the hypothesis of a sphere.

In this case we make the hypothesis carry *more* than is required by the task of describing immediate experience. The hypothesis as it were has a wheel running idly: as long as no further experiences occur, the wheel remains unused and only comes into action when further experiences have to be integrated. (It is as in the case of a differential gear: by turning a wheel a well-defined movement is caused.)

Our hypothesis is thus designed to cover *more* than the reproduction of this one kind of experience (e.g. the measuring of angles and distances without experience through feelers). What, then, does the hypothesis achieve? If we had the experience of a circle coming nearer towards us, we would say, Now we expect to be able to have also a well-defined experience of a different kind.

The hypotheses of physics are constructed in such a way that they connect a very great number of experiences of different kinds. What connects them is an hypothesis.

Here the general principle is the following:

What is verified in various ways is more than what is verified in one way.

That is, if we say that we have verified 'the same thing' in two different ways, then 'the same thing' means more than something that is verified in one way only.

Of course I verify something different by means of every single observation. And there is surely no logical necessity why by verifying one proposition a different one should also be verified. I can e.g. very well imagine that, although I see this hyacinth over there, I shall have no tactile perceptions when I want to touch it or that I get different results in measuring a length by at one time laying a measuring-rod against the object and at another time using gauges. Phenomena are different 'aspects' connected by an hypothesis.

WAISMANN ASKS: I have always understood the matter in this way: If I am to measure the length of a certain distance AB, I can either measure AB by means of a measuring-rod or I can survey A and B from a third point, C, measure the lengths of AC and BC, and then compute the length of AB by means of the cosine-theorem. Have I, then, verified the proposition 'The length of AB is such-and-such' in different ways? That depends entirely on what you want to mean by 'measuring'. If by 'measuring' I mean the procedure of repeatedly laying measuring-rods against things, of surveying, of establishing coincidences, etc., then I am faced with two different reports and it is a matter of experience whether the results tally. It is different, on the other hand, when I use the axioms of Euclidean geometry as my basis and thus describe the results of measuring by means of a language whose syntax is fixed. If in this case a deviation occurred—would I say that the cosine-theorem is false and Euclidean geometry refuted? No, we would adhere to Euclidean geometry and look at the physical behaviour of our measuring-rods for a reason for the deviation. We would say, The yardstick has become deformed, there was a certain field of force, we have measured imprecisely, the ray of light was not straight, etc. That is to say: we construe the propositions of geometry as rules of syntax. A rule of syntax defines when two methods of verification are equivalent.

WITTGENSTEIN: If by 'space' I mean visual space, then geometry is the grammar of the words by means of which I describe phenomena.

But if by 'space' I mean physical space, then geometry is an hypothesis, just like physics; it refers to experiences of measuring things.

⟨*Geometry as Syntax III*⟩

WAISMANN: Sometime, a year ago, when you were explaining these things to us, you said that geometry was syntax. Einstein said: Geometry describes the possible positions of rigid bodies.[118]

If the actual positions of rigid bodies are described by the propositions of a language, then only the *syntax* of this language can correspond to these possible positions. To what extent, then, can we construe geometry as an hypothesis? To what extent can we construe e.g. the three-dimensionality of space as an hypothesis?

WITTGENSTEIN: Geometry is not something self-sufficient, it is brought to completion by physics. Thus it is *part* of an hypothesis. This part I can fix by reserving the right so to adjust everything else that I achieve correspondence with experience. Such a part of an hypothesis that is fixed from the very beginning I call a *postulate*.

There is only one thing in the world we can postulate: our way of expressing ourselves. We cannot postulate the behaviour of facts. Accordingly I can also say that, if I lay down a postulate, I thereby fix

118 See p. 38 and footnote, and p. 61, above.

the syntax by means of which I express hypotheses. I choose a system of representation. Thus there is no contrast at all between the conception of geometry as part of an hypothesis and the conception of geometry as syntax.

I can also construe three-dimensionality as an hypothesis. Were I to change it, then this would at any rate have to be compensated by changes elsewhere. There would be something I should have to re-interpret.

What has here been subtracted must re-appear at some other place.

ADDENDA[119]

Chess[120]

The *meaning* of chess is what all chess-games have in common.

In chess the appearance of the pieces matters just as little as strokes of ink in mathematics. Would it impress my opponent in chess if I said: 'I have a frightening queen with glowing eyes, etc.'?

Playing games and knowledge differ only in respect of their application. If on Mars men waged war in the same way we play chess, the rules of chess would at once acquire a serious significance, and the general staff would concern themselves with chess in the same way as they now do with maps.

---

119 It becomes clear from the third of these addenda that they are due to Wittgenstein and not to Waismann. Perhaps they contain what Wittgenstein said when Waismann asked him about points discussed before. See editor's Preface, p. 23.
120 A repetition, without essential changes, of p. 104 (part of Wittgenstein's discussion of 'What to say at Königsberg').

Apropos of Königsberg[121]

What does a mathematical question mean?

Nowadays it looks as if a text-book of mathematics contained two entirely different elements: the calculus and something that looks as if it contained the justification of the calculus. The second element, however, disappears as soon as we reach the calculus. What disappears is apparent description.

With a machine it only matters that the cogs interlock but not what colour it is painted. The same holds for set theory. The word 'infinite' is just as inessential as the coat of paint on a cog-wheel. Only the calculus is essential.

Definition of Number[122]

In Cambridge I explained the matter to my audience in this way: Imagine I have a dozen cups. Now I wish to tell you that I have got just as many spoons. How can I do it?

If I had wanted to say that I allotted one spoon to each cup, I would not have expressed what I meant by saying that I have just as many spoons as cups. Thus it will be better for me to say, I can allot the spoons to the cups. What does the word 'Can' mean here? If I mean it in the physical sense, that is to say, if I mean that I have the physical strength to distribute the spoons among the cups—then you would tell me, We already knew that you are able to do that. What I mean is obviously this: I can allot the spoons to the cups because there is the right number of spoons. But to explain this I must presuppose the concept of number. It is not the case that a correlation defines number; rather, number makes a correlation possible. This is why you

121 Seven paragraphs which literally repeat the first part of 'What to say at Königsberg' (see pp. 102ff. above) are not printed here.
122 The ideas in this addendum seem to be new, as far as the conversations in Vienna are concerned. Waismann wrote several expositions of this argument; the last one, together with a statement of his indebtedness to Wittgenstein, appeared in *Einführung in das mathematische Denken*, 2nd edition, Vienna, 1947, pp. 77–80 (cf. p. 168), English translation by J. Benac, *Introduction to Mathematical Thinking*, New York, 1951, pp. 107–113 (cf. p. 245).

cannot explain number by means of correlation (equinumerosity). You must not explain number by means of correlation; you can explain it by means of possible correlation, and this precisely presupposes number.

You cannot rest the concept of number upon correlation.

Frege once said, 'A straight line is already drawn before it gets drawn.'[123] This dictum sounds very paradoxical. It is connected with Frege's distinction between 'objective' and 'real.'[124]

What Frege means is evidently that it is possible to draw a line. But possibility is not yet reality. A straight line is drawn only when it has been drawn. And this is how it is with numbers too. When Frege and Russell attempt to define number through correlation, the following has to be said:

A correlation only obtains if it has been *produced*. Frege thought that if two sets have equally many members, then there is already a correlation too. (Just as: if two points are given, then there is already a straight line connecting them). Nothing of the sort! A correlation is there only when I actually correlate the sets, i.e. as soon as I specify a definitive relation. But if in this whole chain of reasoning the *possibility* of correlation is meant, then it presupposes precisely the concept of number. Thus there is nothing at all to be gained by the attempt to base number on correlation.

If Russell laid his cards on the table, then by correlation he would have to mean something that is given by a *list*. Russell thought that there always was a correlation, namely by means of identity.[125] (?) If identity drops out, however, nothing remains.

---

123 Cf. *Grundgesetze der Arithmetik* I, Jena, 1893, p. 88, where Frege holds that when we correlate two concepts, we do something similar to drawing an auxiliary line in geometry. Such an act of drawing something is far from being an act of creating something. 'Rather, we only make ourselves aware of . . . , only grasp what has already been there.' (I owe this reference to Prof. P. T. Geach.)

124 E.g. *Grundlagen der Arithmetik*, Breslau, 1884 (*The Foundations of Arithmetic*, Oxford, 1950) p. 35.

125 If two (of course finite) equinumerous lists are given, then it is possible to generate a correspondence between them by means of the identity relation. I have not been able to find precisely this remark in Russell's works. But cf. footnote p. 243 infra.

V

Monday, 21 September 1931 (first Argentinierstraße, then in the street)[126]
WITTGENSTEIN SHOWS TYPED SHEETS FROM HIS MANUSCRIPT TO
WAISMANN AND MAKES REMARKS ABOUT CERTAIN SIGNS.[127] A word
which is underlined in this way: ——— means: Wittgenstein is in
doubt about whether it is to be retained or not.[128] Although he would
not at all mind putting down a different word, he has because of some
obscure feeling chosen this precise word, even though this sometimes
produces terrible German. The sentences are quite higgledy-
piggledy. They are meant for Wittgenstein who will carry them with
him to England, in order to continue working on them. They are an
extract from his manuscript-books (90 pages so far).

INTENTION, TO MEAN, MEANING

WAISMANN HAPPENS TO READ OUT THE FOLLOWING SENTENCE:
'Were you thinking of Napoleon when you said that?'
'I was thinking of what I was saying.'[129]

WAISMANN ASKS: Does this mean to say that a proposition transcends
what it says and refers to other things?

126 The town house of the Wittgenstein family. At that time Wittgenstein's oldest
sister, Hermine, and his brother Paul lived there. It is likely that Schlick was not
present on this occasion, but had already left for America.
127 Very probably the first pages of *EM* (vW no. 211) where many topics of this
conversation are discussed.
128 This was Wittgenstein's usual procedure.
129 This passage occurs in Wittgenstein's *MS. vol.* VII (1931), (vW no. 111), in
EM (vW no. 211), p. 17, and, later, in *BT* (vW no. 213) §53.

WITTGENSTEIN. I will explain it to you. In this work I again and again concern myself with the question, What does it mean to *understand* a proposition? This is connected with the general question of what it is what people call *intention, to mean, meaning*. Nowadays the ordinary view is, isn't it, that understanding is a psychological process that accompanies a proposition—i.e. a spoken or written proposition? What structure, then, does this process have? The same, perhaps, as a proposition? Or is this process something amorphous, as when I read a proposition while I have a toothache?

I now believe that understanding is not a particular psychological process at all that is there in addition, supplementary to the perception of a propositional picture. It is true that various processes are going on inside me when I hear or read a proposition. An image emerges, say, there are associations and so forth. But all these processes are not what I am interested in here. I understand a proposition by *applying* it. Understanding is thus not a particular process; it is operating with a proposition. *The point of a proposition is that we should operate with it.* (What I do, too, is an operation.)

The view I wish to argue against in this context is that understanding is a *state* inside me, like, for instance, toothache. The best way of seeing that, on the contrary, understanding has nothing to do with a state is to ask, 'Do you understand the word Napoleon?' 'Yes, I do.' 'Do you mean the victor of Austerlitz?' 'Yes, I do.' 'Have you been meaning this all the time, without interruption?' It obviously does not make sense to say that I have been meaning this all the time without interruption in the way I can say that I have been having toothache all the time without interruption. Now I can say that I am aware of the meaning of 'Napoleon' in the same way I know that $2 + 2 = 4$, that is, this knowledge does not have the form of a state but that of a disposition. My using the past tense—'I meant the victor of Austerlitz'—does not refer to an act of meaning but to my pronouncing the proposition at the time. It would not make sense, however, to suppose that I understand the word 'Napoleon' at a certain time. For then I should have to be able to ask, *When* do I understand it? Already at the sound of the first N? Or only after the first syllable? Or only at the end of the complete word? Curious as it may sound, all these would be real questions.

Understanding a word or a proposition is calculating. (?)

WAISMANN: This use of the word calculus is surely unusual. Previously you yourself always attached great importance to the distinction between a calculus and a theory? You used to say, 'What is the difference between a calculus and a theory?' It simply is this, that a theory describes something, whereas a calculus does not describe anything; it is there.[130]

WITTGENSTEIN: You must not forget that I am now not talking about propositions but about dealing with signs. I am saying that our way of using signs constitutes a calculus, and I am saying this deliberately. For there is not a mere analogy between our way of using words in a language and a calculus; I can actually construe the concept of a calculus in such a way that the use of words will fall under it. I shall presently explain how I mean this. Here I have a little bottle of benzine. What purpose does it serve? Well, it is used for cleaning. Now there is a label glued onto it saying 'benzine'. What purpose, then, does the label serve? Surely I use benzine for cleaning, not the label. (It is of course clear that instead of this label there could be a different one.) Now this label is the point of contact of a calculus, that is, the point where it gets applied. For I can tell you, 'Get some benzine!' And in virtue of the label there is a rule in accordance with which you can proceed. When you get the benzine, this is again a step within the calculus defined by these rules. I call the whole business a calculus, since now there are two possibilities: that you proceed according to a certain rule or that you do not proceed according to this

130 See pp. 126 and 133ff. above.

rule; for now I am in the position to say, for instance: 'Well, what you have brought is not benzine at all!'

The names we use in everyday life always are labels like this, which we put on things and which serve us as points of contact of a calculus. I can, for example, put a label carrying the name 'Wittgenstein' on myself and one carrying the inscription 'Waismann' on you. Instead of this I can also do something different: I point my arm first there, then there, then over there, and say: Mr. Müller, Mr. Waismann, Mr. Meier. In this way I have again created points of contact of a calculus. I can for instance say, 'Mr. Waismann, go to the Fruchtgasse!' What does that mean? There is another little label hanging there saying 'Fruchtgasse'.[131] Only because of these things can I determine whether what you are doing is right or not.

WAISMANN: The meaning of a word is the way it is used. If I give a name to a thing, I by no means establish an association between the thing and the word; I indicate a rule for the use of the word. The so-called 'intentional relation' dissolves into such rules. In reality there is no relation here at all, and if people talk about such a relation, this is just an unfortunate mode of expression.

WITTGENSTEIN: Yes and no. This is a complicated business. In a certain sense you may say that there is a relation. For it is a relation of exactly the same kind as that between two signs that stand next to one another in a diagram. I point e.g. my arm at you and me and say: Mr. Waismann, Mr. Wittgenstein. (?)

I could surely also use a calculus in which Mr. Meier and Mr. Waismann as well as the Fruchtgasse and the Stephansplatz are intersubstitutable, just as 3×5 and 15 are intersubstitutable.

What I am doing with the words of a language in *understanding* them is exactly the same thing I do with a sign in the calculus: I

131 Waismann lived in the Fruchtgasse.

operate with them. It does not make any difference that in the one case I perform actions, while in the other I merely write down and delete signs, for what I am doing in the calculus is an action too. *Here there is no sharp boundary*.

⟨CALCULUS AND APPLICATION⟩

What is the difference between language (M)[132] and a game? You might say: It ceases to be a game when things begin to become serious, and here seriousness means application. But this would not express it quite correctly. You would really have to say that a game is what is neither serious nor fun. For we call things serious if we apply the results of the calculus to everyday life. I apply e.g. the calculation $8 \times 7 = 56$ thousands of times, and this is why we take it seriously. But, at bottom, this multiplication is not the least bit different from one I merely do for fun. The difference does not lie in the calculation itself, and that is why you cannot tell by looking at the calculus whether it is a serious business or merely serves to entertain us. Hence I cannot say: If a calculus amuses me, it is a game, but only: If I *can take a calculus to be something* that amuses me, then it is a game. The calculus itself implies no relation either to seriousness or to fun.

Think of the game of chess. Today we call it a game. Suppose, however, a war were waged in such a way that the troops fought one another on a field in the form of a chess-board and that whoever was mated had lost the war. Then the officers would be bending over a chessboard just as they now do over an ordnance map. Then chess would not be a game any longer; it would be a serious business.[133]

132 Perhaps 'mathematics'.
133 See pp. 104 and 163, above.

I calculate when I am free by looking it up in a diary. This is just as much of a calculation as $\int \sin x \; dx$.

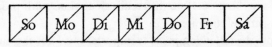

How is it really that I ask a person to come and see me on Friday on the basis of the picture I see here? Once again it must be said: I use the picture like the signs in a calculus, as a point of contact for action. Looking things up in a diary is also a calculus, for I operate with the picture, and if I go to see someone or ask someone to see me on Friday, these are further steps within the calculus.

CONSTRUCTING A BOILER[134]

Why do men think, why for instance do they calculate the dimensions of a boiler and not rather leave it to chance what size they will come out? Will this calculation perhaps save us from an explosion of the boiler? No, the boiler can explode despite the calculation. But men will no more dispense with calculating the dimensions of boilers than they will put their hands into a fire once they have been burnt. Now I wish to say the following: Such a calculation is of course a calculus. I start from certain data, multiply,

and if the number 15 comes out as the end-result, I make the boiler-plate 15mm thick. Of course, I could have performed the

134 Cf. *PI* §466; *EM* pp. 68f, 84.

calculation with whole propositions instead of with numbers—in that case I should have been calculating with propositions. The fact that I calculate with numbers only means that I use an abbreviation, does it not, because the same calculation occurs in 1000 different contexts, that is to say, because 1000 different calculations with propositions have this part in common.

And now the following point is important: if I get the number 15 as my result and, because of that, make the boiler 15mm thick, then the construction of the boiler is *a further step within this calculus* and not something entirely different. [Calculation and engineering belong together. They are different parts of one calculus.] [1]

Now, if I am asked, Had you any right to make the boiler 15mm thick? can you sleep soundly?—then I cannot help replying with a counter-question: What does 'right' mean here? If what you mean by it is that we know that an explosion of the boiler is impossible, then I had no such right. But if by 'right' it is meant that I have calculated the dimensions of the engine in terms of this calculus, then I do have the right. There is no more to be said.

PROOF OF EXISTENCE

If, on one occasion, I prove that an equation of nth degree must have n solutions by giving e.g. one of the Gaussian proofs, and if, on another, I specify a procedure for deriving the solutions and so prove their existence, I have by no means given two different proofs of the same proposition; I have proved entirely different things. What is

---

1] WAISMANN ASKS: I believe that all actions are in this sense calculi. The difference between an action and a mere event is precisely that an action is performed in accordance with rules, i.e. that it is part of a calculus.

WITTGENSTEIN: Perhaps you can put it that way, I don't know.

common to them is simply the prose proposition 'There are n solutions,' and that, taken by itself, means nothing, being a mere abbreviation standing for a proof. If the proofs are different, then this proposition simply *means* different things.[135] The reason for speaking of 'existence' in both cases is that the proof of the existence of the solutions exhibits a certain kinship with the procedure for constructing the solutions. But the words 'there are' in themselves must in this context by no means be understood in the same way as we understand them in everyday life, as when I say, 'There are two men in this room.'

A proof proves only what it does prove and nothing further.[136]

[The words 'there are' belong to a calculus too, only to a different one from that which the same words in ordinary language belong to.]

⟨CONSISTENCY VI⟩

Hidden Contradiction

WAISMANN ASKS: I want to include in my work[137] the points about consistency you made some time ago, but here I meet with a difficulty. You said that in the calculus there was no contradiction whatsoever.[138] Now I do not understand how this can be reconciled with the essence of indirect proof, for the basis of this kind of proof is precisely that a contradiction is produced in the calculus.

135 See p. 109 above.
136 See pp. 33f. and 110ff above.
137 This proves that Waismann was, at that time, meant to publish Wittgenstein's ideas.
138 See pp. 119f. above

WITTGENSTEIN: What I mean has absolutely nothing to do with indirect proof. There is a confusion here. Of course there are contradictions in the calculus. What I mean is only that it does not make sense to talk of *hidden contradictions*.[139] What would a hidden contradiction be, after all? I can say, for example: The divisibility of the number 357567 by 7 is hidden for just as long as I have not applied a certain criterion—the rule for division, I suppose. To turn the hidden divisibility into an open one I need only apply the criterion. Is it the same with contradiction? Obviously not. I cannot bring a contradiction to light by applying a criterion, can I? So I say that all this talk about a hidden contradiction does not make sense, and the danger mathematicians talk about—as if a contradiction could be hidden in present-day mathematics like a disease—this danger is a mere figment of the imagination.

You might now ask: But what if one day a method were found for establishing the presence or absence of a contradiction? This proposition is very strange. It makes it appear that mathematics could be regarded under a certain presupposition, namely the presupposition that such a method will be found. Now I can, for instance, ask if a man with red hair has been found in this room, and this question makes good sense, for I can describe such a man even if he is not present. I can, on the other hand, not ask for a method for establishing a contradiction, for I can only describe it if it is there. If it has not yet been discovered, I have no possibility of describing it, and anything I say is empty verbiage. Thus I also cannot raise the question what would happen, if a method were found.

As regards a method for demonstrating the presence or absence of a contradiction, it is just the same as with Goldbach's conjecture: What is here going in is an unsystematic attempt at constructing a calculus. If the attempt is successful, I shall again have a calculus in front of me,

139 See p. 120 above.

only a different one from the calculus I have been using so far. But I have not proved *that the calculus is a calculus*, and that is something you cannot prove at all.

If anybody described the introduction of irrational numbers by saying that he had discovered that there are further points between the rational points on a line, we would reply to him, You have not discovered new points between the old points, you have constructed new points; you have a new calculus in front of you.

The same must be said to Hilbert if he thinks it a discovery that mathematics is consistent. In reality Hilbert has ascertained nothing, he has stipulated: he has stipulated a new calculus.

If Hilbert says '0 ≠ 0' is not to occur as a provable formula,[140] he defines a calculus by means of permission and prohibition.

CONTRADICTION

WAISMANN ASKS: But you said, did you not?, that no contradiction can occur in the calculus itself, only in the rules. The configurations surely cannot represent a contradiction.[141] Is this still your view?

WITTGENSTEIN: I should say that the rules too form a calculus, only a different one. The main point is that we should come to an understanding about the concept of contradiction. For we cannot reach agreement if you mean by it something different from me.

The word 'contradiction' is taken in the first place from where we all use it, namely from truth-functions, where it means roughly '$p . \sim p$'. Thus in the first place we can only talk about contradiction when we are dealing with statements. Since the formulae of a calculus are not statements, there also cannot be a contradiction in the cal-

140 Op. cit. (see footnote p. 119, above).
141 See p. 124 above.

culus. Yet it is of course possible to stipulate that a certain configuration of the calculus, e.g. '$0 \neq 0$', is to be called a contradiction. Only then there always arises the danger of associating this with contradiction in logic, hence of confusing the concepts 'contradiction' and 'forbidden'. For if I have called a particular configuration of signs in the calculus a contradiction, this means only that the construction of this configuration is not allowed: if in a proof you hit on such a formula, something must be done about it, e.g. the formula you have used as your premise is to be deleted.

In order to avoid these confusions, I should like to propose to use, instead of the word 'contradiction,' an entirely new sign, with which we do not associate anything but what we have explicitly laid down—the sign Z, say. *In the calculus nothing is self-evident*. The occurrence of the formula Z does not mean anything yet—we have first to make further stipulations.

From this it becomes evident that it is wholly illegitimate to regard a 'contradiction' as something that is tabu; it is just as illegitimate as if I wanted to say, If this or that formula occurs, a terrible thing will have happened.

By the way, Hilbert calls the configuration '$0 \neq 0$' a contradiction because he has a conception of contradiction in no way different from ours, i.e. '$p. \sim p$'. For he wants to say that on the one hand we have $0 = 0$ and on the other hand we have $0 \neq 0$ and these two formulae contradict one another just as if we said, when playing chess, 'The bishop may move on a straight line,' and, 'The bishop must not move on a straight line.'

WAISMANN: May I put the matter in a slightly different way? The words 'correct' and 'incorrect' have different meanings according as they are applied to proofs or formulae. A proof has been given correctly if it has been performed according to the rules of the game; incorrectly if it contains a violation of these rules. A formula is correct if it has come out as the result of a correctly conducted proof. But we must by no means say that a formula is incorrect if it is the result of an incorrectly conducted proof. The only thing we may say in that case is that it has not been proved. Thus I must lay down a new stipulation for when to call a formula incorrect. In arithmetic I can do this e.g. by saying, A formula is to be called incorrect if the formula '$0 \neq 0$' can be derived from it. I simply think that if the expressions 'correct' and 'incorrect' are explained in this way, they do not stand in the same relation to one another as affirmation and negation. It may very well be that a formula is correct and incorrect at the same time. For that only means that '$0 \neq 0$' can be derived from the basic formulae.—This is, as far as I can see, where the analogy with the game of chess ceases to apply. For I can only ask if a move has been correct, and in mathematics the corresponding question is if a step of a proof is correct. In arithmetic, on the other hand, we face a problem that does not occur in chess, that is the problem of checking whether a formula is correct or not.

WITTGENSTEIN: You are perfectly right in saying that we need a stipulation for when to count a formula as incorrect. But if we proceeded as you said, we would misuse our words, for 'incorrect' simply is the negation of 'correct'. There is a very simple remedy, however, by just using different expressions. In that case no one can object to our making these stipulations.

How do we go about establishing that a formula is false? E.g. the formula $7 \times 5 = 30$? How do we know that, if $7 \times 5 = 35$, it is not also equal to 31? What would we do if anybody said '$8 \times 7 = 75$'? We would say, 'What are you doing there? That is false!' If he now replied to us, 'Why do you think so? I have simply laid it down this way,' we could only tell him, 'In that case you apply a different calculus from the one usually called multiplication. Your calculus is unknown to us. If we proceed according to the rules we have been given, then $8 \times 7 = 56$ and is not equal to 75, and that is our refutation.'

If anyone said that $8 \times 7 = 75$, he would have just as much or just as little right to do so as if he defined the word 'table' in an entirely new way. A definition is certainly arbitrary. But we may nonetheless say that a definition is false, namely if it does not represent what we actually mean. In this sense the formula $8 \times 7 = 75$ is also false.

⟨Equation and Substitution-rule II⟩

WAISMANN ASKS: In arithmetic an equation has a twofold meaning: it is a configuration as well as a substitution-rule. What, then, would happen if a proof for the formula '$0 \neq 0$' were found in arithmetic or analysis? Then an entirely different interpretation would have to be given to arithmetic, for we should no longer be entitled to interpret an equation as a substitution-rule. Because '0 cannot be substituted for 0' does not mean anything. A follower of Hilbert could now say, Here you see what the proof of consistency really achieves. Such a proof is designed to show us that we have the right to construe an equation as a substitution-rule.

WITTGENSTEIN: Of course, it cannot mean that. First of all: how does it come about that we can construe an equation as a substitution-rule? It is simply due to the fact that the grammar of the word 'substitute' is the same as the grammar of an equation. For this reason there is from the very beginning of a parallelism between substitution-rules and equations (both e.g. are transitive). Imagine I were to tell you: '*a* cannot be substituted for *a*.' What would you do?

WAISMANN: I could not associate anything with that, since this statement is not compatible with the syntax of the word 'substitute'.

WITTGENSTEIN Right, you would not associate anything with that and you would be absolutely justified; for you would be confronted with a new calculus that you are not yet familiar with. If I explain the calculus to you by specifying the rule of grammar and application, then you will also understand the statement '*a* cannot be substituted for *a*'. You will not understand that statement as long as you hold on to the point of view of the old calculus.

If the formula '$0 \neq 0$' could be proved, this would only mean that we were faced with two different calculi: one calculus which was the grammar of the word 'substitute,' and a different one in which the formula '$0 \neq 0$' could be proved. These two calculi would then co-exist. (?)

If you now wanted to ask whether it could not be proved that the grammar of the word 'substitute' is the same as the grammar of equations, that is, that an equation can be understood as a substitution-rule, we should have to reply, There can be no question of a proof here. For how should the assertion that is to be proved read? For my applying the calculus only means that I lay down rules telling me what to do if this or that is a result of the calculus. Am I, then, to prove that I have laid down rules? For there cannot be any other sense to the question of whether I have applied the calculus.

I once wrote,[142] Calculus is not a concept of mathematics.

WAISMANN: Mathematics is not a concept of mathematics.

Indirect Proof I

WAISMANN: At one time you said that no contradiction at all can occur in the calculus.[143] If we take e.g. the axioms of Euclidean geometry and the proposition 'The sum of the angles of a triangle is 181°' as a further axiom, no contradiction would arise from that. For it

---

142 In his *MS. vol.* VII (1931), (vW no. 111), and, later, in *BT* (vW no. 213) §§66 and 109.
143 See pp. 126ff. above.

could be, could it not?, that the sum of the angles has two values, just as $\sqrt{4}$ does. Now if you put it that way, I no longer understand what is accomplished by direct proof. For an indirect proof turns precisely on this, that a contradiction is derived in the calculus. How, then, is it if I lay down as assumption an axiom which has been refuted by an indirect proof? Is not the axiom system so extended inconsistent? For example: in Euclidean geometry it is proved that from a point only *one* perpendicular can be dropped onto a straight line, and this is proved by an indirect proof. For suppose there were two perpendiculars, then these would form a triangle with two right angles the sum of whose angles would be greater than 180°, which contradicts the well-known theorem about the sum of angles. If I now lay down the proposition 'There are two perpendiculars' as an axiom and add it to the other axioms of Euclidean geometry—would I not then get a contradiction?

WITTGENSTEIN: Not at all. What is indirect proof? An action performed with signs. But that is not quire all. There is a further rule telling me what to do when an indirect proof has been given. (This rule may read, for example: If an indirect proof has been given, the assumptions from which the proof starts are to be deleted.) *Here nothing is self-evident. Everything must be said explicitly*. The fact that we so easily fail to do this is connected with the fact that we cannot free ourselves from what the words 'contradiction' etc, mean in ordinary language.

If I lay down the axiom 'Two perpendiculars can be dropped onto a straight line from a single point,' then a schematic representation of indirect proof will surely be contained in that calculus [then we will surely also see in that calculus the schematic representation of indirect proof.] But we will not use it as such.

What would happen if we laid down such an axiom? 'I should arrive at a point where I did not know how to go on.' Absolutely right. You would not know how to go on because you would be faced with a new calculus which you did not yet know. What must happen is the following: a further stipulation as to what is to be done must be made once such a proof has been given.

WAISMANN: But this could be done every time that an indirect proof has been given in an ordinary calculus. You could retain the refuted proposition by changing the stipulation regarding the application of indirect proof, and then our proposition would no longer be refuted.

WITTGENSTEIN: Of course we could do that. We should then have destroyed the character of the indirect proof, and only its schematic representation would remain.

VI

Wednesday, 9 December 1931 (Neuwaldegg)[144]

ON DOGMATISM

One fault you can find with a dogmatic account is, first, that it is, as it were, arrogant. But that is not the worst thing about it. There is another mistake, which is much more dangerous and also pervades my whole book, and that is the conception that there are questions the answers to which will be found at a later date. It is held that, although a result is not known, there is a way of finding it. Thus I used to believe, for example, that it is the task of logical analysis to discover the elementary propositions. I wrote, We are unable to specify the form of elementary propositions,[145] and that was quite correct too. It was clear to me that here at any rate there are no hypotheses and that regarding these questions we cannot proceed by assuming from the very beginning, as Carnap does, that the elementary propositions consist of two-place relations, etc.[146] Yet I did think that the elementary propositions could be specified at a later date. Only in recent years have I broken away from that mistake. At the time I wrote in a manuscript of my book (this is not printed in the *Tractatus*),[147] The

144 See footnote p. 115 above.
145 *TLP* 5.55.
146 Presumably an allusion to Carnap's *Der logische Aufbau der Welt*, Berlin, 1928 (E.T. *The Logical Structure of the World*, London, 1967).
147 This remark (or, these remarks, if the two following remarks are meant) do not occur in the *Prototractatus*. In 6.1251 Wittgenstein says, 'Darum kann es in der Logik auch nie Überraschungen geben' ('Hence there can *never* be surprises in logic either')—cf. 6.1261. 'auch' was added in MS and is much easier to understand if we assume that Wittgenstein intended to precede 6.1251 of *TLP* by the remark here quoted.

answers to philosophical questions must never be surprising. In philosophy you cannot discover anything. I myself, however, had not clearly enough understood this and offended against it.

The wrong conception which I want to object to in this connexion is the following, that we can hit upon something that we today cannot yet see, that we can *discover* something wholly new. That is a mistake. The truth of the matter is that we have already got everything, and we have got it actually *present*; we need not wait for anything. We make our moves in the realm of the grammar of our ordinary language, and this grammar is already there. Thus we have already got everything and need not wait for the future.

As regards your *Theses*,[148] I once wrote,[149] If there were theses in philosophy, they would have to be such that they do not give rise to disputes. For they would have to be put in such a way that everyone would say, Oh yes, that is of course obvious. As long as there is a possibility of having different opinions and disputing about a question, this indicates that things have not yet been expressed clearly enough. Once a perfectly clear formulation—ultimate clarity—has been reached, there can be no second thoughts or reluctance any more, for these always arise from the feeling that something has now been asserted, and I do not yet know whether I should admit it or not. If, however, you make the grammar clear to yourself, if you proceed by very short steps in such a way that every single step becomes perfectly obvious and natural, no dispute whatsoever can arise. Controversy always arises through leaving out or failing to state clearly certain steps, so that the impression is given that a claim has been made that could be disputed. I once wrote, The only correct method of doing philosophy consists in not saying anything and leaving it to another person to make a claim.[150] That is the method I now adhere to. What

---

148 Printed as Appendix B. See editors Preface, p. 22.
149 This remark not only occurs in Wittgenstein's *MS. vols.* (which he is here probably referring to) but also in *BT* §89 and *PI*§128.
150 *TLP* 6.53, roughly.

the other person is not able to do is to arrange the rules step by step and in the right order so that all questions are solved automatically.

What I mean by that is the following: when we are talking about negation, for instance, the point is to give the rule '$\sim\sim p = p$'. I do not assert anything. I only say that the structure of the grammar of '$\sim$' is such that 'p' may be substituted for '$\sim\sim p$'. Were you not also using the word 'not' in that way? If that is admitted, then everything is settled. And this is how it is with grammar in general. The only thing we can do is *to tabulate rules*. If by questioning I have found out concerning a word that the other person at one time recognizes these rules and, at another time, those rules, I will tell him, In that case you will have to distinguish exactly *how* you use it; *and there is nothing else I wanted to say*.

In my book I still proceeded dogmatically. Such a procedure is legitimate only if it is a matter of capturing the features of the physiognomy, as it were, of what is only just discernible—and that is my excuse. I saw something from far away and in a very indefinite manner, and I wanted to elicit from it as much as possible. But a rehash of such theses is no longer justified.

WAISMANN: I too used to think otherwise. My mistake was to think that it was the job of the logical analysis of language to describe the most general traits of reality, as it were, those traits that are common to language and the world and make possible the expression of thoughts. If I say, for example, that every state of affairs is complex, that sounds just like a general description of nature. I have now come to see that it is better not to assert propositions of that kind at all, that it is better to remain exclusively within the realm of grammar. Another example of that is the assertion, for instance, that a colour never occurs by itself but always within a system. Put in this way it again looks as if something were being said about reality antecedently to all experience, whereas it is actually just a point about our symbols. (?) The same difficulty makes itself felt when we talk about the connection between language and the world, for instance, when it has been unclear that a proposition is a logical picture of a fact. Then we are tempted to say that logic pervades the world—and that is metaphysics".

WITTGENSTEIN That is very easy to clear up. When I wrote 'A proposition is a logical picture of a fact'[151] I meant that I could insert a picture, literally a drawing, into a proposition and then go on with my proposition. I could accordingly use a picture in the same way as a proposition. How is that possible? The answer is, just because both agree in a certain respect, and what they have in common is what I call a *picture*. Here the expression 'picture' is already taken in an extended sense. I have inherited this concept of a picture from two sides: first from a drawn picture, second from the picture of a mathematician, which already is a general concept. For a mathematician talks of picturing in cases where a painter would no longer use this expression.

The word 'picture' has one advantage: it has helped me and many other people to make something clear by indicating a common feature and pointing out: 'So that is what matters!' We then have the feeling, 'Aha! Now I see, a proposition and a picture are of the same kind.'

I could also use a measuring-rod as a symbol, that is, insert a measuring-rod into a description and use it in the same way as a proposition. You may even say, In many respects a proposition behaves just like a measuring-rod, and therefore I might just as well have called propositions measuring-rods. (For example, in a colour-statement we lay the whole colour-measuring-rod against reality.)[152]

When the common element of propositions and pictures became clear to me for the first time I constantly used different phrases to point it out and compared a proposition with a tableau vivant,[153] at

---

151 Nowhere exactly, but cf. *TLP* 3, 4.01, 4.03.
152 A picture is compared with a measuring-rod in *TLP* 2.1512 and a proposition in *Nb 1914–16*, p. 32. But these earlier passages show no traces of the idea of a propositional system as is the case on pp. 76ff. above.
153 *TLP* 4.0311.

another time with a model,[154] or said that a proposition represented,[155] showed,[156] how things stand, etc.

I should like to indicate the difference between a dogmatic and an undogmatic procedure by means of an example. First I shall speak dogmatically, and then undogmatically. Thus I say, If a proposition is verified in two different ways, then it has different senses in these two cases. That still sounds odd and could give rise to objections. For someone might say, I do not see at all why a proposition should have different senses in that case and why it should not be possible to verify the same proposition in two entirely different ways. Now, however, I shall express myself undogmatically and simply draw attention to the following point: the verification of a proposition can itself only be given by means of a description. Thus the fact of the matter is that we have two propositions. The second proposition describes the verification of the first one. What, then, am I going to do? I simply lay it down as a rule of grammar that the first proposition is to follow from the second one. Thus I do not talk of sense and what sense is at all; I remain entirely within grammar. If you now say that one sentence has two different verifications, then I will point out that these verifications are described by different propositions; thus, in deriving the same proposition, we *proceeded according to different rules; and I did not want to say anything more than that.*

Thus I simply draw the other person's attention to what he is really doing and refrain from any assertions. Everything is then to go on within grammar.

The point is to draw essential, fundamental distinctions.

154 *TLP* 4.01, 4.04, 4.463.
155 'Darstellen' ('represent') often occurs in the sense required here, but never with 'wie es sich verhält' ('how things stand') as object. Cf. e.g. *TLP* 2.0231, 4.021, 4.031, 4.1.
156 *TLP* 4.022, 'A proposition *shows* how things stand *if* it is true. And it *says that* they do so stand.'

WAISMANN: An example of the confusion of the logical with the empirical point of view is a conception, for example, which is frequently propounded by Hahn, namely that it is only because of the psychological constitution of the consciousness that we happen to have that our thinking is finite.[157] Hahn thinks that there could just as well be a consciousness that would be capable of thinking infinitely many thoughts. I imagine a consciousness, for example, which needs half a minute to think the first thought, a quarter of a minute to think the second one, and so on. When a minute has passed by this creature has thought infinitely many thoughts—that that is not the case is only shown by experience. The reply to that is clear: we are not able to describe such a consciousness, are we?

WITTGENSTEIN: That, too, might be possible. It is just a matter of going into the details of what Hahn thinks and picturing it all to ourselves very exactly. I would ask, How do we establish whether a creature has such a consciousness? What is the criterion for that? We shall then see what the statement means. Let us take another example! (It does not matter that we change our examples, for the difference in grammar is transplanted to every other example.) What does it mean to say, for example, that a string is infinitely long? Does that amount to saying that I cannot reach its end? That cannot be what it means. Let us make the matter clear by means of the following example.

Assume somebody claims, I can quite well imagine a telegraph pole which is infinitely tall. Well, I will ask him: How do you verify that? First, how do you verify that it is 10m. tall? 'I check by means of a measuring-rod.' And how do you verify that it is 100m. tall? 'In the same way.' Thus I now know what the criterion for its being n m. tall

---

157 Probably in oral discussions. Brouwer's proof of the possibility of the division of a map into three countries, so that all three countries border on each other in every point of the boundary, partly rests on similar considerations. This proof was expounded by Hahn in *Krise und Neuaufbau in den exakten Wissenschaften* (several authors), Vienna, 1933, pp. 54–56.

is. I shall now ask, What is the criterion for its being infinitely tall? Again laying a measuring-rod against it? 'It cannot mean that.' Aha! But then the criterion is not of a finite kind any more, and in that case one thing is already clear: that the word 'infinite' has, in any case, a different grammar from a number word. How, then, is that statement to be verified? Well, here too several possibilities are conceivable. The following, for example, is one possibility: I empirically discover a law and now notice that the taller I assume the telegraph pole to be the more exactly I can describe the facts by means of this law. I shall say then, I lay down the hypothesis that the telegraph pole is infinitely tall, since in that case the law serves to reproduce experience exactly.

The word 'infinite,' then, can have different meanings. Here it is just as in the case of the question whether there is only *one* kind of real number. I should say that there are very different kinds of real number because there are different grammatical rules. Brouwer's number,[158] for instance, are of an entirely different kind, since the grammar of '>', '=', '<' is a different one with respect to them. You could also ask, Are the complex numbers still numbers? I can suppose that they are. In supposing this I am doing the following. I am pointing very emphatically to those features which the grammars of the natural numbers, the rational numbers, the real numbers, and the complex numbers have in common. (I could also interpret their common features in such a far-reaching way that I would call a *proposition*, for example, a number, since we could calculate with it, since here too there are, for instance, sums and products.) But in doing so I run the risk of forgetting about the differences. And this is the risk in present-day mathematics, which seeks to remove differences and make everything level. I, on the contrary, endeavour to emphasize the *diversity* of grammatical rules.

158 See footnote p. 73 above.

ON RAMSEY'S DEFINITION OF IDENTITY[159]

Ramsey explains identity in this way:

'$x = x$' is a tautology,

'$x = y$' is a contradiction.

I.e., the symbol '$. . . = . . .$' is a tautology if there is *the same* letter on both sides. In this way, however, this symbol cannot be used at all, for I need the identity-sign, don't I?, in order to express the intersub-

---

Wιττgenstein το Ramsey: *Extract from a letter dated June 1927*
You define '$x = y$' by

$$(\varphi_e) \cdot \varphi_e x = \varphi_e y.$$

$$Q(x,y)$$

The ground of this definition should be that '$Q(x,y)$' is a tautology whenever 'x' and 'y' have the same meaning, and a contradiction, when they have different meanings.

I will now try to show that this definition won't do nor any other that tries to make '$x = y$' a tautology or a contradiction.

It is clear that '$Q(x,y)$' is a logical product. Let 'a' and 'b' be two names having different meanings. Then amongst the members of our product there will be one such that '$f(a)$' means 'p' and '$f(b)$' means '$\sim p$'. Let me call such a function a critical function 'f_k'. Now although we know that 'a' and 'b' have different meanings, still to say that they have not, cannot be nonsensical. For if it were, the negative proposition, i.e. that they have the same meaning, would be nonsensical too, *for the negation of nonsense is nonsense.* Now let us suppose, wrongly, that $a = b$, then, by substituting 'a' for 'b' in our logical product the

---

159 This appears to be a criticism of a lecture given in 1925, reprinted in *Foundations of Mathematics*, London, 1931, p. 53. The extracts from letters printed *under the line* show an earlier stage of discussion. It seems that Wittgenstein's views were communicated to Ramsey by Schlick and Waismann (hence the existing copy among Waismann's papers) and perhaps translated by them. Ramsey answered Schlick who passed the answer on to Wittgenstein (in the letter printed above which is in the possession of Professor H. Hänsel). Later on, in October 1927, Schlick visited Cambridge and no doubt met Ramsey.

stitutability of two different signs. I need not express the intersubstitutability of '$x = x$'. (By the way, the only use we could make of this symbolism consists in its allowing me to replace the words 'tautology' and 'contradiction' by the expressions '$x = x$' and '$x = y$'. If the

critical function '$f_k(a)$' becomes nonsensical (ambiguous) and, consequently, the whole product, too. On the other hand, let 'c' and 'd' be two names having the same meaning, then it is quite true that '$Q(c,d)$' becomes a tautology. But suppose now (wrongly) $c \neq d$. '$Q(c,d)$' is a tautology still, for there is no critical function in our product. And even if it could be supposed (which it cannot) that $c \neq d$, surely a critical function f_k (such that '$f_k(c)$' means 'p', '$f_k(d)$' means '$\sim p$') cannot be supposed to exist, because this sign becomes meaningless. Therefore, if '$x = y$' were a tautology or a contradiction and correctly defined by '$Q(x,y)$', '$Q(a,b)$' would not be contradictory, but nonsensical (as this supposition, if it were the supposition that 'a' and 'b' had the same meaning, would make the critical function nonsensical). And therefore '$\sim Q(a,b)$' would be nonsensical too, for the negation of nonsense is nonsense.

In the case of c and d '$Q(c,d)$' remains tautologous, even if c and d could be supposed to be different (for in this case a critical function cannot be supposed to exist).

The way out of all these troubles is to see that neither '$Q(x,y)$', although it is a very interesting function, nor any propositional function whatever, can be substituted for '$x = y$'.

Your mistake becomes still clearer in its consequences; viz. when you try to say, 'There is an individual'. You are aware of the fact that the supposition of there being no individual makes

$$(\exists x).x = x$$

E

'absolute nonsense'. But if 'E' is to say 'There is an individual', '$\sim$E' says: 'There is no individual'. Therefore from '$\sim$E' follows that 'E' is nonsense. Therefore '$\sim$E' must be nonsense itself, and therefore again so must be 'E'.

identity-sign, then, is supposed to express the intersubstitutability of two *different* signs, then '$x = y$' cannot be a contradiction. If I want to reach a contradiction, I have to add a further rule, say 'xDefy' (which means: 'y' can be substituted for 'x') and now write:

$$x = y. {\sim}x\text{Defy}$$

The case lies as before. 'E', according to your definition of the sign '$=$', may be a tautology right enough, but does not say, 'There is an individual'. Perhaps you will answer: Of course it does not say, 'There is an individual' but it *shows* what we really mean when we say, 'There is an individual'. But this is not shown by 'E', but simply by the legitimate use of the symbol '$(\exists x)..$', and therefore just as well (and as badly) by the expression '${\sim}(\exists x).x = x$'. The same, of course, applies to your expressions, 'There are at least two individuals' and so on.

SCHLICK TO WITTGENSTEIN: *Extract from a letter dated 15 August 1927*

Some time ago I here ⟨in Millstätt, Carinthia⟩ received Ramsey's reply to your letter. I shall copy for you the passages that interest you. First there is a sentence in which Ramsey reproduces the point of your objection; he then continues, 'With this I entirely agree, but it still seems to me that $Q(x,y)$ [this was the abbreviation of $(\varphi_e).\varphi_e x \equiv \varphi_e y$] is an adequate substitute for $x = y$ as an element in logical notation. We always use $x = y$ as part of a propositional function which is generalized, and in any such case we shall get the right sense for the resulting general proposition if we put $Q(x,y)$ instead.

. . .

'I never really meant to suggest that $Q(x,y)$ was a way of saying that x and y were identical. I imagined that Wittgenstein had shown that it was impossible to say any such thing. I only proposed $Q(x,y)$ as a substitute for the symbol $x = y$, used in general propositions and in defining classes.

'He also made some criticisms of my remarks on the number of things in the world, which I think can be answered in the same sort of way, but in any case they are less important.'

Only now have we got a contradiction, since '$x = y$' allows what is forbidden by '$\sim x\text{Defy}$'. But in that case '$x\text{Defy}$' expresses equality.

This shows that the contradiction has to manifest itself as a contradiction between two rules.

CONSISTENCY VII

WAISMANN FORMULATES THE PROBLEM OF CONSISTENCY: The problem of consistency means the following, How do I know that a proposition I have proved by means of transfinite methods cannot be refuted by a finite numerical calculation? If e.g. a mathematician discovers a proof of Fermat's Last Theorem which essentially uses transfinite methods—the axiom of choice, for instance, or the law of excluded middle in the form, Either Fermat's Last Theorem applies to all numbers or there is a number to which it does not apply—how do I know that such a proposition cannot be refuted by a counter-example? That is in no way self-evident. And yet it is remarkable that mathematicians have such confidence in transfinite ways of inference that, once such a proof is known, no one would make an attempt at finding a counter-example. The question then is, Can this confidence be justified? That is, are we sure that no proposition which has been proved by means of transfinite methods can ever be refuted by a concrete numerical calculation? That is the mathematical question of consistency.

I will at once put forward how the matter seems to me to stand, by raising an analogous question about ordinary algebra. How do I know that a proposition cannot be refuted by a numerical example if I have proved it in the calculus with letters? Suppose, for example, I have proved that

$$1+2+3 \ldots +n = \frac{n(n+1)}{2}$$

—how do I know that this formula will stand up to a numerical check? Here we have the very same situation. I think we must say that the reason why a calculation with letters and a calculation with numbers lead to the same result, that is, the reason for the applicability of a calculation with letters to concrete numbers, lies in the fact that the axioms of calculation with letters—the commutative and associative laws of addition, etc.—are from the very beginning chosen in such a way that they allow such an application. This is connected with the fact that we choose the axioms in accordance with a certain prescription, for an axiom corresponds to an induction, and this correspondence is possible because the formulae possess the same multiplicity as the induction, so that we can project the system of induction onto the system of formulae. In this case there is thus no problem, and it is quite impossible to raise the question whether a calculation can ever come into conflict with a numerical calculation. But what is the situation in the case of analysis? Here, on the face of it, there really seems to be a problem.

WITTGENSTEIN: To begin with, what are we really talking about? If what is meant by confidence is a certain mood, I would say, That does not interest me. We are not here concerned with the psychology of mathematicians. Accordingly it is presumably something else that is meant by confidence. In that case it can only be something that can be written down in symbols. What we here seem to be asking for is the reason for the agreement between two calculations. Let us take a very simple example:

$$2+(3+4) = 2+7 = 9$$
$$(2+3)+4 = 5+4 = 9$$

I have here performed two independent calculations and reached the same result both times. Independent here means that the one calculation is not a copy of the other one. I have two different processes.

And what [what would the situation be like] if they did not agree? Then I could do nothing about it. Then the symbols would, to be sure, have a different grammar. The associative and commutative laws are valid because of grammar. In group theory, however, AB is no longer equal to BA; we could hence no longer, for instance, do one multiplication in two ways, but we should nonetheless have a calculus.

The point is this: I must antecedently lay down when to count a calculation as correct. That is, I must specify under what conditions I can say that a formula is proved. If the case then arose that a formula, according to one method, counted as proved, but, according to another method, as disproved, this would not in the least mean that we then had a contradiction and the case was hopeless; we could say that the formula simply means different things. It belongs to two different calculi; in the one calculus it is proved, in the other one it is disproved. So we have at bottom two entirely different formulae before us that only happen to have these signs in common.

Quite a number of things get confused when dealing with the question of consistency.

First it must be asked where a contradiction is supposed to occur: between the rules or between the configurations of a game?

What is a rule? If I say, for example: Do this! and: Don't do this!, then the other person does not know what to do. That is, we do not recognize a contradiction as a rule. We just do not call a contradiction a rule. Or, even more simply, the grammar of the word 'rule' is such that a contradiction is not called a rule.

If now a contradiction occurred among my rules, I ocould say that they are then not rules in the sense in which I usually speak of rules. What are we to do in such a case? That is the easiest thing in the world! We lay down a new rule and thereby the matter is settled.

A board-game would be an example of that.[160] Suppose there is a rule which says that a black piece must jump over a white one. Now if a white piece is standing at the edge of the board, the rule cannot be applied any more. We then simply make a new stipulation for this case and the difficulty is annihilated.

160 Cf. p. 124 above.

But things must be expressed more exactly here. We have here a contradiction (between namely the rules 'A white piece must jump over a black one' and 'No piece may move over the edge of the board'). I now ask, Did we already at the beginning have a method of discovering the contradiction? Here there are two possibilities:

1. In the case of the board-game this possibility undoubtedly existed. For the rule says 'In all cases . . .,' doesn't it? If that means 'At this point, and at that point, and . . .,' then from the beginning there has obviously been the possibility of my discovering the contradiction, and if I did not see it, then it was my fault—perhaps I was too lazy to inspect all the cases, or I forgot about one case. In this case there is no serious problem here. Once the contradiction is there I simply make a further stipulation and by means of that remove the contradiction. A contradiction can always be annihilated.

I can always decide, however, if a contradiction is present by scrutinizing my list of rules. In the case of Euclidean geometry, for instance, that is a matter of five minutes. The rules of Euclidean geometry do not contradict one another, i.e. no rule occurs which invalidates another formerly established rule ('p' and '$\sim p$'), and with that I am content.

2. But now we assume the second possible case, that we have no such method. My list of rules, then, is in order. I see no contradiction. I now ask, Does any danger still remain? Out of the question! For what are we afraid of? [1] Of a contradiction, of all things? But I am given a contradiction only by a method for discovering it! As long as a contradiction is not there it does not concern me. I can accordingly stay quite calm and do my calculations. Would the discovery of a contradiction in mathematics, then, make all the calculations cease to exist that have been established by mathematicians in the course of several hundreds of years? [2] Should we say that they were not

---

1] We need not be disconcerted. There is no reason whatsoever for being disconcerted.

2] What puzzles us is the thought, Cannot a contradiction occur at some point? Here I ask, What does *at some point* mean? Even if a contradiction occured half a year later—would everything I have calculated be illegitimate because of that?

calculations? Absolutely not. If a contradiction is going to occur, we shall manage. *Now,* however, we need not worry about it.

What is really meant is something entirely different: we have the notion of a certain model and we want to *assimilate* the calculus *to this model*. (Cf. infra.)[161]

Insertion from dictation.[162]

CONSISTENCY VIII

I want to object to the *bugbear* of contradiction, the superstitious fear that takes the discovery of a contradiction to mean the destruction of the calculus. [1]

Ishould like to ask: Why this narrow-mindedness? Would not

1] Imagine I am told that my brother Paul was found dead in a forest. What am I to do? Am I to call the police? Here too we ask in the same way, What are we to do?

161 Perhaps this refers to p. 201 infra.

162 In December 1931 Schlick was in America. Waismann, however, saw Wittgenstein and took notes for Schlick. Perhaps the 'Insertion from dictation' in his own note-book corresponds to all, or a part of, those notes. There is a 'Diktatfür Schlick' among Waismann's papers (evidently Wittgenstein's work at roughly that time) which deals with the understanding of a proposition. It does not coincide with the present insertion and is not identical with anything in Wittgenstein's posthumous papers. It is now with Wittgenstein's papers in Trinity College, Cambridge (vW no. 302). See editor's Preface, p. 24.

163 This remark appears on the verso facing the title 'Insertion from dictation.' It is of general significance for what precedes the title as well as for what follows it. The only brother of Wittgenstein's who was still alive at that time was in fact called Paul.

calculi with a contradiction have their own particular charm?[164] It will probably be said, No, such a calculus would be trivial. [1] For from a contradiction every formula follows: you can write down any arbitrary formula, and with that the calculus loses all its interest. To that I would reply, In that case the calculus consists, does it not?, of two parts, of one part that goes as far as the discovery of the contradiction, and of a second part in which it is permitted to write down any formula. The first part is the interesting thing. It will be asked, Does the calculus come to an end? *When* does it come to an end? A very exciting question!

Let us take Euclidean geometry! Here the axioms are rules, i.e. propositions of grammar. (If I say, for example, 'It is possible to draw a circle with an arbitrary radius around any arbitrary point,' this means, If I make a statement referring to the circle around this point, then this statement has a sense, whether it is true or false. This shows that that axiom was a rule of grammar.) The rules for inferring new propositions from the axioms are the rules of logic. I now ask, *Where* in that case could a contradiction be looked for?

Let us assume that an empirical measurement of the sum of the angles of a triangle yielded a result of 182°. Now someone comes along and proves that the sum of the angles is 180°. To that it will be

---

1] We do not want to have '$p . \sim p$' in our list of rules. That is, we do not regard '$p . \sim p$' as a *rule*. (The grammar of the expression 'rule' is such that '$p . \sim p$' does not count as a rule.)

We can imagine all this very much simplified, e.g.

$$'c \rightarrow p' \text{ is the whole game.}$$

But now it is furthermore said, 'And no contradiction must ever follow from a rule.' This we again fail to understand. Let us take the Euclidean axioms. The axioms are rules, that is, propositions of grammar. The rules according to which the game is played within geometry are the rules of logic. Where then could a contradiction be looked for?

'Make this stick 5m. long.' 'Make this stick 3 + 3m. long.' Would it be like that?

164 See p. 139 above.

said, He already had a rough idea of how great the sum was and he has now shown that it really comes quite close to that result. What would it be like, however, if the measurement deviated considerably from the value 180°? Then it would entirely depend on how I *interpreted* the matter. I could take *both* to be sums of these angles. But we must be clear about the fact that the measurement and the proof by no means contradict one another. The measurement is just what it is. It is not invalidated or refuted by the proof. If I introduce measurement as an admissible method into geometry, then we just have a structure before us that is altogether different. It cannot surprise me at all that I then get different values for the sum of the angles, for I have now simply made different stipulations as regards the size of an angle, i.e. the expressions 'angle' and 'sum of the angles' are ambiguous; they are governed by different rules of grammar.

The situation is the same as if I wanted to say that a straight line could be drawn through any three points. I should then simply mean something different by the words 'straight line' from what is usually meant by them in geometry. Now the words 'straight line' already have an established grammar, so that I should see a contradiction where my grammar of the words 'straight line' deviates from the usual one. (It is in the same sense that I use the identity-sign as a synonym of 'substitutable for'.)

Let us return once more to the sum of the angles of a triangle. Suppose we could at one time prove that the sum of the angles is 180° and at another time that it is 182° (and in fact from the axioms in both cases)—what then? I should say that we have simply laid down two different stipulations as to when to regard a measurement as correct. At one time I used to say that the axioms of geometry were the standard according to which we judged the quality of a measurement.[165] The rule $a + \beta + \gamma = 180°$ is such a standard. If I have

165 See p. 62 above.

specified such a rule, I have simply introduced two standards, standards, to be sure, in *different senses*. Imagine, for instance, that at one time I use a measuring-rod with fixed graduating lines and at another time a measuring-rod with fixed graduating lines 1, 2 . . . 9 but a movable graduating line 10. That would then be a measuring-rod in an entirely different sense. Of course I do not know whether we would ever use such a measuring-rod. But who can forbid me to call this too a measuring-rod? The two propositions: The sum of the angles of a triangle is $180°$, and: The sum of the angles of a triangle is $182°$, would be two such different measuring-rods or standards, and the only problem now is how to apply them. I could even imagine how to apply such rules [1]: The one rule I use, for example, when measuring angles by a *mechanical* method (protractor), the other one when measuring them by an *optical* method.

Where, then, must we be rigorous? In respect, I believe, of the logical rules. [2] There, however, we can be rigorous, can't we? It is

---

1] We cannot use a contradiction as a rule. I do not *call* a contradiction a rule, since this is just what the grammar of 'rule' is like.

2] What will count as a list of rules is connected with the grammar of the word 'list of rules' in the way that the identity-sign is connected with the words 'substitutable for'. If you want to find a reason, for example, for requiring that it be, say, transitive, you can point out that the word 'substitutable' has the same grammar. But the reason for this grammar cannot be specified. Similarly, with the grammar of the word 'list of rules'. The reason why no contradictions must occur is simply this: that only what does not contain a contradiction is called a rule. There is no further reason to be given.

Consistency is to be required only where it is a matter of what is called an *obvious* contradiction. A hidden contradiction does not violate the grammar of a 'list of rules'. For it is hidden only because the method of application of my list of rules is not at all settled as yet.

very easy to show that Euclidean geometry does not contain a contra-diction in that sense. It will now be said that it does not contain an obvious contradiction. To that I reply, Quite enough as far as logic is concerned! For everything else depends on overt rules, which I would change in order not to obtain a contradiction.

Were a contradiction to be discovered, this would happen because of rules which I still have to lay down and which I can abolish afterwards. It appears as though ruin were imminent. But that could happen only if there were an overt contradiction. Logic is not against a hidden contradiction. It does not say that a contradiction must never occur; it says, You must prevent this from happening, that is, you have to arrange the rules you are going to lay down in such a way that no contradiction will arise. For the present, however, everything is all right, perfectly all right, and there is no danger at all.

In other words, if a person is shown the axioms of Euclidean geometry and asked, 'Is this a list of rules?' he will say, Yes. If you now go on asking him, 'Is there a contradiction contained in it?' the answer will be 'No'. 'Can a contradiction develop from it?' 'I don't know; it depends on what you are going to do with it. Can you already specify how it is to develop? If not, you are not clear about it yet, you will than have to prepare yourself so that no contradiction will develop from it.'

In logic we are rigorous against contradiction in so far as we do want to have a list of rules and not a list which is not a list of *rules*. Furthermore, in logic the only contradiction is one between 'p' and '$\sim p$'. From this it follows that it turns entirely on the calculus

---

Well, then I have to settle that method, and I have to do it in such a way that no contradiction will result. But this kind of contradiction, too, can only be avoided when it arises. Before it arises and before I have any method of generating it, it is not only impossible to avoid it, but there does not even exist anything that I might have to avoid and I can hence also not make provision for avoiding it. There is no reason whatsoever for being concerned.

provided by logic, whether something is logically permitted or forbidden. All other interpretations and transformations do not concern logic.

Let us suppose that I have the proposition 'q' and lay down the rule '$q . \sim p \equiv q$' (i.e. '$\sim p$' follows from 'q'). This is a rule I can lay down, or I can refrain from doing so. Let us suppose I formerly obtained 'p' as a result, then logic would say, You must not lay down that rule. ('q' = 'The sum of angles is 180°' ⟨and⟩ 'p' = 'The sum of angles is 181°' stand in juxtaposition. Only when I lay down the rule '$q . \sim p \equiv q$', *only then* is there a contradiction; before this there isn't!) Thus the contradiction will arise when I lay down the rule which yields the result 'p' and '$\sim p$', and that is something I certainly must not do.

What is misleading is the belief that everything happens through compulsion, that we are sliding into an abyss willy-nilly without any possibility of being rescued. Is it not true that we are compelled to follow the path we do? In a certain sense, it is. But by what? By an analogy—not by the calculus, but by certain implicit conditions which we want to make the calculus fit. E.g., it would otherwise cease to be geometry (the sum of angles is to have only one value). It is some other characteristic that guides me here. Contradiction as such is something I can always avoid.

It is different if there is a certain formula within the calculus which I call a contradiction. This, of course, is something I can do. If, however, I say that this formula must not occur, then in doing so I have laid down a further rule, and hence changed the game. The question whether such a formula occurs is a purely mathematical problem. It has nothing to do with something's being logically permitted and logically forbidden.

An Analogy—'The Expansion' of π

Suppose I am calculating with decimal numbers which never contain four sevens in a row. So far this is nonsense. There is no way for me, is there?, to find out what I am allowed to calculate and what not. I could, on the other hand, lay down another rule. I could say: If four sevens in a row ever occurred, I would not use this number any more.

What does it mean to say 'If it ever occurred'? That does not really yield the picture of a calculus, since it as it were depends on time. The first condition was only a pseudo-condition. It means nothing at all. I cannot say, I shall only calculate with this number *if* . . .—unless I have a criterion for determining whether this condition is satisfied. Otherwise it means nothing.

The two things that get confused here are the *law* governing π and the *expansion* of π. I can certainly say, I shall only write down such expansions of π as do not contain any four sevens. But I cannot say, The only numbers I want to calculate with are those which are governed by a *law* in which no four sevens occur, and this is the confusion here.

To this analogy there corresponds the case where it is said that the game comes to a kind of end whenever a certain configuration arises that I call a contradiction. In that case I have simply defined the game in this way from the very beginning. A contradiction in the sense of one that makes the game impossible is not in question here at all.

⟨*The Concept of a Calculus*⟩

What I want to object to in this context is the view that we can define what a calculus is. One calculus is just as good as another. We can only describe a calculus, not require anything of it.

The word 'calculus' has different meanings: there are different calculi just as there are different lists of rules. By this I do not mean different calculations, but different *kinds* of calculi. The concept *calculus* itself is ambiguous.

The following is what always gets confused. People say, I do not know whether a contradiction will occur. We feel like replying to that, It does not matter whether *I* know that; what matters is whether the *calculus* knows it. And in this respect calculi behave in very different ways.

⟨*Proof in Geometry and Arithmetic*⟩

If I consider the equation $25 \times 25 = 625$, the proof is given by means of multiplication. The calculation is the proof. But proofs also occur, for instance, in Euclidean geometry, e.g. the proof of Pythagoras' theorem. Is this, then, a proof in the same sense as the proof of the equation above? What we find striking here is that, whereas I have a method which I can apply mechanically for proving the equation, I have no such method for proving Pythagoras' theorem. If I confront a person with an assertion of Pythagoras' theorem, he will not immediately see how to prove it. He will first have to look for the proof. But then the word 'proof' means something completely different in arithmetic and geometry, and we now see how calculi can differ according to the kind of proof involved.

In all these investigations there is the risk that the mathematicians may pretend that the difference is merely a *psychological* one—as though the difference consisted entirely in the fact that in geometry a proof requires *more effort* than in arithmetic. But this is roughly the same mistake as saying that we cannot write down all the infinitely many numbers of the series—as if that were *our fault*. In reality an infinite number series *means* something different from a finite series. And the situation here is the same. The difference I have in mind is a logical difference. The question is not whether it is more or less easy for me to find a certain proof, but whether *the calculus* recognizes *a method* of conducting proofs. (The word 'recognize' is to be taken in the sense in which we say that the calculus with rational numbers 'recognizes' different possibilities from the calculus with integers.) *That* is the difference and not the degree of difficulty.

We shall make the question clear to ourselves little by little. To reach the main point we shall proceed in this way: What does it mean to divide an angle into two parts? To this we have to reply that that depends on what is permitted as a verification. If a check by measuring counts as a verification, then bisection has a different sense from the case where a proof from the axioms of geometry is regarded as a verification. The word 'bisection' has thus an entirely different sense, for an empirical bisection *means* something completely different from a construction by means of ruler and compasses. You can by no means say that both are methods leading to the same end.

There is a relation, however, that obtains between those two, namely that I can apply the geometrical construction as I do apply it, that is, to the actual division of an angle into two halves. If, for any reason, this were, however, not the case, geometry could nonetheless be concerned with a procedure called the 'bisection of an angle,' although it could not be used for an actual division. [1] But then there would be no risk of confusing the two concepts of bisection either.

I can apply the empirical method to trisection too. For it makes good sense to draw two lines on a sheet of paper so that measuring shows that the distances between them are equal. In this sense accordingly I can speak of the trisection of an angle. I cannot, however, say that any longer if it is the construction that is meant. The view probably is that we can also talk of the construction of a trisection, by analogy with bisection. Here, however, we must ask, 'What does "analogy" mean here?'[166] Again it is surely only a word. If I wanted to say, e.g., I have five senses—by analogy I imagine a sixth sense—would I have said anything by that? (The same applies to

---

1] The two procedures would then have nothing to do with one another. There would be no application.

166 See p. 143 above.

Helmholtz's remark that in his best moments he could imagine four-dimensional space or that four-dimensional space was conceivable on the analogy of three-dimensional space.)[167] This is to *misuse* the word 'analogy' and the same applies to speaking of the construction of the trisection of an angle. In this case we mostly imagine ourselves somehow drawing auxiliary lines, using compasses and describing curves, laying rulers against points and connecting them, making these lines intersect, and the like. But construction does not consist in these overt performances; *method* is the essence of construction. If I am talking of the *method* of bisection, however, I cannot at all by analogy talk of the method of trisection; I cannot construct this analogy at all.

It might now be asked, why is it that we reach the same thing by means of construction and by empirical trial? To this I would reply that it is not the 'same thing' at all. The word 'bisection' is ambiguous and that is all.

If I regard construction as my criterion, I can by no means check the division of angles by measurement. The case is much rather this: if measuring yields a difference, I shall say, The compass is faulty, that was not a straight line, etc. For construction is now my *standard* according to which I judge the quality of a measurement.

I can hence not learn anything about the result of an empirical measurement from axioms and constructions. (The two have nothing whatsoever to do with each other.)

This is an illustration of what is important for me here: a proof by means of *transfinite* methods and a proof by *numerical calculation* by no means need to lead to the same result. I can only say: If they do not agree, then there is by no means a conflict between different proof methods; we have simply proved entirely different things. What those two have in common is the appearance of the formulae they lead

167 Helmholtz said exactly the contrary (*Vorträge und Reden* II, Brunswick, 1903, pp. 8 and 28). The reference must be to some other mathematician.

up to or, say, an identity in the wording by which we represent the formulae. A formula will then simply be ambiguous, and that is all that follows. Of course there is a problem here, but it is a *mathematical* problem and not a philosophical one; it is not a question of life or death for mathematics.

What I should like to object to in this context is the view that we can *prove* that a system of rules is a calculus.

GENERALITY IN GEOMETRY

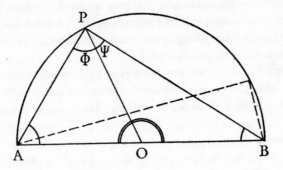

Thales' theorem:

$$\varphi = A$$
$$\psi = B$$
$$\varphi + \psi = \tfrac{1}{2}(\varphi + A + \psi + B)$$
$$\overline{}$$
$$= \tfrac{1}{2}(\sphericalangle AOP + \sphericalangle BOP)$$
$$= \tfrac{1}{2} \times 180° = 90°$$

You can ask, Does the proof for one figure prove the theorem for another figure at the same time? Or do I only prove it for the one figure and we subsequently extend it to the other triangles? Some mathematicians were silly enough to believe the latter alternative. The mistake involved is the following: we are not dealing with pencil-strokes on paper (it is even a *question* whether the theorem applies to the drawing), the sketch itself is a symbolism, i.e. we

206

operate by means of strokes and pencil-marks according to certain rules, and these rules are the essential thing, not the strokes. We could also say that the strokes here are not meant as strokes, as part of reality, but as pieces of a game for which we have laid down certain rules. The proof is thus not *about* the figure drawn; this figure is a notation in terms of which we express the proof or part of it in a very simple and perspicuous manner.

We must distinguish: an example as a particular case and an example as an arbitrary instance of a general proposition. These two things are different.

$$2\ 3\ 4 = 4\ 5\ 6$$
$$.\,.\,.\,2\ 3\ 4\,.\,.\,. = .\,.\,.\,4\ 5\ 6\,.\,.\,.$$

I tend to forget that here there are also dots.

People pretend that something could be inserted between generality and a particular case, namely an example. But either it is the example itself and nothing else that is meant by an example, or I already read generality into the example. In that case, however, the example is already an *expression* of generality. And this is the situation here. For generality lies in the *rules* that I had laid down before I started to play the game (hence before anything was proved). In these rules points, straight lines, etc. occur as variables.

I should like to say: the lines and dots on paper form a *calculus*, and the drawn figure on the basis of which the proof is conducted is itself essentially a *part* of the calculus.[168]

INDIRECT PROOF II

An indirect proof has the form: $p.q \rightarrow \sim p$. There are now two possibilities of construing it: I can either drop 'q' (which is the usual case) or 'p'. Example: proof that $\sqrt{2}$ is irrational.

$$\sqrt{2} = \frac{m}{n}\ .\ .\ .\ q$$

168 In the note-book there follows a piece on proof and hypothesis in arithmetic which is also to be found in one of Wittgenstein's *MS. vols.* too.

$$\frac{(m,n) = 1 \ldots p}{(m,n) \neq 1 \ldots \sim p}$$

We now say: *Therefore* there is no rational number whose square is 2. Thus we drop 'q'. There is in fact a second possibility remaining. We could drop 'p' and would then have to alter the grammar of '$\sqrt{2}$'. I would then be in a situation where I simply must not mean by '$\sqrt{2}$' what we mean by it now.

Does the calculus acknowledge a method of discovering future contradictions?

A contradiction is found—have I had from the very beginning a method of discovering it? If so, then only an oversight has occurred; I have forgotten to check all the possibilities. If not, then no possibility of a contradiction comes into question, for a contradiction is given only by a method of discovering it.[169]

169 The rest of this note-book (approximately 16 pages shorthand) consists of material which is either in Wittgenstein's *MS. vols.* (extracts from which have been and will be published) or in *PR*.

VII

1 July 1932 (Argentinierstraße)[170]

Conversation about the view that a proposition can only be compared with a proposition; e.g. a prediction of an eclipse of the sun only with a report of an astronomer; but no confrontation of a statement with reality.

WITTGENSTEIN: Of course there is such a thing as confronting a proposition with reality. If I say, 'There are six people sitting there,' then there is such a thing as a confrontation by looking there and comparing:

There, there, there, there, . . . (WHILE SAYING THIS WITTGEN-STEIN ALTERNATELY LOOKS TO THE LEFT AND TO THE RIGHT.)

In my manuscript[171] I speak of 'collating'.

List of people: Reality:

—
—
—
—
—
—

As regards ostensive definition and *its* remaining within language the situation is completely different. In that case there is no confrontation of a sign with reality.

In the *Tractatus* logical analysis and ostensive definition were

---

170 There is reason to suppose that the topic of this conversation was brought up by an article by Carnap ('Die physikalische Sprache als Universalsprache der Wissenschaft,' *Erkenntnis* 2, 1931, pp. 432–65 (E.T. *The Unity of Science*, London, 1934)) which talks about *comparison with a report* ('Protokoll') and claims that *ostensive definition remains within language* and discusses *hypotheses*.

171 This word occurs in *BT* several times.

unclear to me. At that time I thought that there was 'a connexion between language and reality.'[172]

HYPOTHESES III

On a field of ruins fragments of columns, capitals, pediments are dug up and it is said, That was a temple. The fragments are completed, gaps are filled up in the imagination, lines are traced. This is a likeness for an hypothesis.

An hypothesis differs from a proposition in virtue of its grammar. It is a different grammatical structure.

It used to be held that an hypothesis was a proposition except that its truth was less firmly established. It was thought that where an hypothesis is concerned, we had not yet checked all the cases and so we were less sure of its truth—as though the distinguishing criterion were an *historical* one, as it were. According to my conception, however, an hypothesis is from the outset a completely different grammatical structure.

172 For an apparent allusion to ostensive definition see *TLP* 3.263; for logical analysis see *TLP* 3.2–3.201; for the connexion of pictures and reality see *TLP* 2.1511.

If I were to describe the grammar of an hypothesis, I would say that it follows from no single proposition and from no set of single propositions. It will—in that sense—never be verified.

That is not the view of Poincaré,[173] who suggests that he understands hypotheses to be definitions.

173 Poincaré held this view as far as the principles of mechanics were concerned (*La science et l'hypothèse*, Paris, 1920, p. 122), but not with respect to all kinds of hypotheses (ibid. p. 180f.).

APPENDIX A

TOTALITY AND SYSTEM

Points in space form a 'set' in an entirely different sense from, say, books or hats. We all feel that there is an essential difference here, and this difference must be susceptible of clear formulation.

The difference is connected with the difference between the words *'having a sense'* and *'true'*. The set of hats in this room is given by a property (propositional function). Knowing the property concerned we do not yet know whether anything falls under the property, and, if something does, how many things fall under this property. This is something only experience can teach. What corresponds to the extension of the property is a *class of true propositions*.

What is a point in space? We come to know this by observing how signs meaning points in space can be used with sense. In our propositions a point in space occurs in a very different way from an object of reality, in that it is always only part of a description dealing with objects of reality. I can describe the position of a body by specifying its distance from certain other bodies. A possible state of affairs corresponds to that description, no matter whether the description is true or false. A point in space hence represents a possibility, namely the possibility of the position of a body relative to other bodies. The expression of this possibility is that the proposition describing that position has a sense. To the totality of points in space corresponds a totality of possibilities, thus a *class of propositions with sense*.

A class of true propositions is delimited in a completely different way from a class of propositions with sense. In the first case the limit is drawn by experience, in the second case by the syntax of language. Experience delimits the propositions from the outside, syntax from the inside. The *domain of sense* of a function (i.e. the totality of values of *x* regarding which *fx* has sense) is delimited from the inside by the nature of the function. And the class of points in space is in the same way delimited from the inside, by the syntax of statements about space.

What is wrong with Russell's conception is that he, to begin with, constructs the points in space from actual events. For such a 'space' extends only as far as our knowledge of actual events. Now, the totality of points in space is the totality of possible positions of a body, and we survey these possibilities from the outset. We cannot add a point in space, nor can we discover one. We can discover things only *within* space and time.

And that, after all, agrees with our natural feeling. If a man were locked up in a room for the whole of his life—would that be a reason why he should not know that space extended beyond the room? How does he know it? Russell would have to reply, 'That is an hypothesis.' It is clear, however, that that reply is nonsense. For what we know is only a *possibility*, isn't it?, and that possibility *cannot* be an hypothesis.

Experience cannot give us the system of possibilities. Experience only teaches what is there, not what can be there. Possibility is not an empirical concept, but a concept of syntax.

Russell's chief mistake is that he time and again tries to reduce possibility to reality. He thus confuses a *description* and the *syntax* of that description.

Space is the possibility of Where, time the possibility of When, and number the possibility of How Many.

If you connect space and time—or number—with the accidental properties of the world, then this already shows that you are on a completely wrong track.

Space, time, and number are *forms* of representation. They are designed to express every possible experience and for this reason it is wrong to base them on actual experience.

Even if no class of this or that number happened to exist in our world, it would still make sense to consider such classes. We must not exclude any possibility from the beginning; that, however, is done if, in accordance with Russell, you define the numbers as classes of *actual* properties.

If Russell were right, then the two statements 'At time *t* event *A* occurs' and 'At time *t* event *B* occurs' would have the same sense.

Second, what is wrong about Russell's conception is that he thinks he could first construct points in space from real events and then bring the points in space thus constructed into an order. In reality points in space are ordered from the outset, and it is impossible to imagine them without that order.

We need not know anything about actual events in order to understand a spatial specification. If a proposition suffices to describe the position of a body, then that proposition must already contain *everything* relating to that position, and what does not occur in that proposition cannot have any significance for the specification of that position.

Can we describe a point in space by specifying which objects are in that spatial position? No, we cannot! For we do not know how to reach that point in space.

It is of the essence of a spatial specification to *point out the way* of reaching a spatial position. To specify a point in space is to specify a method of reaching that point in space.

But the specification of a point in space must then already contain its relations to other points in space, and that means: *the relations between points in space are internal*. If we are to introduce points in space correctly, we must introduce them and all their relations at one stroke.

Concerning time the situation is the same. If I know *which* events occur at a time, I do not yet know *when* those events occur. A temporal specification is a specification of When and not a specification of the simultaneity of occurrences.

The difference between the set of chairs in this room and the set of points in space can be traced back to the difference between 'function' and *'operation'*.

Just take the logical particles—they are enough to show that there are sets of a completely different kind. We know the operation which generates all logical particles. Once we have perfectly grasped just *one* logical particle we know *all* logical particles. The discovery of further logical particles is inconceivable. In a certain sense all of them are there at the same time. They form a system whose scope and limits we can survey perfectly clearly from the outset.

I distinguish between an *'empirical totality'* and a *'system'*.

The books and the chairs in this room are empirical totalities. Their extension depends on experience. The logical particles, the numbers, the points in space and time are systems. It is inconceivable to discover a new logical particle, a new number, a new point in space. Here we have the feeling that everything springs from *one* root. If we know the principle on which a system is based, then we know the *entire* system.

An empirical totality is traceable back to a *propositional function*; a system to an *operation*.

The logical particles are truth-operations. Thus the meaning of the word 'or' is the operation that turns the sense of the propositions 'p', 'q' into the sense of the proposition 'p or q'. This operation is expressed by the structure of a truth-function. Truth-functions can be constructed systematically. The numbers come into existence through repeated applications of the operation $+1$.

Operations occur when we are dealing with propositional forms that are ordered according to a formal law. Thus the statements

$$aRb$$
$$(\exists x)aRx.xRb$$
$$(\exists x,y)aRx.xRy.yRb$$

are ordered according to a formal law. An operation is the transition from one propositional form to another. It generates one propositional form from another. If we know the operation in question, we can, starting from one propositional form, generate all others.

An operation is completely different from a function. A function cannot be its own argument. An operation, on the other hand, can be applied to its own result.

In mathematics we must always be dealing with systems, and not with totalities. Russell's basic mistake consists in not having recognized the essence of a *system* while representing empirical totalities and systems by means of the same symbol—a propositional function—without drawing any distinctions.

We know a certain point in space if we know the way which leads to that point. That way is given by a propositional form (e.g. 10 steps ahead, then 5 steps to the right). The totality of possible ways, thus the totality of propositional forms, corresponds to the totality of points in space. The propositional forms are constructed by us, and this is why we can survey all the possibilities. We can foresee only what we ourselves produce, which justifies our feeling that we cannot discover a point in space. For it means that we cannot discover a propositional form.

This also clarifies why the relations between points in space are *internal*. The relations between points in space are relations between those propositional forms that correspond to points in space. Every propositional form stands in an internal relation to every other one.

The infinity of space is the infinity of mathematical induction.

It is surely clear that we express nothing *factual* by saying that space is infinite. What we know *a priori* is—here and everywhere—the *form* in terms of which we express our experiences.

Here the question arises whether we need experiences to establish syntax. To that we have to reply, There are two completely different concepts of 'experience'. The kind of experience we need for establishing the truth of a statement is completely different from the one we need for understanding the meaning of a word. Only the first kind of experience is expressed by propositions.

There is in fact something that mathematics and logic have in common. What is right about Russell's idea is that in mathematics as well as in logic we are dealing with *systems*. Both systems are due to operations.

What is wrong about it is the attempt at construing mathematics as a part of logic.

The true analogy between mathematics and logic is a completely different one. In mathematics, too, there is an operation that corresponds to the operation which generates a new sense from the senses of given propositions, namely the operation which generates a new number from given numbers. That is, *a number corresponds to a truth-function*.

Logical operations are performed with propositions, arithmetical ones with numbers. The result of a logical operation is a proposition, the result of an arithmetical one is a *number*.

The analogy between logic and arithmetic ceases to apply for the reason that arithmetic considers *equations* between numbers. *Equality is not an operation*. In $7+5 = 3+9$, $7+5$ and $3+9$ are expressions of operations, but equality, i.e. the indication that different operations lead to the same result, is not the expression of an operation. In logic it would not be a truth-function that would correspond to an equation between numbers; it would be the statement *that two truth-functions mean the same*. There is, however, no such statement.

It seems, to be sure, that there is such a statement, namely the *tautologous statement $p \equiv q$*. This is how people come to hold that a tautology corresponds to an equation. That, however, is not the case.

We express a thought in different ways. Thus e.g. $p \supset q$ says the same as $\sim q \supset \sim p$. In order to establish that, we only need to write down the two statements as truth-functions; then the mere appearance of the two functions will *show* that they agree in every line. We can, however, also show it by constructing the equivalence of the two statements, $(p \supset q) \equiv (\sim q \supset \sim p)$, and establishing that it is a tautology. Does the tautology, then, *say* that those two statements mean the same? No, the tautology only shows what has shown itself without bringing tautologies in, namely that the structures of the two truth-functions agree; it only shows it in a different way.

Tautology is hence only a method for facilitating the recognition of the agreement of two truth-functions. The essential thing is not a tautology, but *what is shown by a tautology*.

The fact that $p \equiv q$ is a tautology *shows* that p and q mean the same. The fact that $p \supset q$ is a tautology *shows* that p follows from q. The fact that $\sim(p.q)$ is a tautology *shows* that p and q contradict one another.

The characteristic feature of the use of a tautology is that we never use a *tautology* to express something in virtue of its propositional form; we only avail ourselves of it as a method for making evident the logical relations among other statements.

If we were blind, a telescope would not make us see anything; if language did not already show all its logical features, tautology would not teach us anything.

In mathematics the proof of an equation corresponds to the method of tautology. The very feature that we employ in tautologies—namely their making evident the agreement between two structures—this very same feature is also employed in the proof of an equation. If we prove a numerical calculation, we transform its two sides until their equality *shows* itself. This is in fact the same procedure as that on which the use of tautologies is based. Mathematics and logic share this feature, that a proof is not a proposition, that a proof *points* something *out*. Logic uses *propositions* to point something out, mathematics uses *numbers*.

To a certain extent it is true that mathematics is based on intuition, namely the intuition of symbols; and in logic it is the same kind of intuition that is employed when we use a tautology.

A proposition is not a sign for a state of affairs; it describes it. Imagined states of affairs too can be described by a proposition, which is why it is not a name. Syntax is the totality of rules that specify in what combinations a sign has meaning. It describes nothing, it sets limits to what is describable. A symbol is what can be perceived of a sign plus the rules of its use, of its syntax. An understanding of a language presupposes knowledge of the meaning and syntax of signs. Philosophy is the clarification of the syntax of language. It yields an understanding of propositions.

The form of a proposition is obtained by turning its words into variables while leaving their meaning out of consideration. A subject-predicate proposition has a different form from a relational proposition; a symmetrical relational proposition has a different form from an asymmetrical one. A state of affairs is a combination of things. The signs of a proposition go proxy for things, not for the form of a state of affairs, which is exhibited by the form of a proposition. A concept needs to be explained, the form is exhibited by a description. To have a form is to be a picture; to think or speak is to depict. Concepts are expressed by signs. A form, a propositional picture, shows itself. A form is not a generalization, nor is it a property that is common to a class of propositions. Symmetry and asymmetry show themselves in propositions, they are contained in a description—they are not properties like yellow and hard, which are designated and expressed by a propositional function. It is not states of affairs that are asymmetrical, but the combination of signs by means of which they are represented. Symmetry does not relate to reality, but to the syntactical form of a description or reality; it indicates the features a symbolism needs to have to depict a state of affairs. Words signifying forms are not concepts; they are instructions for the construction of a symbolism, i.e. of logical pictures.

---

174 This section comes from Mr. Stein's notes; see editor's Preface, p. 20.

WHAT IS A NUMBER?

Definitions are signposts. They indicate the path leading to a verification.

The requirement of verifiability is the requirement that all symbols be defined and that we understand the meaning of the indefinable symbols.

What a definition explains is the use of a sign in propositions. A definition explains the *sense* of propositions.

A definition is a transformation-rule. It specifies how to transform a proposition into other propositions in which the concept in question no longer occurs.

A definition reduces one concept to another or to several others, which again are reduced to others, and so on. The direction of this reduction process is fixed by a certain method of verification.

Definitions which do not fulfil that purpose are without significance.

According to the Frege-Russell abstraction principle the number 3 is the class of all triplets. Here we have to ask, Does that definition indicate the way leading to verification?

Is the statement 'There are 3 chairs here' verified in such a way that the class of those chairs is compared with all other triplets in the world? No, it is not! If, however, we can understand the sense of the statement without verifying it in that way, then the statement *by itself* must already contain everything essential and the listing of triplets cannot be of any consequence for the number 3.

If I asked the question 'How many chairs are there in this room?' and received the answer 'As many as in that room,' I should be entitled to say, 'That is not an answer to my question. I asked how many chairs there were and not where there were equally many.'

The Russellian definition fails to achieve the very thing that matters. A specification of number must contain a method for reaching that number. And that is exactly what the definition lacks.

To be sure, it is true that all classes that allow a one-one mapping have the same number of members. But the specification of those classes is not the specification of a number. Either we construe classes intentionally, as properties (propositional functions), in which case a specification of equivalent classes does not tell us how many objects fall under them. Or we construe classes extensionally, as extensions, in which case the description of such a class already contains a picture of the number in question and it is again wrong to wish to define a number through such classes.

To specify a number is to specify How Many and not to specify equinumerosity.

And can we seriously believe that to specify the essence of the number 3 is tantamount to specifying the properties under which three things fall? A world is no doubt conceivable in which those properties would always be satisfied by four things. Would the number 3 be the number 4 because of that? The following is clear: we must deal not with the extensions of actual properties but *with that which enables us to describe them*.

The class of triplets differs from the number 3 in roughly the same way in which a brain process differs from a state of consciousness.

Hence, what is wrong with the Frege-Russell definition is that it does not specify a method of verification. If people say 'But it does: the verification consists in our comparing one set with another set, namely with the set of our number signs,' then we have to reply to that, That is no verification, for the following reason. If I say that I have mapped a set onto a part of the series of number signs—i.e. that I have counted— then by that I of course do not mean the class of actual number signs on paper; I mean the number symbols. But in that case the series of number signs is not defined through a property: what we have before us is a *law for constructing* a series of signs, and it is this law—not the actual properties—that enables us to derive all the preceding number symbols from the specification of *one* number symbol, to reconstruct the whole series. (The order of our number words is based on their syntax and not on their actual properties.) But in that case the procedure will not *mean* a mapping of one set onto another in the sense of the definition; it will not mean a mapping *onto* the number signs *qua* signs but *by means* of the number signs *qua* symbols, and hence a *representation* of the number concerned.

But is it true that, syntactically, a number word occurs as the property of a class? We are no doubt able to understand a sign of this kind:

|||| plums

If, however, this sign is adequate to communicate its meaning, then the sign must contain *everything* that needs to be considered regarding the communication, and what it does not contain cannot be essential for its meaning. The sign contains a *picture* but not the specification of a *property* or a *relation*.

Is this sign perhaps to be understood in such a way that it means, The class of plums is mapped one-to-one onto the class of strokes preceding? Certainly not. I would have mapped one class onto another one if and only if I had said: The class of plums can be mapped onto the class of strokes that are on page 223 of this book, hence if I had *described* the class of strokes by a property. It is clear that here the strokes do not occur as a described class—as a class *about* which we talk—but that they occur in the same way as the word 'plums', i.e. as part of a proposition. Here the strokes function as a *symbol*, not as a *class*.

Thus Russell's argument rests on a confusion of sign and symbol.

Numbers are forms. The expression of a number is a picture that occurs in propositions.

The proposition 'There are two things with property f' can be represented as follows:

$$(\exists x,y).fx.fy. \sim (\exists x,y,z).fx.fy.fz$$

Here the number 2 occurs as a depicting feature of our symbolism.

Russell, too, had to employ this principle of picturing when introducing particular numbers. In order to introduce the number 2, he needs to employ a symbolism which itself has the multiplicity which it is designed to define. But then the multiplicity and not the definition is the decisive thing.

A definition *defines* something and *shows* something. It is what a definition shows that corresponds to a number.

Can a form be defined? Can e.g. the subject-predicate form be defined as the class of all subject-predicate propositions? The subject-predicate form itself would surely have to occur in such a definition—we would hence already need to know what the subject-predicate form is, in order to understand the definition. It is clear that here we are not dealing with actual propositions but with what makes it possible to form propositions.

If a form were definable, we could not understand it without a definition. But the possibility of expressing a sense rests on the very fact that we understand a form without its being explained to us. A proposition shows its form. The wish to define the very thing on which the possibility of all communication and information rests does not make sense.

What is mistaken in this conception is based on construing a form as a *property*. The subject-predicate form is taken to be a general property that all subject-predicate propositions have.

The property *fx* is a generalization of the property *fx.gx*. Generalizing leads from one property to another one.

A form is expressed if the constant parts of a proposition are transformed into variable ones. This transformation into variables is something entirely different from generalization.

The whole Frege-Russell logic is based on the confusion of concept and form. The numbers are not concepts. You do not obtain them by means of generalization.

Frege and Russell looked for the essence of number in a wrong direction. They believed that the number 3 was the result of a kind of generalization from 3 chairs, 3 plums, etc. And in that way they came to invent the principle of abstraction so as to express the peculiarity of that generalization.

The number 3 is not the general feature of triplets.

The number 3 does not originate in generalization from particular triplets, any more than the form of a picture originates in generalization from particular pictures.

The number 3 is the common form of triplets, not their common property.

The form 3 can only be transposed, it cannot be defined.

Forms have nothing to do with generality. A form is neither general nor specific.

The propositions of arithmetic are not *general laws* that are applied to concrete cases. In saying '2 plums plus 2 plums equals 4 plums' and '2 chairs plus 2 chairs equals 4 chairs' I do not apply the proposition $2 + 2 = 4$ to different cases; it is always *the same* application that I have before me.

What is mathematical is the same everywhere. For mathematics there is no 'problem of application'.

That is connected with the fact that one form cannot fall under another (super- and subordination exist only for concepts). *The method of representing numbers is the method of picturing.* A number shows itself in a symbol.

In speaking of 5 men I can represent the men by strokes. But those men's being 5 is not represented; it manifests itself in the fact that the number of strokes is 5. Here the number sign is immediately conceived as a picture.

The usual way of representing the numbers by means of the system of figures rests on exactly the same principle. At first blush the number 387 does not seem to be a picture of the quantity it means. We must, however, take into account that in addition to the signs there are the rules of syntax too. The signs 3, 8, 7 are defined. If we reduce them to their definitions, that is, if we analyse these signs step by step, then they assume the very multiplicity they mean; e.g. $3 = 1 + 1 + 1$. Second, the position of figures, too, depicts something. Our number signs contain the possibility of being transformed into other signs that are pictures in an immediate way. That is, our number signs, together with the rules of syntax, are instructions for the construction of picture-like symbols.

There must always remain a clear way back to a picture-like representation of numbers leading through all arithmetical symbols, abbreviations, signs for operations, etc. The symbolism of the representation of numbers is a system of rules for translation into something picture-like.

To define a number can mean two different things. If it is held that to define 3 is, roughly, to specify a class of classes, then the reply must be that 3 is not definable in that sense. But if by a definition the *arithmetical* definition, $3 = 2+1$. $2 = 1+1$, is meant, then 3 can of course be defined. (The words 'symbolize,' 'define,' have completely different meanings according to whether they are used in the context of concepts or forms.)

A number word symbolizes in a completely different way from a concept.

The definition of a concept points the way to a *verification*, the definition of a number word (a form) points the way to a *construction*.

And that is the basis of our understanding the meaning of a number sign jotted down at random that has not been explained to us.

Could there be an arithmetical notation that gave every number a proper name? No, there could not. Arithmetic introduces a limited number of proper names (figures) and expresses all other numbers by means of the multiplicity of representation. Wherever we have to represent an unlimited number of possibilities by means of a limited number of means, the method of representation is based on our using signs as pictures.

Infinity is not a picture.

'Infinite' is not an instruction for the construction of a picture. Infinity is hence not a number.

If you say that there might be creatures other than us who could represent infinity, then the proper reply is, Do you think that we could describe such a creature? And here it makes itself manifest that such an assumption gets us nowhere.

The difference between finite and infinite is a logical difference. It has nothing to do with the empirical nature of our consciousness.

We cannot leave our logical world to consider it from the outside.

The sense of a proposition is the method of its verification. A method of verification is not the means of establishing the truth of a proposition; it is the very sense of a proposition. In order to understand a proposition, you need to know the method of its verification. To specify it is to specify the sense of a proposition. You cannot look for a method of verification. A proposition can only say what is established by the method of its verification.

A question is an invitation to look for something. An answer is reached at the end of a thought-movement. The direction of a thought-movement is defined by the logical place of the answer. Questions differ if their answers are different. To understand a question means to know what kind of proposition the answer will be. Without an answer our thoughts do not point in any direction; there is no question. We cannot look for something if we do not look for it in a certain direction.

A word, an expression, a symbol, only has a meaning in the context of a proposition. In order to obtain a clear notion of the meaning of a word it is necessary to attend to the sense of the propositions in which it occurs, to the way they are verified.

ON INFINITY

A general statement which is verified by complete induction must be general in a completely different sense from a statement that is verified by particular cases. In those two cases generality must mean different things as must also, accordingly, the expression 'class'.

The expression 'class' has as many different meanings as there are different methods of verification.

If you tried to say 'There are infinitely many chairs' in the way in which you can say 'There are infinitely many prime numbers,' then your statement would not be false; it would be senseless. For there is no way of verifying this statement. This shows that those two con-

175 This section comes from Mr. Stein's notes; see editor's Preface, p. 20.

cepts of class obey completely different rules of syntax, and hence are entirely different concepts.

The conception on which the misleading present-day mode of expression of set theory is based is that we can understand the meaning of a class without knowing whether the class is finite or infinite, that that is something we establish only later. How many chairs there are in this room is an accidental determination of the concept 'chair in this room'. We cannot foresee that number. 'Finite' and 'infinite,' on the other hand, do not signify accidental determinations of the concept of a class. We cannot imagine the same class finite at one time and infinite at another. The truth of the matter is that the word 'class' means completely different things in the two cases. It is not one and the same concept at all that is qualified by the addition of 'finite' or 'infinite'.

Russell promoted this mistaken idea by creating a symbolism which represents both kinds of classes in exactly the same way. He was thus entirely prevented from recognizing the true significance of the difference in question.

A correct symbolism has to reproduce an infinite class in a completely different way from a finite one. Finiteness and infinity of a class must be obvious from its syntax. In a correct language there must not even be a temptation of raising the question whether a class is finite or infinite.

'Infinite' is not a quantity. The word 'infinite' has a different syntax from a number word.

In language infinity always occurs in the same way, namely as a qualification of the concept *possible*. We say, for example, that a stretch is infinitely divisible, that a body can move infinitely far, etc. Here we are talking of a possibility, not of reality. The word 'infinite' qualifies that possibility.

What does the statement 'A distance is infinitely divisible' mean? This proposition is about the possibility of dividing things. If I say 'This distance can be divided into two parts' that means that the statements that the distance *is* divided into two parts has a sense, no matter whether it is true or false. Here the number word 'two' can be replaced by any arbitrary number word. We can hence form a series of statements that say, the distance is divided into two parts, the distance is divided into three parts, etc. The series is ordered in accordance with a formal law. We can emphasize this formal law by specifying the operation which, from one propositional form, generates the successor of that form. What we know *a priori* is that the operation can be performed, that is, we know that a newly formed proposition also has a sense. And that we know because of the logical structure of the statement concerned.

It is clear that those propositional forms do not form an empirical totality; they form a *system*. This system is given by its initial term and by the operation in question.

If we now say 'The distance is infinitely divisible'—does that mean that the statement 'The distance *is* divided into infinitely many parts' has a sense? No, it does not, since there is no such proposition. First, it is not verifiable. Second, in a correct system of signs it cannot be written down at all. (This will be shown at a later stage.)

The possibility of indefinitely continuing the series of corresponding propositional forms corresponds to the possibility of indefinitely continuing a division. If we now say 'The possibility of division is infinite,' that means 'The possibility of constructing propositional forms that describe that division is infinite.' *An infinite possibility is represented by an infinite possibility*.

The concept 'infinite' is hence a qualification of the concept 'possible'. It is not expressed by a statement about infinity's having a sense, since there is no such statement. Infinite possibility does not mean 'possibility of infinity'. The word 'infinite' characterizes a possibility and not a reality.

The infinite divisibility of a distance is something purely logical. It is, after all, clear that *that* possibility cannot be arrived at from experience.

Infinite divisibility, continuity of space and time—they are none of them hypotheses. They are insights into a possible form of description.

Cannot experience teach us that space and time have a discrete structure? If in the process of continuously dividing a rod we meet with certain limits for physical reasons, then this is a fact of experience, which will be described by a proposition. In that case the negation of the proposition must have a sense too, and that means; we must also be able to describe possible experiences following on a further division. If the hypothesis of the existence of molecules has a sense, it presupposes the possibility of a further division. Here it is possible to see that the infinite divisibility of space is nothing factual. The possibility we need here is a *logical* possibility, that is, the possibility of a description, and that must not depend on actual experiences.

It is clear that here we are not dealing with an hypothesis; we are dealing with what enables us to put forward hypotheses.

We could, for all that, draw logical limits to divisibility. That would mean changing the syntax of our representation. It would of course not mean that we exclude certain experiences from the outset; it would mean that we renounce the possibility of representing those experiences by that symbolism.

We cannot ask, Is nature continuous or discontinuous? That question does not make sense. Every discontinuity can be construed as an apparent one, but the same applies to every continuity. That shows that this is not a matter of facts but of stipulations about the representation of facts.

It seems that in some cases infinity can appear in the form of an hypothesis. We could e.g. state the hypothesis that the fixed stars are distributed in Euclidean space according to a certain law, ranging into infinity. Does such an hypothesis mention infinite experience? That has to become clear from the way of verifying the hypothesis. 'Infinitely many fixed stars' makes sense only in the context of a law according to which we represent our experience (law of gravitation). In that case, however, they form part of the mode of representation of that law. That means: we can construct a series of descriptions in which 1, 2, 3, 4, . . . fixed stars occur and state that the more fixed stars we assume the better the approximation of those descriptions to our actual experience. Every single one of those statements makes sense and can be verified without appealing to the law of gravitation. The assumption of infinitely many fixed stars for its part cannot be verified by itself but only in connexion with the law of gravitation. In that case, however, an assumption of infinitely many fixed stars must have a completely different *sense* from an assumption of 100 fixed stars; it cannot be an independent statement at all; it is part of a *system of representation* by means of which we describe reality.

If we measure the ratio of circumference to diameter in a series of empirical circles, we shall obtain numerical values that are more or less close to π. *The number π is not a result of actual measurements*. If the measurements yielded a different value from that ratio, we would not say, The number π is equal to a different value, but we would say that our measurements are inaccurate. That is, we adhere to the number π and regard it as the standard according to which we judge the quality of an observation. Euclidean geometry rests on a stipulation. The number π represents an infinite law which accompanies our actual observations. However accurately we may measure, the accuracy of the number π will keep abreast with our measurements. Here we are talking of an infinite possibility and not of an infinite reality.

The propositions of geometry relate to an infinite possibility of the accuracy of measuring. They do not describe actual measurements; they specify how we judge actual measurements.

If we speak of infinitely many fixed stars, then that means that we specify an infinite law according to which we describe our actual experiences. That law is a stipulation and not a statement. We stipulate how we want to interpret actual experiences. That law suffices for every conceivable accuracy of measuring, and that is what the infinite possibility of that law lies in.

'Infinitely many fixed stars'—that is a matter of stipulation, not of experience.

Would it not be possible, following Dedekind, to express symbolically that a class is finite or infinite? The Dedekindian definition says that a class is infinite if there is a unique mapping from it onto a proper sub-class. That statement has no significance as long as no method of verification is given. If the method of verification consists in assigning members of the class and members of the sub-class to one another by means of enumeration, then *no* class has that property. In that case finiteness is already contained in the rules about how to verify statements about such classes, and hence in the syntax of a class. If a different method of verification, however, is admitted—namely induction—then the very words 'all,' 'class,' and 'sub-class' *mean* something completely different and we again cannot ask whether a class is finite or infinite.

---

176 Cf. p. 69, above, and footnote.

APPENDIX B

THESES

by Friedrich Waismann
(ca. 1930)

The only value the following sentences have is that of elucidations. The only value the following explanations have is that of paraphrases. The purpose of these elucidations and paraphrases is the logical clarification of our thoughts. They result not in propositions, but rather in a correct understanding of propositions.

1. States of Affairs, Facts, Reality

Everything that can exist or not exist is a state of affairs.

The existence and non-existence of a state of affairs is called a *fact*.

Reality is the existence and non-existence of states of affairs. (The non-existence of a state of affairs is also a delimitation of reality.)

Reality consists of facts, not of things. The sum-total of reality is the *world*.

A fact can have parts which, on their side, are also facts. Every particular state of affairs can exist or not exist, independently of the remaining states of affairs. Such a fact is called *composite* (e.g. my visual field).

Two facts can, consequently, have a fact in common.

Two facts can, however, also agree in a different way, e.g. The fact 'This patch is yellow' and the fact 'That patch is yellow.' The two facts have the colour yellow in common, which does not by itself constitute a fact. Yellow is a feature of facts but not an independent one.

It is possible to analyse a state of affairs by specifying the features in respect of which it agrees with other states of affairs. That analysis can be performed only in thought, not in reality. Every feature appearing in a state of affairs is also called an *element* (member, part) of that state of affairs.

In a state of affairs its elements are concatenated. A state of affairs is a combination of elements.

That a state of affairs is *complex* means that it has something—a feature—in common with other states of affairs.

Every state of affairs is complex.

A state of affairs can be analysed in only *one* way.

What can exist or not exist is a configuration of elements.

Elements are what is unalterable, subsistent in the world; states of affairs are changing and unstable.

The multiplicity of states of affairs is due to this: that the same elements continually form new configurations—continually form new states of affairs.

The existence of unalterable elements is not an hypothesis. If there were no unalterable elements, no kind of description whatever would be possible.

The way elements are concatenated—that is the *structure* of a state of affairs.

Form is the possibility of structure.

An element is something dependent. An element only occurs in the context of a state of affairs.

If I know an element, I do not yet know in what state of affairs it occurs, but I do know in what context it *can* occur; i.e. I know the form of the state of affairs in which it occurs.

Colour occurs only in connexion with something spatial, pitch only in connexion with degree of loudness, etc.

The possibility of its occurrence in states of affairs is already contained in an element. That possibility is called its *form*.

An element already *has* a form; this cannot be added to it subsequently. We cannot *look for* the form of an element.

The totality of possible situations is delimited by the totality of elements.

2. Language

We picture facts in and to ourselves. The pictures we produce are our *thoughts*.

What is grasped of a thought is its *sense*.

The sense of a thought is the existence or non-existence of states of affairs.

The object of a thought is hence always a fact, never a thing (member, element).

A thought can depict any state of affairs, an existing one and a non-existing one as well.

By means of thoughts we reach beyond reality.

In a *proposition* a thought finds an expression that can be perceived by the senses.

Language is the method of so representing our thoughts that they can be perceived by the senses.

Facts that can be perceived by the senses are called *signs*.

Language must extend as far as our thoughts. It must hence be able to represent not only real facts, but possible ones as well.

By means of language we communicate. That is only possible, however, if we understand the sense of a sentence without its being explained to us. If it were necessary to explain the sense of a combination of signs to us on every occasion, we should not be able to express a new thought. Language must have the capacity of expressing a new sense by old signs.

Accordingly, if a sign system is to be a language, we require of it that we can express any thought by means of it and that we can understand the expression of that thought without its being explained to us.

The procedure language employs to achieve that is the following. It uses signs that go proxy for the elements of a situation and represents the situation itself by means of a combination of the signs in question.

Thus it reconstructs the structure of a situation by combining signs in the appropriate way.

A proposition—like a model—shows us how the elements of a situation are connected.

That is why we understand a proposition without its being explained to us.

A *propositional sign* is what can be perceived of a proposition.

A propositional sign must have as many distinguishable elements as the corresponding situation. Both must have the same *multiplicity*.

A very good illustration of that is provided by taking the proposition of a language as instructions for doing something. By using words, I can, for instance, guide somebody around my room, by saying, 'Take three steps straight ahead! Now two to the left! Now stretch out your arm! etc.' Hence it is evident that language must have the same multiplicity as those movements.[177]

A proposition *describes* a state of affairs, and that description consists in nothing but tracing the form of reality in a propositional sign.

A sign only *tells* us something insofar as we see that form in a propositional sign; only in that case do we *understand* a proposition.

A propositional sign is itself a fact. It consists in this, that signs (words) form a context of a particular kind—a particular configuration.

It is not the case that 'A proposition tells us that a fact has this and that structure,' but rather, '*That* the signs of a proposition are combined to form a fact of a certain structure expresses that that state of affairs exists.'

Only a fact can express a sense.

A proposition is not a class of words. A proposition is articulated.

That is why what is logically simple cannot be expressed. You cannot say what red is or what the nature of sweetness consists in. What can be described is always complex.

The possibility of all communication and information rests on the depicting character of our language.

Could we communicate by means of a language without propositions? Could we, for example, construct a language in which signs

177 Cf. p. 95 above, and *PR* pp. 57ff.

would go proxy for the facts themselves? It would be absolutely possible to have such a system of signification. We would only need to introduce a new sign for every state of affairs. In that case the sense of a sign would still be perfectly determinate, but it would then no longer be possible to understand the sense of a sign by merely looking at it. We could not understand it without its being explained to us. What we should have before us would be a system of *signals*, not a language.[178]

Such a system, to be sure, is adequate to refer to a limited number of facts, but we could not communicate by means of it.

A signal *names* a situation; a proposition *describes* it.

A proposition consists of words.

A *word* is whatever the sense of a proposition depends on and propositions can have in common.

A proposition has a *sense*; a word has a *meaning*.

If you know how to use a word, you know its meaning.

A word occurs only in a proposition, just as elements occur only in states of affairs.

Propositions are what is changing and alterable; words are what is firm and unalterable.

The meanings of words we have to lay down. The sense of a proposition, however, *results from* the words.

The form of a proposition is prefigured in words. A property word, for example, requires a completely different kind of complement from a relational word. If I know the meaning of a word, then I also know in what combinations it can occur and in what combinations it cannot. It is by no means possible for me to discover a new possibility later on.

The stipulation of the syntactical character of a word will hence consist in indicating the form of propositions in which it occurs (e.g. 'x is yellow,' 'x is to the right of y'). The addition of variables marks the way a proposition is to be completed.

178 Cf. pp. 86f. above.

Nothing can be added to a saturated expression,[179] to a proposition. A proposition is a termination, a limit, to the combining of signs.

A word, together with variables, represents the possibility of a proposition.

In specifying the schematic pattern of this proposition we fix the *form* of a word.

The addition of the variables, however, does not by itself enable us to recognize the form of a proposition. We must furthermore specify the values the variable is allowed to take.

What distinguishes a variable from a constant? It is simply the fact that certain rules of substitution hold for the sign of a variable. The specification of these rules *determines* a variable.

Specifying a form hence includes laying down the values over which a variable is allowed to range.

Propositions with the same external structure—e.g. *'xRy'*—can hence still have completely different forms, according to what we have laid down about the variables.

The form of a word is the possibility of its occurrence in a proposition. Every such possibility must already be contained in the word. If all words are given to us, then all possible statements are given too.

A combination of words (signs) is called an *expression*.

A word too is an expression.

An expression which becomes a proposition only when further signs have been added to it is called *unsaturated*.

An expression can combine with other expressions only as long as it is unsaturated. (Unsaturatedness is the force, as it were, which holds together the parts of a proposition.)

Whether an expression is unsaturated follows from the form of the words.

Once all variable places are filled in, once everything that was open is saturated, then a proposition is generated.

179 In Frege's terminology an expression for a function was unsaturated, in contrast with an expression which stood for an object. Not only ordinary proper names but propositions too stand for objects (truth-values) and are saturated expressions.

3. Syntax

We can picture facts to ourselves.

A picture represents the existence or non-existence of a state of affairs.

What a picture represents is its *sense*.

The agreement of its sense with reality constitutes the truth of a picture.

A picture can be true or false only if it is different from what it depicts.

A temperature curve can be a true or false picture of fever; it has the multiplicity of fever. It cannot, however, be even a false picture of a landscape, for that has a different multiplicity.

What a picture, even an incorrect one, must have in common with what it depicts is its *form*, i.e. the possibility of structure.

A *true* picture also has its *structure* in common with what it depicts. A picture can depict everything that has the same form; it cannot, however, depict anything else.

Syntax consists of rules which specify the combinations such that in them alone a word makes sense. It is by syntax that the construction of nonsensical combinations of words is excluded.

Our ordinary languages have a syntax.

Maps, musical notation, temperature curves also depict reality; they, however, make do without syntax.

How is this difference to be explained?

A map can depict reality truly or falsely, but never in a nonsensical fashion. Everything a map represents is possible.

A description by means of verbal language, on the other hand, can be nonsensical. I can say, for instance, '*A* is to the north of *B*, and *B* is to the north of *A*'. Such a proposition does not tell us anything, as it does not have the form of the fact it is supposed to represent.

Syntax is hence connected with the possibility of nonsense. ('Non-sense' is not the opposite of 'sense'. You can indeed say, 'This proposition expresses a sense,' but not, 'This proposition expresses a nonsense.' It is the use of signs that is nonsensical.)

Syntax hence becomes requisite where the nature of signs is not yet adjusted to the nature of things, where there are more combinations of signs than possible situations. This excessive multiplicity of language must be confined by artificial rules; and these rules are the syntax of language.

The rules of syntax assign to combinations of signs the exact multiplicity they must possess in order to be pictures of reality.

You could say that a system of signs which is perfectly suited to its purpose renders syntax superfluous. And conversely—syntax renders such a system of signs superfluous. Each of them *deputizes for* the other.[180]

The fact that the form of a system of signs can deputize for syntax is important, for it shows us that the rules of syntax describe nothing.

You need not first invent an 'ideal language' in order to depict reality. Our ordinary language already *is* a logical picture as soon as you know how each word signifies.

The point is only to make the rules of syntax into a system.

The rules of syntax are *rules dealing with signs*.

The difference between a rule dealing with signs and a statement is the following. In a proposition signs stand for things. A proposition speaks about reality by means of, or through, signs. It represents reality.

A rule dealing with signs, however, deals with signs themselves. Here signs are not representatives of objects. That is the reason why a rule dealing with signs does not sketch out a picture of reality—it is neither true nor false.

Signs occurring in a proposition are 'transparent,' as it were; occurring in a rule dealing with signs they are not.

180 Cf. p. 80 above.

A rule dealing with signs is a stipulation about the use of signs. Hence it has a meaning only in the context of the notation used.

At first blush a rule dealing with signs looks just like a proposition. (This is why such a rule is frequently confused with a proposition.) In saying, for example, that one point of my visual field cannot have two colours at the same time I am giving a rule of syntax and not an induction. For the proposition does not run, 'A point never has two colours at the same time,' but rather, 'A point *cannot* have two colours at the same time.' Here the word 'can' means *logical possibility* whose expression is not a proposition but a rule of syntax. (A rule delimits the form of description.)

That becomes very clear if we imagine the visual field described, not by means of words, but by means of a mathematical symbolism, for instance by representing the colour parameter as a function of the parameter of place (and time). The fact that a point can have only *one* colour at a given time is then already expressed by the *form* of description.

In order to give our ordinary language the multiplicity of mathematical language we only need to add the rule that propositions which ascribe to a point different colours at the same time are to be excluded.

That makes it clear how we can decide whether a proposition of ordinary language signifies a statement or a rule dealing with signs—by looking to see whether we can make the proposition in question disappear by translating it into a language of adequate multiplicity. If it disappears, it is a rule dealing with signs, for it then depends *only* on the notation, and that is arbitrary.

4. Symmetry, Asymmetry

One case in which it is easy to confuse a rule dealing with signs and a statement is the formulation of the symmetry (asymmetry) of a relation.

Russell[181] defines these properties in the following way: xRy is

---

181 Whitehead and Russell, *Principia Mathematica* I, Cambridge, 1910, p. 32.

symmetrical if $(x,y).xRy \supset yRx$

asymmetrical if $(x,y).xRy \supset \sim yRx$

Here the question to be asked is whether the propositions aRb, bRa express different facts or only one.

The proposition 'a is simultaneous with b' obviously represents the same fact as 'b is simultaneous with a.'

We must hence distinguish between *essential* (logical) and *accidental* (empirical) symmetry and asymmetry.

Where symmetry means logical symmetry it cannot be expressed by writing

$$(x,y).xRy \supset yRx$$

for that already presupposes that xRy has a different sense from yRx. That proposition describes empirical symmetry.

In order to indicate that the asymmetrical position of the signs 'a' and 'b' is of no consequence, we lay down the rule that aRb is to mean the same as bRa. By means of that we emphasize that a certain feature of our symbolism is inessential, that it does not depict anything.

If we use a symmetrically constructed propositional sign from the very beginning, we could do without this rule dealing with signs.

Logical asymmetry is to be formulated in such a way that the logical product of the proposition aRb and bRa becomes a contradiction. (Again, that comes about in virtue of a rule dealing with signs.)

In all these cases it is a matter of giving to a system of signs the multiplicity required for depicting something.

5. Identity

If we at one time refer to the same object as 'a' and, at another time, as 'b,' then more signs occur in our language than are necessary for depicting the facts. We must then explain that this surplus of signs does not mean anything, that the difference of signs is not a depicting feature of the symbolism. That is explained by means of the rule '$a = b$,' which deals with signs. If I know the meaning of the sign 'a,' the rule tell me what is meant by 'b'.

This rule consequently does not speak of reality. It does not say that the objects referred to by '*a*' and '*b*' stand in the mutual relation of identity; it deals with those signs themselves. It is a stipulation about the use of those signs.

Identity is misunderstood as soon as people take the signs to have their meaning. In that case it looks as though '*a* = *b*' were a proposition talking of things by means of, or via, those signs.

We see that identity is a mere rule dealing with signs from the fact that it disappears as soon as we use a language which represents every object by means of *one* sign.

Russell tried to formulate identity in the following way. 'Two objects, *a* and *b*, are identical if they have all their properties in common.'

$$a = b. = :(\varphi):\varphi!a. \supset.\varphi!b:\text{Def.}$$

This proposition does not capture the essence of identity. For in order to understand it, I must have given the signs '*a*' and '*b*' a meaning, and when I give them a meaning I know whether they mean the same or not.

The same must be said about F. P. Ramsey's attempt.[182]

Russell's mistake did not consist in giving a *false* formulation of identity, but in giving a *formulation* at all. It is nonsensical to wish to formulate by means of a proposition the very same thing which is the condition for understanding that proposition.

By the same token Russell's attempt at defining by means of identity the class which consists, e.g., of the two things *a* and *b* is also a failure.[183]

6. *Verification*

A person who utters a proposition must know under what conditions the proposition is to be called true or false; if he is not able to specify that, he also does not know what he has said.

182 Cf. pp. 189ff. above.
183 Cf. e.g. *Introduction to Mathematical Philosophy*, 2nd edition, London, 1920, p. 12.

To understand a proposition means to know how things stand if the proposition is true.

One can understand it without knowing *whether* it is true.

In order to get an idea of the sense of a proposition, it is necessary to become clear about the procedure leading to the determination of its truth. If one does not know that procedure, one cannot understand the proposition either.

A proposition cannot say more than is established by means of the method of its verification. If I say 'My friend is angry' and establish this in virtue of his displaying a certain perceptible behaviour, I only *mean* that he displays that behaviour. And if I mean more by it, I cannot specify what that extra consists in. A proposition says only what it does say and nothing that goes beyond that.

The sense of a proposition is the way it is verified.

Sense itself is a method of verification; that method is not a means, not a vehicle.

I can, to be sure, say 'I shall drive to A' or 'I shall walk to A'; in that case we have two vehicles for doing the same thing, that is, with respect to spatial distance. I cannot, however, say, 'I shall verify this proposition in this way *or* that way.' A method of verification, after all, is not something that is added to a sense. A proposition already *contains* the method of its verification. You cannot *look for* a method of verification.

To say that a statement has sense means that it can be verified.

It can never be a question of experience whether a statement has sense. For experience only teaches whether a proposition is true or false. In order to establish whether a proposition is true of false, however, I must have given it a sense.

Whether a proposition has sense can for that reason never depend on whether it is true.

If two propositions are true or false under the same conditions, they have the same sense (even if they seem different to us.)

If I lay down under what conditions a proposition is to be counted as true or false, I thereby lay down the *sense* of that proposition. (That is the basis of the truth-functions.)

Is it *always* possible for me to doubt whether a proposition is verified? Could it not be the case that verifications only make it probable? But if I cannot specify under what conditions the proposition is to count as verified, I have not given the proposition a sense. A statement that cannot be verified definitively is not verifiable at all.

Absolute doubt is unjustifiable.

A proposition that cannot be verified in any way has no sense.

There are no unanswerable questions.

What is a question? It is a request to look for something. A question introduces a movement of thought, as it were, at the end of which the answer is to be found. The direction of that movement is determined by the logical place of the answer. If no answer exists, then there is no direction in which you can look for anything; hence there is no movement of thought, and that means that *there is no question*.

You can only ask where you can look for something. And you can only look for something where there is a method of looking for it. To look for something means to look systematically.[184]

A statement has sense, not because it is constructed in a legitimate way,[185] but because it can be verified. Hence every verifiable statement is constructed in a legitimate way. If I specify a method of verification, I thereby lay down the form of the proposition in question, the meaning of its words, the rules of syntax, etc.

In order to learn what a sign means, you have to ask, 'How is a proposition in which that word occurs to be verified?'

The same word can have different meanings in propositions that are verified in different ways. In that case we are simply dealing with different symbols that happen to have the same sign in common.

Thus in everyday life the word 'yellow' means something completely different from what it means in physics. For in the one case a proposition about yellow is verified by looking, in the other case by measuring its wave-length. (If that difference is disregarded, it will

---

184 Cf. pp. 34ff., above, and passim.
185 Probably an allusion to R. Carnap, cf. e.g. his 'Überwindung der Metaphysik etc.' in *Erkenntnis* 2 (1931), p. 227 (E.T. as 'The Elimination of Metaphysics etc.' in *Logical Positivism* (ed. A. J. Ayer), Glencoe, Ill., 1959).

seem as though the colours as we see them were something incomplete, as though infra-red, for instance, were their complement.)

7. Definition

A *symbol* is an applied, rule-governed sign.

A sign is what can be perceived of a symbol. (So one and the same sign can be common to two symbols. The sign will then symbolize differently in those two cases.)

The way a sign is used is its *meaning*.

A meaning is what all symbols that can represent one another have in common.

Thus negation, for example, is the common rule according to which the proposition $\sim p, \ p/p, \ p \supset \sim p$, etc, are constructed.

To give a meaning to a sign means to lay down a rule for its use.

There are two ways of giving a sign meaning: 1. By means of *ostension*. In this case we explain the use of a word in statements by construction various propositions by means of that word and each time pointing to the fact in question. In that way we become aware of the meaning of the word. (Ostension really consists in two acts—in an external action, pointing to various facts, and a thought-operation, namely learning what they have in common.) 2. By means of *definition*. In this case the meaning of a sign is explained by means of signs that already have a meaning.

A definition remains within language. Ostension steps outside language and connects signs with reality. A definition can be expressed in language, and ostension cannot.

What ostension and definition have in common is that both specify rules for the use of signs.

You know the meaning of a sign if you understand the sense of the propositions in which it occurs.

To define a sign thus means to explain the sense of propositions in which it occurs.

A definition thus consists in the specification of a rule which tells how to express by means of other signs the sense of a proposition in which the sign in question occurs.

A definition is a translation rule—it translates a proposition into other signs.

Translation preserves the sense of a proposition.

A definition is a rule dealing with signs—it is neither true nor false.

A definition must be *complete*.

Once we have introduced a sign by means of definition, it must have been introduced for all combinations. We must not define a sign piecemeal by first explaining its meaning for one class of cases and then for a different class. (Thus Russell, for example, regards negation in front of an elementary proposition as an indefinable primitive sign and then explains it again when it occurs in front of a general statement.)

A definition explains the meaning of a sign by means of other signs. In this way one sign points to another, that sign in turn points to yet another, etc., and in this way signs are arranged in an order.

A sign signifies via all the signs by means of which it has been defined.

If we analyse the signs in a statement, replacing them by other signs in accordance with their definitions and replacing those others by yet other signs, etc., the verification-path becomes visible step by step.

Definitions are signposts. They show the path leading to verification.

We used to say that a proposition contained the method of its verification. That is true in the sense that a proposition contains the definitions of the signs out of which it is constructed and that those definitions guide us in verifying it.

A verification-path cannot lead to infinity. (An 'infinite verification' would no longer be a verification.)

To be sure, a proposition can lead back to other propositions, and those back to yet other ones, etc., but ultimately we must reach propositions that do not indicate further propositions, but point to reality. Or rather, a proposition with sense talks about reality via the whole chain of definitions.

If it were otherwise, no proposition could be verified. There would then be no connection between language and the world.

The propositions that deal with reality immediately are called *elementary propositions*.

It is not an hypothesis that there are elementary propositions. The requirement that elementary propositions should exist is the requirement that our statements have sense. The fact that we understand the propositions of our ordinary language already guarantees that there are elementary propositions.

The elementary propositions are what give all other propositions sense.

We can understand the propositions of our ordinary language without knowing what the elementary propositions look like. Just as we understand most expressions without knowing their definitions, or just as we move without knowing how every particular movement is brought about.

One could ask, How is it possible that we understand the propositions of our ordinary language if we do not know the elementary propositions? The answer is that to *apply a rule* does not mean to *know about the rule*. We can, for example, introduce new signs and analyse the familiar signs by means of definitions. In the latter case definitions only *elucidate* the sense of propositions. The propositions themselves, however, can be understood without our knowing how the definitions are to be formulated.

In the same way logical analysis elucidates the sense of propositions by analysing their signs; it is, however, not through analysis that they first acquire sense. Once we have completely analysed a proposition, we must in the end have the feeling that that was the very thing we had always meant when uttering the proposition. (An analysis must never surprise us.)

If the sense of our statements was not already fixed—how would we then know *which* analysis was the right one?

What a strange view to think that only logical analysis *explains* what we mean by the propositions of ordinary language! Do I, accordingly, not know what I mean when I say 'Today it is colder than it was yesterday'? Do I have to wait for the result of logical analysis? But it is just the other way about, isn't it? Our statements already have sense, and it is that sense that determines their logical analysis.

But can we not be wrong? Is it not possible that we imagine we mean something by a proposition which turns out to be senseless on a closer look? No, for a statement has sense if there is a method of verifying it. And *vice versa*, if we know how to verify a proposition, then the proposition does have sense. We can only be in the dark about that as long as we go by the external linguistic structure of a proposition.

To analyse a proposition means to consider how the proposition is to be verified.

It is by means of elementary propositions that language *touches* reality.

To specify the elementary propositions means to specify the states of affairs in the world.

It is clear that statements about bodies (tables, chairs) are not elementary propositions. Nor will anybody believe that in talking about bodies we have reached the ultimate elements of description.

Phenomena (experiences) are what elementary propositions describe.

I can say, to be sure, 'This conductor is charged with electricity, *since* the electroscope displays a deflection.' But I cannot say 'This patch in my visual field is yellow, *since* . . . .'[186] If, in order to verify a proposition, I can no longer appeal to other propositions, this indicates that the proposition is elementary.

The *form* of elementary propositions cannot be specified *a priori*.

The form of elementary propositions must conform to the form of phenomena, and that is something we cannot foresee.

Hence if you ask, 'Will the elementary propositions turn out to

186 Cf. p. 97 above.

have subject-predicate form? Or will they turn out to be two-place relations?,' that shows that you have not yet understood the nature of elementary propositions.

Our principle must be that there *must not be any hypotheses about elementary propositions*.[187]

You can specify the form of elementary propositions only when you have got it.

One thing is clear. The logical structure of elementary propositions need not have the least similarity with the logical structure of the propositions of our ordinary language. Remember, for instance, that we can describe the visual field by means of a mathematical symbolism whose multiplicity is no less complex than the equations of physics. Here we see that we are no longer talking about subject and predicate, two-place relations, etc.

The signs occurring in elementary propositions are called *primitive signs* (elementary signs).

The primitive signs cannot be analysed by definitions.

The meaning of primitive signs can only be indicated by pointing.

Signs that signify directly are primitive signs; all other signs signify indirectly, via primitive signs.

Primitive signs constitute the *limits* of definition.

That there is such a limit is proved by the fact that there is a limit to the verification-path. That limit makes itself manifest in the primitive signs.

When is it *possible* to define an applied sign? That is a question of logic and not merely a question of expediency.

The definition of a sign must conform to the verification-path. Hence it depends on that path how a meaningfully used sign is to be defined.

A sign can be defined only if the propositions in which it occurs cannot be verified directly, and hence only if we have not yet reached the end of the verification. If you pretend that *every* sign is definable,

---

187 Cf. p. 182 above.

as if it were a mere matter of our being skilful at inventing definitions, as it were, you are barking up the wrong tree.

If you ask, for example, 'Can the colour word "yellow" be defined?,' the answer must be that it depends entirely on how a statement about that word is to be verified. If I verify it by looking, I cannot define the word 'yellow'. And if I nonetheless tried to do so, I should have defined something, but not what the word means in *that* context.

Assuming I could reproduce every colour by means of specifying the way in which it can be obtained by mixing the colours red, yellow, blue, green, white, and black, then I would call such symbols, which are all on the same footing, *elements of representation*.[188] These elements of representation are the primitive signs. The primitive signs must have such a nature that any state of affairs can be described by means of them.

For example, I see a red patch in front of me. Am I now to say that red is a property of that patch? Or should I rather say that it is a property of red that it is in that place? What is an object and what is a property here? That question is completely pointless. The truth is that our traditional linguistic forms (noun, adjective, etc.) completely lose their significance as soon as we apply them to the actual phenomena.

A state of affairs, a phenomenon, is a combination of elements. But there is nothing in that combination which indicates that there is something thing-like, something property-like in it.

The first question that arises here is, What can be meant by such a distinction?

Frege held that what connected the words within a proposition—as it were, what was propositional about a proposition—was its predicate. He called possible predicates *concepts* and distinguished accordingly between concept and object.[189]

---

188 Cf. p. 43 above.
189 None of these expressions occur literally in Frege's writings, but cf., e.g., 'On Concept and Object,' in *Translations from the Philosophical Writings of Gottlob Frege*, op. cit., pp. 42–55.

It might then be thought that in describing the phenomena we encountered an analogous difference, i.e. that there was something in a state of affairs which constituted its form, which connected the other elements, as well as something thing-like which was to be connected. The predicate would then signify the form-like part of a state of affairs and the other elements of a proposition its thing-like part.

Thus this whole distinction arises when we ask, What connects the elements of a state of affairs? But have we any right to ask this question? The elements are not connected with one another *by anything*. They simply are connected, and that concatenation just is the state of affairs in question.

After all, does the other conception explain anything? If cement is needed to hold the elements together—what is it that connects the cement and the elements?[190]

Form is the possibility of structure and structure is immediately generated by the connection of the elements.

Now you can no longer ask whether the primitive signs mean something thing-like or whether they represent properties or relations. Which simply shows that the categories of ordinary language do not suffice for the description of phenomena.

Elements are simple. For that reason they cannot be described.

What can be described? Whatever is complex. The description of a complex will consist in a specification of the way its components are related to one another. If those components too are complex, they can be described in the same way, etc.

Here the question arises whether that process can be continued indefinitely.

Suppose that were possible. Then every sign occurring in a proposition p would signify a complex, and that complex could in turn be described by means of a further proposition q. Can I then ever be sure

---

190 An argument used by F. H. Bradley (*Appearance and Reality*, 2nd edition, London, 1897, p. 33) who is referred to in the earlier version of *Theses*. Russell alludes to the argument in *Our Knowledge of the External World*, Chicago and London, 1914, p. 17.

that a sign used to describe something has a meaning? No, for I should have to check every time whether that complex *existed*, i.e. whether proposition *q* was true. It would hence depend on experience whether a sign had a meaning. But then no description at all would be possible.

Every description presupposes that something unalterable exists in the world, something which is independent of the existence or non-existence of states of affairs. The elements simply are what is unalterable in this way.

The existence of simple elements, far from being an abstract and theoretical result, is something we ought all, really, to know. And it agrees with our natural feeling too. I can describe a table by specifying what colour it has. But I cannot also describe the colours red, yellow, etc. Can my knowledge of colours change in the course of experience? Does it make sense to say, 'The oftener I see the colour red the more of its properties I come to know'? Clearly there is here some kind of completeness in our knowledge. And that means that, as regards the elements, there is nothing more for us to learn.

(To be sure, it is by means of experience that we become acquainted with colours. But that is not experience of a state of affairs.)

There is one and only one complete analysis of a proposition.

The analysis of a proposition makes evident the way the proposition is connected with reality.

The connexion is established by the primitive signs.

A proposition is connected with reality only if it is possible to analyse it far enough to obtain its primitive signs; only in that case does it have sense.

If the meaning of a sign can neither be elucidated by means of ostension nor reduced to other signs by means of definitions, the verification-path is blocked.

The totality of primitive signs sets a *limit* to language.

8. Objects

Elementary propositions describe the context of our experience. All other propositions are merely an expansion of that content.

Here arises the question of how we can obtain the propositions of our ordinary language from the elementary propositions.

The purpose of our ordinary language is to describe what goes on in the world around us. Its end is not to reproduce the logical structure of phenomena. It does, however, speak of the events in our environment by talking of objects (things, bodies), ascribing properties to them, or relating them to each other, etc.

We now have to ask which symbolism it is that represents an object.

Russell held that an object—e.g. a table—is the class of its aspects.[191]

'A class of aspects' can mean two kinds of thing.

1. A number of aspects enumerated by means of a list. That is obviously not what we mean when we are talking of a table.

2. A property of aspects, hence a common feature which can occur as part of an aspect (e.g. a colour). It is clear that we do not mean that either.

Our ordinary language is enough to show that the symbolism which represents a table must be of a completely different nature from that of propositional functions. For ordinary language treats words for objects in a completely different way from words for properties and relations. The words 'white,' 'greater than,' 'between' demand a very definite propositional form. For that reason we can reproduce their logical forms by means of the symbols fx, xRy, $P(x, y, z)$.

A noun, on the other hand, requires no definite propositional form—it has all the forms language assigns to it. That difference must have a reason, and a correct conception of objects must clarify that reason.

---

191 Cf. e.g. *Our Knowledge of the External World*, Chicago and London, 1914, pp. 89ff.

The truth of the matter is that the concept of an object is connected with *induction*.

Induction appears in the form of hypotheses.

By an *hypothesis* we here mean not a statement but rather a law for constructing statements.[192]

Only particular statements can be true or false, an hypothesis cannot.

Its justification lies in what it accomplishes, i.e. in the simplification it leads to.

Even if the statements to which it leads are false, an hypothesis is not refuted. We can retain it in its previous status by introducing a new hypothesis. If an hypothesis requires new auxiliary hypotheses all the time, it becomes impracticable and we drop it.

Simple, plausible, probable—with respect to an hypothesis these words mean the same.[193]

There are hypotheses of mathematical form. The laws of physics are such hypotheses.

If I describe, for example, the behaviour of a gas under different pressures and constant temperature I can connect those observations by means of the law '$p.v = $ const.'. On the basis of that law I can construct any number of pairs of numerical values for p and v, and to every such pair of numbers there corresponds a description. The equation is a method for constructing any number of such descriptions.

A law of nature comprises not only the observations that have been made to date. If you tried to say that it comprised infinitely many observations, then that would express nothing at all, since that proposition could never be verified.

A law of nature is not constructed by means of the *sense* of particular descriptions—it is hence not a truth-function of those propositions. It

192 Cf. p. 99 above.
193 Cf. p. 100 above.

is, rather a mathematical law which connects the numbers occurring in those descriptions. (Hence a general implication is not the expression of a natural law.)

Physics constructs a system of hypotheses, which is represented by means of a system of equations.

The concept of an object involves an hypothesis, for we assume as an hypothesis that the particular aspects we perceive are connected in a law-governed manner.

When I say, 'All the different pictures I see belong to one object, say, to a table,' that means that I connect the seen pictures by means of a hypothetically assumed law. On the basis of that law from given pictures I can derive new pictures.

If I wanted to describe the particular aspects, that would be tremendously complicated. The structuring achieved by our language consists, therefore, in assembling all those innumerable aspects in a hypothetically assumed connection.

The simplification is of the same kind as when I say with regard to the following figure that I see parts of an ellipse.

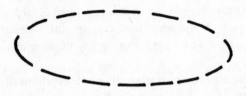

The language of everyday life uses a system of hypotheses. It does so by means of using nouns.

Aspects are spatially and temporally connected.

An object is the way aspects are connected.

An object is a connection of aspects represented by an hypothesis.

The following, is a simile to clarify this. An object is similar to a body in space—the particular aspects are the cross-sections made when we cut through it.[194]

194 Cf. p. 100 above, and *PR* p. 282.

What we observe are always only particular cross-sections across the connected structure of a law.

If I know a number of cross-sections, I can connect them by means of an hypothesis. In the same way I can connect some aspects by means of an hypothesis. What connects them is nothing other than the object in question. An hypothesis is justified if it proves to be confirmed, that is to say, if by its means I can predict the appearance of new aspects.

Here the dispute about whether an object 'consists' only of perceived or of possible aspects is also settled. For an object does not consist of aspects at all; it is only that we use a method by means of which we derive statements about aspects.

Russell does not represent the nature of objects correctly when he conceives of an object as a *class*. For a class does not help us at all to obtain a statement about a further aspect. A class has nothing to do with induction—an object, however, is essentially connected with induction.

Particular aspects are what is changing and unstable; it is the form of the connection of aspects that is unalterable and remains. That unalterable connection is signified by *one* word.

It has after all always been felt that there is something in an object that is unalterable and enduring, and that has been expressed by the proposition that an object is the bearer of its properties. And that is correct, too, if by a bearer is meant the unalterable form of a connection of aspects.

It is not an accidental fact that our description of an object always remains unfinished. The possibility of such a description must already be contained in the nature of an object—in the form of an hypothesis.

Here we see quite clearly that an object behaves quite differently from an element of a state of affairs. Now we also see how easily philosophical mistakes are engendered by making the category of objects apply to elements too—i.e. by carrying the logical form of nouns over to elements—and thereby being tempted into wishing to describe an element in the same way as an object.

All logical forms of our ordinary language—subject-predicate structure, the structure of relations—are very closely connected with objects and becomes inapplicable as soon as we attempt to describe the phenomena themselves.

The proposition 'Orange lies between yellow and red,' for example, sounds just like the proposition 'This table stands between this chair and that window.' and that is why it so easily appears as though such a proposition described those colours. Here the use of the noun form continuously misleads us.

The same holds for propositional functions. The symbol 'fx' is taken from the case in which 'f' signifies a predicate and 'x' a variable noun. When we advance to elementary propositions propositional functions (classes) become worthless.

The hypothesis of an object connects facts of *different kinds*.

The word 'table' makes us think, not only of the connection between different visual images, but also of the connection between those and tactile sensations. An object is something that connects all those facts.

An hypothesis is designed to comprise *more* than the reproduction of *one* kind of experience. When we have a particular experience (see the visual image of a table, for instance) we, on the basis of an hypothesis, expect to be able to have particular experiences of a different kind (tactile sensations).

An hypothesis contains, as it were, idly turning wheels. They remain unused as long as no further experiences occur, and they become active only when it is a matter of representing further experiences.

That also explains how it comes about that we seem to be able to verify the same proposition in different ways.

I say, for example, 'There stands a clock.' If I were now asked how I knew that, I could answer 'I have seen it,' or 'I reached out and touched it,' or 'I heard it tick.' Here it seems as if I verified the same propositions in three completely different ways.

But that is not the way things are. What I have verified are different cross-sections through the same hypothesis. Only we do not describe a particular cross-section; rather we immediately represent the phenomena in question in the context of the whole hypothesis.[195]

If one kind of experience were inaccessible to me, had I been blind from birth, for instance, then the hypothesis of an object would also have *meant* something different—something less—to me.

Hence if you say that 'the same thing' can verified in different ways, then 'the same thing' means more than something that is verified in only one way.

A noun does not occur only in propositions of a single form.

The logical form of a noun is hence not to be represented by 'fx', 'xRy', etc., but rather by means of the entire complicated system of syntactical rules that hold for the words in question.

Here our natural language proves superior to Russell's artificially produced symbolism. The symbolism of propositional functions is very useful as long as it is a matter of representing certain simple logical relations—inference, for instance. But it fails when it is a matter of the logical clarification of concepts by means of which we really describe reality.

Does the following question make sense? How many aspects is it necessary to have seen before the existence of an object is safely established? No, it does not. No number of aspects can prove that hypothesis. Whether we accept the hypothesis or reject it—that depends entirely on what the hypothesis will accomplish.

And that is how we in fact behave. What should I do, for example, if this book dissolved into nothing as soon as I had a close look at it. Or if I had visual images without the corresponding tactile perceptions? I should say. '*There was no book there*; I only *believed* I was seeing one.'

195 Cf. p. 159 above.

And that means that I dispense with the hypothesis of the existence of the book. And when I say that the book is there, that means that I adhere to the hypothesis of the existence of the book.

Here you can see that it makes good sense to speak of the *reality* of objects.

It is striking that the predicate 'real' attaches to the objects and not to the phenomena, which are the only things that are given.

The explanation of that lies in the fact that a phenomenon is something which occurs but once, whilst the hypothesis contained in an object points to the future. An object affects our expectations. That is why we call it real.

The world slips away from a person who does not hope for, or fear, anything. The world becomes 'unreal'

It is by no means to be taken for granted that the expectations connected with an hypothesis about the existence of an object are fulfilled every moment. Realists have a dim feeling of that and utter it in an unclear form by saying, Objects are real. And they are right, after all, if by the word 'real' they mean not something metaphysical, but the confirmation of an hypothesis.

Belief in reality is belief in induction.

9. *Logical Space*

Elements are form and content.

Different elements can have their form in common. They are then different only with respect to their contents.

Elements of the same form make up a *system* (e.g. colours).

If you replace the elements of a state of affairs by elements of the same form in every possible way, a class of states of affairs will result, every single one of which can exist or not exist. The totality of these existent and non-existent states of affairs is called *logical space*.

Logical space is the possibility of the existence and non-existence of states of affairs.

Facts lie in logical space.

All facts of the same form lie in a single logical space.

Let us imagine a white sheet of paper covered with a network of lines. I can describe every mesh of the network by specifying two point-numbers. The elements in a state of affairs correspond to the point-numbers and the states of affairs themselves to the meshes of the network. If a state of affairs then exists in reality, we imagine the corresponding mesh filled in black. The distribution of black patches on the white sheet of paper then is a picture of reality in logical space.

(This analogy is accurate only on condition that facts are independent of one another. If that is not the case, some further restrictions about the distribution of patches need to be introduced.)

Reality is as it were an island amidst possibility.

How do we know that colours form a system? If e.g. somebody had seen only red all his life—would he then not say that he knew only one colour? To this we have to reply that, if everything he saw was red and he could describe that, he would also have to be able to construct the proposition 'That is not red,' and that already presupposes the existence of other colours. Or else, by saying that, he means something that he cannot describe, in which case he does not know colours in our sense at all; in that case he cannot be *asked* whether red presupposes a system of colours either. Hence if the word 'red' has a meaning, it already presupposes a system of colours.[196]

And it is the same with every sign that is used meaningfully. If the sign '*a*' occurs in the proposition '*fa*,' that already presupposes other propositions of that kind, e.g. the proposition '*fb*'. For if only the state of affairs *fa* existed, but not the state of affairs *fb*, then it would be superfluous to mention '*a*', and *superfluous signs mean nothing*.

That shows that every proposition is part of a system of propositions.

196 Cf. pp. 66 and 88f. above.

INDEX

PR indicates that the numbers thereafter refer to pages of *Philosophical Remarks*. Not all topics in that book or in Waismmann's "Theses" are listed here, but only those also touched on in the conversations recorded in this volume.

"All" 38 ff., 44 f., 51 ff., PR 116 ff.;
  ~ numbers, 81, PR 150 f;
  ~ propositions, 96;
  ~ real numbers, 110 ff.
analogy, 110, 143, 204 f.
appearance)(reality 59, PR 270.
application, ~ of a calculus 125 f., 129,
    139 f., 170 ff., 193;
  ~ of a game, 163;
  ~ of a language, 104;
  ~ of mathematics, 34 f., 225, PR
    130 f., cf. geometry
axioms, 33 f., 103 ff.,
  ~, independence of, 128 f., 145 ff.;
  ~ and information, 62;
  ~ and rules, 119;
  ~ as a standard, 190 f.

Calculus, 114, 120, 178 ff., 202 f.,
    206 f.;
  ~ and application, 106, 125 ff.,
    139 f., 170 ff.;
  ~)(prose (theory), 129, 133, 149,
    164, 168
colour-system, 42 f., 63 ff., 65 ff., 78,
    89, 184, 241, 261, PR 51 ff.,
    75 ff., 105 ff., 273 ff.
comparison with reality, 86 ff., 209
compositeness of a proposition, 90, 97,
    107
concept)(form, 224
consistency, 38, 119 ff., 130 ff., 137 ff.,
    142 ff., 173 ff., 192 ff., 196 ff.;
  ~, proof of, 121 f., PR 189
contradiction (cf. tautology), 148 f.;

~, hidden, 120, 173 f., 195 ff., 208
~ between rules, 192
correlation (equinumerosity), 103,
    164 f., 222, PR 140

Decidability, 37, 129
discovery, ~ in grammar, 63, 77 f.;
  ~ in logic, 103, 129 f., 248;
  ~ in mathematics, 63, 175, PR 120,
    190;
  ~ in philosophy, 182 f.;
  ~ of a point in space, 241, 216;
  ~, Sheffer's, 122 ff., 145, PR 182.,
    191 f.

Einstein on geometry, 38, 162
elementary propositions, 42 f., 73 ff.,
    93, 248 ff., PR 106 ff.
elements, 234 f., 260 f.;
  ~ of representation, 43, 45, 251 ff.
equation, ~ and substitution rule,
    151 ff., 178., PR 143;
  ~ and tautology, 35, 105 ff., 158,
    218 ff., PR 126 ff., 203
ethics, 68 f., 92 f., 115 ff., 142

Formalism, 103 ff., cf. Frege and Weyl
Frege, ~ on concept, 238, 251;
  ~ on consistency, 130 ff.;
  ~ on correlation, 165;
  ~ on formalism, 105, 138;
  ~ on meaning, 150 f.;
  ~ on objects, 41

Games (chess) and mathematics, 103 ff., 119, 131 ff., 150 ff., 163, 170
generality in geometry, 206 f., *PR* 125
geometry, double meaning of ~, 100;
  ~ Euclidean and non-Euclidean, 127, 143, 144 f., 179 f., 195 ff.;
  ~ and physics, 71, 162;
  ~, rough, 56 ff., *PR* 268 ff.;
  ~ as syntax, 38, 61 ff., 162 f., *PR* 216;
  ~ and visual space, 55–60

Heidegger on being and anxiety, 68
Hilbert, ~ on consistency, 119 ff., 137 ff., 175;
  ~ on independence, 147;
  ~ on metamathematics, 136
Husserl on the synthetic a priori, 67, 78 f.
hypothesis, 97, 99 ff., 159 ff., 162 f., 188, 210 f., 214, 229, 250, *PR* 282 ff.;
  ~ and verification, 255 ff.

Identity, 165, 189 ff., 242 f., *PR* 141 ff.
induction, 33 f., 45, 53, 71, 82, 94, 98 f., 109 f., 134 ff., 227, 232, 255 ff., *PR* 150, 187, 201, ff., 283 f.
inference, 64, 91 f.
infinite, 73, 114, 187 f., 202 f., 217, 226 ff., 247 f., *PR* 146 ff., 206 ff.;
  ~ not an adjective, 102 f.;
  ~, Dedekind's definition of the, 69 ff., 103, 232, *PR* 151
intention, 166 ff., *PR* 63 ff.
internal)(external, 54 f., 157., 215, *PR* 122
interpretation, 113 f., 140

Language and the world, 50, *PR* 81, 98, 104
law and extension, 202, *PR* 221 f.

limits of language, 68, 93
looking for something, 227, 234, 244 f., *PR* 67, 77, 170 ff., 175, 184 f.;
  ~ ad infinitum, 114;
  ~ in mathematics 34 ff.;
  ~ and a method of doing so, 88, 127, 144, 174

Mathematics, cf. discovery; no logical propositions in ~, 46
memory, cf. remember, 98, *PR* 61 f.;
  ~ as a picture, 48, 87 ff., *PR* 81 f.;
  ~ and time, 53 f., 55
metamathematics, 121, 133, 136, *PR* 180
multiplicity, 39, 43, 79, 80, 85, 97, 107, 127, 135, 152, 156, 223, 226, 234, 236, 239 ff., 242, *PR* 57 f.

Noise, "Was that a ~ ?" 107 f., *PR* 55, 121
number, types of ~, 36, 71 ff., 84, 102 f., 109 ff., 175, 188;
  ~s, Brouwerian, 72 f., *PR* 210;
  ~, definition of, 164 ff., 221 ff.;
  ~s, real, 71 ff., 109 ff., *PR* 223 ff.

Objects, 41 ff., 43, 254 ff., *PR* 72, 119, 169, cf. elements
operation)(function, 216 f.
ostensive definition, 209 f., 246, *PR* 54
other minds 49 f., *PR* 88 f.

Phenomenology, 63, 65, 67 f., 101, *PR* 51, 53, 84, cf. primary language
physics, 63, 101, cf. geometry
pictorial (representational) character of propositions (of language) 84, 185, 239, *PR* 57, 61, 77 ff.
picture (depiction), 48, 55, 81, 240;
  ~, incomplete. 39, 52, 54, 90, *PR* 115 ff.

positive)(negative propositions, 85 ff.,
    90 f., *PR* 57
primary)(secondary language, 45, *PR*
    51, 58, 84, 88, 100, 103, 158,
    168, 267
probability, 93 ff., 98 f., 245, 255, *PR*
    289 ff.
proof 172 f.;
    ~ and analysis, 122, *PR* 179;
    ~ and application, 35;
    ~ and calculation, 133 f.;
    ~ in geometry, 206 f.;
    ~, indirect, 143, 179 ff., 207 f.;
    ~ and induction, 33 f., 110 f.,
        134 ff., *PR* 183;
    ~ in mathematics 33 f.;
    ~ and proposition, 33 f., *PR* 192,
        233;
    ~ and seeing, 146, 148;
    ~s of the same thing, two, 109,
        205 f., *PR* 73, 179;
    ~ not a vehicle, 33, 109, 112

Ramsey on identity, 189 ff., 243, *PR*
    141 ff.
red, "The world is ~" 66 f., 88 f.,
    261
religion, 117 f.
remember, "I can *merely* ~ " 48, *PR*
    81 f., 84
rule, 33 f.;
    ~ and application, 154 f.;
    ~ and configuration in a game, 119,
        124 ff., 132, 145, 156, 175, 178;
    ~ and contradiction 124 ff., 194 ff.;
    ~ and statement (proposition) 128,
        240 f.
ruler (standard), proposition (system of
    propositions) as a ~ 63 f., 74, 79,
    87, 89, 185, *PR* 76 f., 110 ff.;
    ~, π (axioms) as a, 198 f., 231
Russell, ~ on "all", 39;
    ~ on axioms, 123 ff.;
    ~ on correlation, 165;

    ~ on identity, 243;
    ~ on the infinite, 114;
    ~ on logical propositions, 106;
    ~ on objects, 41, 254

Solipsism, 45 ff., *PR* 85
space, a form of representation, 214
standard, cf. ruler
subject-predicate form, 41, 43, 46,
    224, 249 f., 258, *PR* 119
symptoms, 107, 159
syntax, 47 ff., 63, 66, 74, 76 f., 78, 92,
    103 ff., 114, 126, 162, 213 f.,
    220;
    ~ and sign, 80, 225, 240
synthetic a priori, 67 ff., 78 ff.
system, ~ of propositions, 63 ff., 89 ff.,
    261, *PR* 59;
    ~)(totality, 216, 218

Tautology, cf. equation, 105 ff., 131,
    189 ff., 218 ff.;
    ~ and contradiction, 140;
    ~ and inference, 91
theory, 168, 253, cf. calculus;
    ~ in ethics; 116 f.;
    ~ and games, 133 ff., 150 f.;
    ~ in mathematics, 129
trisection of an angle, 36 f., 143 f.,
    204 ff., *PR* 177.

Understanding, 167 ff., 243

Verification, 71, 97 f., 126, 221, 226,
    PR 174;
    ~ and definition, 247;
    ~, different, different sense 46, 48,
        53 ff., 70 f., 98, 158 ff., 186,
        204 ff., 245., 258., *PR* 62,
        287;
    ~ of an hypothesis 211;
    ~ and induction, 232;
    ~ and physics, 158 ff.;

Verification—*contd.*

~ as the sense of a proposition, 47, 79, 227, 243 ff., *PR* 66 f., 200 f., 282, 289

Weyl, ~ on formalism, 103;

~ on mathematics, 37, 81 ff.

wheels turning idly, 47 f., 65, 258, *PR* 51